★ UNCOMMON

CONQUEST
TO NOWHERE

ANTHONY HERBERT

CONQUEST TO NOWHERE
An Infantryman in Wartime Korea

ANTHONY HERBERT
as told to Robert L. Niemann

Cover copyright © 2014 by Uncommon Valor Press,
Steve W. Chadde, Series Editor

Printed in the United States of America.

ISBN-13: 978-1951682477

Also available for kindle.

TYPEFACE: Athelas 10/12.5

UNCOMMON VALOR SERIES

Conquest to Nowhere is part of a series entitled *Uncommon Valor,* taken from the quote by Admiral Chester W. Nimitz, U.S. Navy: "Uncommon valor was a common virtue," referring to the hard-won victory by U.S. Marines on Iwo Jima. The intent of the series is to keep alive a number of largely forgotten books, written by or about men and women who survived extreme hardship and deprivation during immensely trying historical times.

Each book in the series is meticulously reviewed to ensure a quality reading experience either on paper or on your kindle device.

Steve W. Chadde
SERIES EDITOR

This book is dedicated to
Clarence Saddler . . . a real hero
—Tony Herbert

CONTENTS

. . .within a lusty mortal span
 of dynasties unbound,

becomes a man immortal
 and Heaven his domain

to tell of barren conquests
 and infinite turmoil

and reign on humble specks of folk
 of those who toil and play,

who naked in the eyes of God
 a tranquil world possess. . .

—John Sakoutis

CHAPTER ONE
"A Speck of Dust In the Eye of Time"

THE CAPTAIN made an effort to lift his head from his chest so he could speak. In his condition, it required super-human strength, but his energy lay on the frozen ground in a pool of blood. He was tied by the wrists and suspended between two houses in a Korean village. Propping my rifle against one of the buildings from which he hung, I moved forward. I strained, reaching up, but unsuccessfully. He was out of my reach. His breath came in a rasping, gurgling sound as he muttered weakly, *"Water."*

I was certain it was useless to cut him down. Death was inevitable for him. The captain flinched as another flash of pain ran through his body. The motion caused him to swing ever so slightly, like the delicate branches of a willow tree.

Around him were other men who had fallen prisoner of the Chinese. Their voices calling to us, asking to be shot, asking to be cut down from their crucifixion, blended with the cold winter night's wind, to form a holocaust of horror. Weird sounds of the night mingled with their pleas. In the rich moonlight, the bodies cast grotesque shadows as they hung suspended by their hands in doorways, between buildings or from the eaves of the Korean houses. To my right hung a corporal, his head pounded in until it resembled nothing human. Suspended behind him was a man with a slash in his abdomen that permitted his entrails to free themselves of their bondage. They were spilled onto the ground, still pulsating, though he scarcely breathed.

Moving quickly from one body to another, not believing our eyes, it became obvious that all of them had been attacked in the same way. Each of the twenty-one men hanging by their arms had been disemboweled by his captors. Six were living, and we hastened to cut them down."

"Don't move me! Don't! Shoot me, for chrissake, shoot me!" one of them cried out.

"I *can't* shoot you, fella. Just take it easy—you'll be alright," I replied. A Turkish soldier stepped into my interlocked fingers and I boosted him up so he could begin cutting the rope which had dug into the man's wrists.

"It's no use—he began, but didn't complete the statement. The rope holding his right arm, parted. He swung like a pendulum, striking the wall of the opposite building. He screamed and then passed out, swinging by his left arm. His feet were almost touching the ground. The Turk balanced himself with his hands on my head and I walked to where the other rope was tied. We cut it and he fell onto the ground in a motionless heap.

I argued with myself, "Better give him a morphine syrette. At least it'll make it easier for him when he comes to." I inoculated the thought and cultivated it to good yield. "It's not good to give morphine with a stomach wound."

Something within me answered, "It's too late to worry about that. You don't think he's going to live, do you? I think you'd better give it to him. He's got to have *something.*"

My Turkish friend motioned for me to go with him, and we moved to the six living men, cutting them down, one by one. The captain was last. Again he asked for a drink of water. I opened my canteen and handed it to the Turk who once more climbed onto the improvised ladder, and lifting the captain's head, held the canteen to his lips. The water ran into his mouth, and seconds later, gushed forth from a slit in his exposed stomach. It ran down his leg, dripping onto the ground. Almost immediately, he died.

In a matter of minutes he was joined by the remainder of his company, and the entire twenty-one men, spiritually, were together again.

The faces of the men bore testimony of the agony of their tortured death. They were masks of horror. The Chinese had not been content with slashing across their prisoners' stomachs with bayonets. Footprints in the snow showed that after the entrails of some of them had fallen out of their bodies, they had been ground into the ice by heels of rubber sneakers or American combat boots, possibly taken from these men themselves. None wore shoes. Their pants were missing, too.

Suddenly a noise startled us. A rustling sound from within the room of the house to our left. Maybe nothing—maybe something. Cautiously, we moved to the doorway. A cat scurried from the building, ran through my legs and disappeared into the night. My heart pounded, dangerously near the breaking point. I wanted to leave the town and try to get back to the 23rd wherever it was.

I began to worry; about being AWOL from my outfit, about being caught by the Chinese and strung up the same way, and about how we could ever get back to our troops. The Turks were checking the rest of the town. I could not speak Turkish, and they could not speak English. I worried.

I began staring at the face of the body nearest me. The face of a youth not more than nineteen. It looked familiar. I walked to him, and raising my rifle, caught his forehead with the barrel and pushed skyward. The eyes that saw nothing, stared at me. I was mistaken. I did not know him. Because of that, I felt a relief, then a sense of pity. I felt pity for a meaningless structure of flesh and bone. A dead substance that had been important to someone—at one time or another.

I wondered? Did he die with a question in his mind? A question of *why?* Not *why* the war was existing, but rather *why,* if he had to die, did it have to be this way? If I were to get it this very night, I felt, I would die with some questions answered—and others not.

I hadn't expected this kind of war. It wasn't like the movies depicted it; not at all. I felt violent—about many things. Then the fragments of the unexplainable thoughts churning through my brain reassembled into no particular order. I remembered myself when I was full of questions and ideas. . .some still to be answered. Why would a man ask to get into such a mess? I wished that my legs were long enough to reach out and kick myself right square in the ass.

The first time I tried to get into the Army was during World War II when I was fourteen. I recall my brother, Bud, with his chest full of ribbons earned while battling the Japanese in the Pacific. Bud was in the Navy, a torpedoman. It seemed like a rather tame job, but the way he'd describe how they'd track a sub and blast it out of the water with depth charges or torpedoes, seemed to put more color in the naval war. So until I was about fourteen, I wanted to be in the Navy.

On Saturdays, a bunch of us would go to the local theater and spend the whole day there, seeing the same movie. Then I changed my mind about the Navy, and decided that if I were going to be a soldier, I had to be in the infantry.

Movies where the soldiers were caught in a barrage of artillery, or in hand to hand combat, bayonets flashing, was *real* war! My older brother, Chuck, was a company commander in the infantry. I can appreciate much more since I've seen war, just how big a job he had. I would listen to his stories of war and arrive at one conclusion: *We were destined to have another war in my lifetime, and I was to be in it!*

Finally when the agonizing desire became too much for me, I went to nearby Pittsburgh and joined the Marine Corps. Tony Spiegel was with me, and everything came along fine. The sergeant in the recruiting station needed recruits at the time, I guess. Anyway, we were in.

We were with a group of men in the railroad station, waiting for the train to take us to Parris Island, S. C., when who should walk up to us but the high school principal. He looked at us two short-lived Marines and said, "Your mothers are looking for you two."

Tony and I glanced at each other.

"Mr. Gessman, how did you know we were here?"

"That doesn't matter," he answered, "come on home."

"But our train leaves in just a few minutes!"

"Are you going to come or am I to have him arrest you!"

We then noticed a policeman standing by the platform master's window. There was no further argument; we went with him.

A "trial," with members of the draft board sitting as a tribunal, winking at each other, dealt out a verdict; no punishment, except to be returned to school and Mr. Gessman's supervision.

Finally, the whole story of how I had told the draft board that I was eighteen, was revealed. The clerk had figured that if I was crazy enough to say I was old enough to be drafted, she was just crazy enough to register me. I had told my mother I was just going south for the summer to train dogs for the Army's canine corps. Dad never interfered in things like that. He let me decide for myself. Sometimes he was right, sometimes not. It wasn't very long before I approached my folks again on the subject of going into the service. I had the draft card, and asked them to approve my enlistment.

"Don't you think you should stay home and finish high school first, son?" Dad asked. A coal miner for most of his life, he had spent the early part of it in the mines of Lithuania. He could never understand why anyone would want to abandon an education that in the Old Country would have been impossible to obtain.

My only argument was, "I can take the Army's tests and get my diploma at the same time. I can get two birds with one stone."

"Sounds good, but you know as well as anybody, you'll never do it," Mom chimed in. In my own mind, I knew it, too.

We discussed that for the better part of an evening, until just to get me to shut up, they agreed.

CHAPTER TWO

Periodically during basic, we were called into the orderly room and told that certain schools were open for assignment. None of them were infantry. I held out for that. I was advised that only an idiot would insist on the infantry. That was quite a compliment, considering I was alone in griping for it.

One day Bob Hisey kept me from telling the captain, the lieutenant, and the whole orderly room what I thought of them. Taking me by the arm, he pulled me outside.

"Don't let them get you down, Herb. What the devil, we'll be finished here before long, and you can go to any damn outfit you want. But frankly, I think you're nuts myself."

Hisey was a good kid who got along with everybody and would help you every chance he got. Then there was his friend, "Tex" Harrington, a guy with a devilish sense of humor.

"Tex" was a big gangling guy from New York. We called him ^'Tex" because he had worked in Texas for about two months, but to hear him explain their relationship, one would be led to believe he had sponsored it for statehood.

Bob went to the movies one evening, and as soon as he was gone, Tex told us he was going to play a joke on him.

"What kind of a joke?" we asked.

"I dunno. How about nailing his boots to the floor?"

"Nah," we argued, "he might get into trouble if he turned them in to supply full of holes."

"So what if he does? Anyway, the supply room will get them before basic's over the way we've been walkin'."

He assumed the characteristic look he usually acquired when conjuring up these seemingly harmless little gags. Convinced of its harassing possibilities, he hopped off his bunk in one lithe motion.

"Dammit, I'm gonna do it! He didn't think of me getting restricted last week-end because he put shaving cream in my boots just before inspection. He's had it! Be back soon's I get some nails."

We decided to switch Hisey's boot with Harrington's while the latter was gone. A few minutes later, he returned.

"How about one of you watching at the door?" he asked, "I don't want to be doing this if someone comes in."

"How many nails did you get?"

"A whole mess of 'em. I told the carpenters we were building a new broom rack. That lousy Hisey'll never get 'em loose."

Tex picked up the hammer and moved the bed so he could nail the boots in their place. He put some of the nails into his mouth and got one inside the boot.

"Think I should?"

"Why not? He put bricks in your pack last week too, remember?"

"Yeah," he said, and started to hammer.

We enjoyed watching him do that to his own boots, and each time he'd get one in, he'd look up at us and snicker. We were all laughing, and the more we'd laugh, the more he enjoyed it—adding more nails with mounting incentive. Then he cut the laces at the bottom so they'd pull out when Bob tried to pick the boot up. Pushing the bed back into place, he stood surveying the scope of his handy-work.

"Hell, the boots are shot now anyway; I may as well do it up right." Taking his knife out of his pocket, he opened it and slit the threads holding the toe onto the sole.

I couldn't sleep in anxiety of Hisey's return from the movie. When he came back I told him what had happened, and how we had switched boots with Tex. He could hardly wait for morning.

When the CQ came into the room and flicked the light on in the morning, Tex was the first one awake. He was out of bed, waiting for Bob to fall victim of the prank. Instead, when Bob did get up, he walked over to Tex's bed and retrieved his own boots.

Tex snatched them from his hands.

"Where the hell do you think you're going?" he shouted.

'Take it easy, fella. I'm just getting my boots."

"What the hellaya mean, *your* boots?"

"These are mine. Take a look."

He turned the top of the boot down. Tex's eyes nearly left their sockets.

There was Hisey's name, big as life.

"So where the hell are mine?" he demanded, furiously.

"Probably under *my* bed, wouldn't you say?"

Tex rushed over, and in his excitement, momentarily forgot they were nailed down. He tried to lift them, and his hand slipped off, striking the bed rail. A white welt appeared across his knuckles.

"You mean these are *my* boots?"

" 'Ppears that way, son," Hisey chuckled, " 'Ppears that way."

"You lousy bastard!" Tex screamed, helplessly.

As the whistle came to fall out, Tex looked as if he were going to cry. When his name was called out at roll call, we explained that he was in the barracks. The platoon sergeant investigated, and there was Tex, crying like a baby, kicking at the anchored boot. The sergeant further peppered his fury trying to explain that the boots really didn't cost twenty dollars. They were only sixteen-fifty!

* * *

At the completion of basic, some of us were assigned to the Second Infantry Division at Fort Lewis, Washington. All men over six feet tall were singled out for MP training, and logically enough since I didn't want to be in the military police, I was selected. It took some diligent talking to convince the CO that I shouldn't be an MP, and eventually I was transferred to the 23rd Infantry Regiment.

After serving for a year and a half, I was discharged and returned to school in Herminie, Pennsylvania. I got my diploma this time, Pop was happy, and I was getting ready to reenlist.

Four months later while I was a student in a radio-repairman's school at Fort Monmouth, the war in Korea began. I was shaving when Henry Crosse, a friend from Chicago, came running into the latrine with the news.

"Cheez, Herb, have you heard?"

"Heard what?" I was ready for a gag.

"War has broken out in Korea!"

My head whipped around, but my razor stood still. Blood oozed out of a nick in my chin.

"You mean we're actually at war?"

"As soon as the United Nations decides we are. According to the news reports, there's not much doubt about it. The guys in Japan have already been alerted. What do you think?"

"I think it's time we got out of here." I said. Wiping the blood from my chin, I gathered my toilet articles and bolted out the door.

Henry followed me to my bunk. I put the shaving articles back in the foot locker and got my clothes from their hanger, all in a panicky rush.

"Do you think it will last long, Herb?" Henry asked.

"No I don't. That's why we've got to work fast if we're going to get over there. It can't last long. Those people aren't equipped for fight."

"Who do you mean? I don't even know where Korea is."

"It's next to Japan, I think it's an island. Once our troops and equipment get going, there'll be nothing left of it. Come on, let's go!"

"Where we going?"

"Where do you think? You want to go to Korea, don't you?"

"Yeah, but school won't be finished for another month. You can't go until it's over."

"Why not? What's to stop us from asking to be released from the school and going over as riflemen? It's up to you, but I'm certainly going to try for it. Whattya say?"

"Okay," he said, "I'm with you."

We requested that the commander of the school release us for duty in Korea. Denying the request, his excuse was that Korea would not be a war. He insisted that before we could get through all the required processing, the fracas would be over. Disappointed, and inclined to believe him, we went to the PX for a beer.

"He's crazy," I mused, "it can't be over that quickly." The more I thought about it, the more convinced I became that I was right.

Some of the other fellows from the class joined us and the Korean War became the main topic of conversation.

"Who could I go see about it?" I asked of no one person in particular. I tossed an empty beer can at a barrel sitting nearby. It hit the edge with a metallic ring and dropped to the dusty ground, spun around and lay still. I felt as inert as the can.

"Why don't you go see Chaplin?" I was asked

Figuring they were giving out with the old gag of, "Go see the Chaplain," I left in disgust. Crosse followed me.

"Why don't you finish your beer, Henry? I just want to think a little bit."

"I was finished anyway. It was that warm 3.2 stuff and not very cold, either. I can't stand that damn stuff when it's warm. Why don't they get 6% beer if they're going to sell anything?" He tried to make conversation, but wasn't very successful.

"I think I've got the answer!" I exclaimed.

"What's that?"

"They're always giving us the devil for not doing this and not paying attention to class. They always threaten to wash us out of the school!"

"So what?" He looked puzzled.

"I'm about to get tossed out of radio-repairman's school, old buddy!"

The next day was rough. Perhaps it was worse for the instructors than it was for me, but I asked idiotic questions, gave them a hard time when they answered me, and just generally fouled up. They put up with it for two days, until the afternoon of the third day, when the lieutenant who was giving the class called me to his rostrum.

"Herbert, what's happened to you here anyway? You were getting along fine until this week. Much more of this and you're going to find yourself out of the school entirely."

"I couldn't care less, sir." I hated being like that with him. He was a good Joe and had helped me a lot in the past. But I had to get kicked out. Time was of the essence.

"I think you should go to see one of the faculty advisors," he said, writing a name on a piece of paper. "Take this to school headquarters."

"Who am I to see?"

"The sergeant whose name is on the paper."

I looked at the paper—and the name was there. Sgt. Chaplin, room 413-B, school headquarters. "Go see Chaplin," the boys had said.

I felt like a fool.

Sgt. Chaplin glanced at the slip and asked me what the trouble was.

"I haven't got any troubles Sergeant, except I don't want to be a radioman. I just don't like it here."

"Didn't you ask to come here?"

"Yes I did, but a man can change his mind, can't he?" I replied.

"Sure he can, but you're in a field of occupation now that can go a long way in the Army. That is if you get good enough at it."

"But Sergeant, you can't make a man a good repairman if he doesn't want to be one can you?"

"That's true, but your past performance here proves you have the stuff in your head. It looks like you're trying to flunk out."

"Are you kidding? Hell, I'd never do that," I lied.

"Then what do you plan to do if you do flunk out of here? Where do you expect to be assigned?"

"Probably back to the infantry."

"You'd better take advantage of a break to be in the signal corps," he said.

"Take advantage of the break? I don't want to be in signal, I want to go back to the infantry."

"You must be crazy."

"Crazy or not—that's where I want to go."

"Then the best way for you to go is to finish the school and request it afterward. You've only got three more weeks anyway, and your previous work would carry you through. Why don't you just settle down and complete the course?"

"I guess I might as well, since you're not interested in flunking me out. But remember, you can't make me like it, even if you can make me do it."

The next three weeks dragged by. It was pretty much a review of things we'd been taught before, so it wasn't much trouble to get through, even though my thoughts were in Korea and the fighting there. Finally, graduation day came.

"Gentlemen," the colonel on the graduation stand was saying, "you have just completed one of the toughest courses the signal corps has to offer."

I turned toward Crosse, standing in the rank behind me. He smiled through the perspiration streaming down his face. The course wasn't half as tough as standing in the hot sun listening to the colonel.

"The parade I've just seen indicates that we have here, some of the sharpest men this school has ever turned out. Mentally or physically, you'll stand up against the U. S. Army's finest."

I looked at some of the men around me, wearing wrinkled khakis with large spots of sweat marks on the backs of their shirts. Each had about an inch of perspiration stain around the band of his cap. Most wore GI issue, and there's nothing more unsightly than the GI issue. I thought to myself, If this is the best the signal corps has to offer, I know darned well I want back in the infantry.

With all his words of praise expended, the colonel embarked on passing out certificates of achievement. Chaplin came up to me when it was all over and asked, "Do you still want to be a rifleman?"

"More than ever, why?"

"No question about you being made happy. You're such a piss-poor radioman, you'll wind up being a rifleman anyway."

Thanking him, I went into the barracks and packed my clothes as Crosse and I talked over plans of meeting in Chicago.

He said, "Orders for FECOM will be down this afternoon. Got the word from the company clerk. What do you think, Korea?"

"What else?"

"Guess you're right. Do you think we'll wind up in a radio outfit?"

"Beats the hell outta me. I think we can work our way out of it if we do, though. That is if you want to."

"I don't know, I've been thinking about that. I'll have to kick it around before really deciding. Anyway, are we going to get together in Chicago"?

I told him I'd call him at his home, and maybe stop by for a day or two before we went on to Camp Stoneman.

"That's a deal," he answered.

CHAPTER THREE

PENNSYLVANIA is hot in the summertime, and this was August. The coolest spot in town was on a hill overlooking the high school. On the seventh day at home, my blue tick hound, "Jim" and I went to an orchard where we had spent so many hours during past hunting seasons. After walking in the orchard for an hour or so, we sat under a tree at the crest of the hill, watching the sun disappear behind the tipples of the mines at the town's edge.

Suddenly, "Jim" got up and started sniffing the ground.

"Got something?" I asked.

His ribs were sliding under his skin as he sniffed for the scent. He got it and began running the crazy zig-zag pattern of a dog on the trail of game. For about twenty minutes, "Jim" followed the trail with a fervent desire, but his anxiety gradually succumbed to fatigue. We settled down at a point from where we had an almost perfect view of the town.

Frankly, I don't believe "Jim" ever did have a scent, but mentally, he was almost human. We had spent many days hunting together, and possibly *he* realized more than any human did, just how much I enjoyed it. Perhaps he wanted to share some of that excitement with me before I left. Maybe he felt it would be the last time we would do it together, and just invented the imaginary chase. I think he did.

The lights of the town were beginning to flicker on. We watched them multiply, one by one. "Jim" was still panting.

"How about an apple, fella?" I asked, rising to my feet.

He chased his tail a couple of times, registering approval, and I picked one up from the ground to see if he'd take it. He just sniffed and backed away.

"You haven't changed a bit, have you?" I picked one from the tree.

That's the only way he'd ever eat them in the past, from the tree. If I'd pick it for him, he'd eat it, but never one from the ground. I bit into mine, and it gave a loud 'crack.' It was so sour that I made a face, but "Jim" was crunching away on his, apparently unconcerned about its pungent taste.

It was dark by the time we had eaten two or three apples. Walking back to town, I decided I couldn't wait any longer. I had to leave for California.

My mind travelled back to years before. To the movies and books I would spend hours with. The war stories from the days of King Arthur; Robin Hood; the Civil War; fiction and truth. But truth and right had always triumphed. From the days of white chargers, streamers flying in the air, meeting their armored counterparts on the field of battle to the more recent days of jets, creating great sounds as if a cannon had erupted its contents when the pilot would pull it out from a power dive, it was always war.

Those were the thoughts in which I was engrossed upon arriving in Pittsburgh the next day.

"Nothin' to worry about," my brother-in-law had told me the night before when I asked if it hurt to get wounded. Foolish question. "When you get it, you're so happy that you're alive to know about it and when you learn that friends of yours are okay, everything's right with the world. No sweat fella, just play it cool and take care of yourself."

I sat on the hard bench at the station. The calls of trains and the sounds of the whistles of those arriving and departing plunged me into thought again. Like a train racing through the night, they gained momentum.

"It must be like Europe," I told myself, "with towns and roads and everything."

My imagination ran wild. I visualized tanks roaring down from the north, followed by thousands of screaming, slant-eyed barbarians.

I saw the United Nations rally to drive them back. Then the whole war collapsed. It was over, just like that! I insisted that it couldn't be. It couldn't end before I was able to vent myself of these deep-rooted longings. I was at the point of becoming frantic, when the train for Chicago was announced.

The trip to Henry's home town went along much too slowly, but at last we arrived at Stoneman. The wheels of processing turned more rapidly there than they had anywhere since I had come into the Army. Outwardly I was collected, but inside I was like a jigsaw puzzle scattered by a hurricane wind—to be assembled elsewhere—or to be scattered even more greatly.

A ten day trip on a transport ship with thousands of men aboard was spent just lying around. At night we would hear World War II veterans talking about the war. Many of them had been called away from their families with little or no notice. Some had volunteered, but most hated to think of taking the same chances they'd taken in World War II, all over again.

One night Crosse and I were lying on the deck, after tying our fatigues to a rope and tossing them overboard so they could be washed by dragging behind the ship. A corporal was nearby with a portable radio and the news was being heard from the States.

"Did you hear that?" Henry asked. "We've made an amphibious invasion at Inchon! Do you suppose the Russians will get into it now?"

"Hard telling, but there's no doubt that they're the ones in back of it. They'll probably be right behind the Koreans."

"Don't worry," he said, "you'll get there in time. It's gonna last a lot longer than it'll take us to get there."

"Could be, but the President said it's just a 'Police Action,' remember?"

In the background, a hillbilly who had smuggled his guitar on board the ship was strumming away, just as he had since we left California, still singing in his twangy, nasal hillbilly voice, the song, "Temptation." The temptation to break the guitar over the ship's rail was a growing one. Besides, the anxiety and boredom of the trip was beginning to get me down. We moved to the opposite side of the ship.

Henry started the conversation.

"How many of these men do you think will make it?"

"You mean of the men aboard?"

"Yeah."

"Beats the hell outta me. Some of them will get it, no doubt. The way the war, pardon me, 'Police Action' is going, damn good percentage, I guess."

"Do you think you'll get back. . .or me?"

I half laughed when I answered, "Snap out of it Crosse, you're not going to the guillotine at sunrise, you know."

"Same thing," he said, and rising to his feet, he stumbled off into the darkness of the passageway, down into the hold of the ship.

I stayed up on deck for awhile, watching the giant swells of water breaking behind us, putting distance between us and home, and taking us closer to Korea. A goony bird was rising above the crest of the swells and down into the cavernous openings created by them. Moonlight shimmered on the salty wash as the ship rolled and lurched forward each time the propellers made full contact with the water. I resented this state of suspended animation. The ship was my enemy—and I rebelled against it. When it got the best of me, I went below.

*   *   *

After breakfast in the morning, we were back up on deck. We went to the fantail of the ship, enjoying its elevator-like motion.

"Should we pull them in now?" Henry asked.

"Pull what in?"

"Our fatigues. They should be good and clean by now."

"Hell's fire, I forgot all about them."

We walked over to where the rope had been tied the night before, and dragged it in. There was nothing left on it but threads bearing a resemblance to Army fatigue-green. We looked at each other.

"Cut the jokes. Where did you put them?" Cross wanted to know.

"Tell you where I put them? What have you done with them?" I replied.

"I suppose you're gonna tell me now that you didn't come over here last night after I went to bed, and take them off the rope."

"I sure as hell didn't!"

"A fish got them, huh?"

"How the hell should I know? I didn't pay any attention to them. I turned in right after you did."

"Well, what happened to 'em?"

We asked one of the deck hands who was nearby if he had seen them. He broke with laughter when we explained what had happened.

"Why man, they wouldn't last ten minutes with those screws churning the water up the way they do! If they'll push a ship this size, think of what they'll do to fabric. They've just been washed to pieces. As the cat would say: 'Man! That's one mad Bendix!'"

He continued laughing as the ship's loudspeaker blasted out for me to report to my compartment. When I got there, the compartment sergeant was waiting for me.

"Why aren't you in the mess hall?" he demanded.

"Whattya mean, I don't get it."

"You name's Herbert, isn't it?"

"Yes, why?"

"Your name's here on the KP roster. You're AWOL."

"AWOL? Where in the hell am I going AWOL on a ship? I'm restricted to the damn thing all the way across the Pacific!" I blurted. "You weren't at the mess hall, so you're AWOL, get it?"

"Do you mean that out of all the guys on this ship, a PFC should be getting KP this soon?"

"Right, now get movin'.."

"I'm not about to go on KP, Sergeant."

"What?"

"I'm not going on KP. What's so complicated about it?"

"You're already in a jackpot fella, and it can be a helluva lot worse if you don't get up there."

"Well, I'm not going."

"Okay, you wait right here. We'll see whether you do or not." He left, and since I was tired, I lay down on my hammock until a two-stripe Navy petty officer came up to me, asking the sergeant if I were the guy. When the sergeant said I was, the petty officer pointed his finger at me and said, "You *will* go on KP. . . *now.*"

I looked at him and answered, "You *will* go straight to hell."

'That could be, too, soldier, but you're coming with us to the troop commander's office. He wants to have a talk with you."

An hour later I was back on deck with Crosse.

"What'd they want?" he asked.

"They wanted me to go on KP."

"Aren't you going?"

"Not no, but *hell no.*"

"You can get busted for that, you know."

'Now he tells me."

He enjoyed it when I explained that I thought because it was a Navy ship, they couldn't order the Army to do things like that. What I didn't know was that the troops were actually commanded by a major. He could, and *did* bust men. I had an empty sleeve to prove it. About an hour passed before I felt sorry I had been that way and went to the sergeant, apologizing. I volunteered for night KP and pulled it for the balance of the trip. It was miserable trying to sleep in the daytime in the hold, but I was occupied and I felt better about it.

Yokohama, Japan was the only stop we made, and then a short hop to Camp Drake for processing. The ship docked to the music of a band and cheering crowds of people on the pier.

We were all out on deck with our packs on, sitting on the baggage waiting for our names to be called out. The hillbilly with the guitar was still at it. We'd stand in one spot for a few minutes; move a step, stopping again. Then one man's name was called several times.

The sergeant came back from the head of the line, holding the roster in his hand. The boy with the guitar fell silent and jumped to his feet, putting the string of the handle around his neck. The guitar hung across his chest. The sergeant was furious.

"Are you the jerk that's holding up this line?"

"I didn't hear my name, Sarge, honest," the boy pleaded.

"Well get the hell up there, no one can get off the ship until you do! I oughtta break your neck!"

With that, he grabbed him by the arm, dragging his victim toward the gangplank. The boy half ran, half stumbled with his bags. The guitar was sticking out from both sides and as they passed between the line of men and a steel girder, it caught with a hollow 'twang.' Strings flew in all directions.

The last we saw of our guitarist friend was while he was trying to determine if had all the pieces, shouting vile things at the sergeant over the laughter of everyone on the ship and trying to keep in line with his baggage.

CHAPTER FOUR

THE PROCESSING through Camp Drake was accomplished in two days. We were briefed by a staff of people who were veterans of the Korean War, and a sergeant on the stage told us of his experiences there and what we could expect.

"Winter is coming to Korea," he said, "and most likely when it does, it will be different from any weather you've known before. Many of you have been used to being out in the cold for periods of time, but it's not the same as being exposed to it 24 hours a day."

He explained how we might have other complications, such as a greater number of enemy than we've ever heard of.

"Yeah, we know it's rough, Sarge. Tell us a war story," a wise guy called out from the rear of the theater.

The sergeant waited a moment or two before continuing, "I'm not trying to tell you a war story, but World War II was a gentleman's war compared to this one."

"Hey, get your steel pots on, he's gonna tell us a war story!" another heckler shouted.

"You're going to find out what it's like soon enough. I've been in both of them and I've been wounded in both of them. I know what they're like." He began weeping a little, and the audience liked it. "I don't want you to think I'm crying because of what you've been saying Ito me," he said, "I'm crying because you think you know so much. I've seen it happen before. I'm crying because I know what's going to happen to a bunch of smart-alecks like you who won't listen. It's bound to happen when you won't listen, when you talk too much. I can only wish you the best of luck."

And with that, he left the stage, his arms hanging at his sides. A captain came out, finished the instruction and we were through with Japan. We embarked for Korea.

The day before we landed in Inchon, I was talking with a swabbie working on the ship, about how damn crowded it was.

"Gawd, man, this is nothing. . .we have three times as many coming back as we have going over," he said.

"That's impossible," I replied, "you couldn't get that many in this tub."

"The hell you say. . .we've had six times this many on board."

"Where could you put that many?"

"Very simple," he stated, gesturing with his hands, "they come back in boxes, six-by-three-by-three. We just stack them up *'this high.'* " He laughed, showing yellow, decayed teeth. He looked the type.

*   *   *

Three days after leaving Yokohama, we were in Inchon Harbor. Even from two miles out, loading onto LCTs to move to the beach, we could hear artillery. My pulse raced and my head hammered to think the fighting was that near. Rumors were spreading that Inchon was becoming a battlefield again. My orders read that I was to go south to an air-ground liaison group as a radio-repairman. I felt guilty, being a rear-echeloner.

The sounds of artillery were set to a tempo, a tempo suggesting urgency. The call came to gather equipment and load onto the boats that were to take us in. About six hundred men crowded and jammed their way into each one. There was no room to sit down, no room to do anything but stand for what seemed like hours. It was cold and the spray broke over the bow, drenching us. As soon as we were free from the confines of the barge, we raced to the beach and gathered around the fires in an effort to dry off and get warm.

Hour upon hour was consumed in getting men assigned to units and loaded onto trucks for departure. One name at a time. Leave it to the Army to louse things up if it's at all possible. Always the hard way.

After a while, when the captain who had been calling the names sat down on a duffel bag for a break, I walked over to him. A clip-board was on his lap, and he rubbed his eyes.

"Captain, do you have any idea how much longer we'll be here?" He glowered at me. "What a helluvva question! Do I know how long you'll be here? How in the name of hell should I know? I just call out the names as I see them. Settle down and wait your turn." He shot my optimism right then and there, but I wasn't about to give up that easily.

"But Captain, they've got me down for an air-ground liaison group in Pusan. I don't wantta go there, I wantta go to a front-line outfit; the Second Division."

"Well don't worry about it. This whole stinkin' place is frontlines. They're shooting everywhere. You should be glad as hell to get such an assignment. There are a lot of men up there on the lines who are giving their lives just to stop fighting. How about that?" he shot back.

"I know that, but I'm an infantryman, and I want back in my old outfit. Isn't there something you can do?"

"Impossible. I'm in the Army the same as you. I only carry out orders like anybody else. When you get to your outfit in Pusan you can get your orders changed to the Second then. Now go away and stop bothering me."

I was both humiliated and furious. There were so many guys trying to keep *out* of the war and *getting* it, and I couldn't get there by asking. I returned to my equipment and waited some more. Around us were French, Greeks and English who had been hospitalized and waiting to go back to their units. The steady hum of activity crowded out the more distant sounds of battle. As soon as a truck was loaded, it moved out, taking men to their organizations. I tried a cup of coffee. It was ice cold. I spat out the mouthful I had taken. I paced and waited, waited and paced. Still my name wasn't called. Finally, they stated that no more shipments would be made that night and we were taken to our sleeping quarters. We were assigned to squad huts in Ascom City—five men to the room. Crosse and I were in the same one.

The hut was typical of Korean houses—mud walls and dirt floors. We had no blankets, so overcoats were our only cover. Two men who had been wounded, shared our room with us. About three o'clock in the morning, after tossing and turning before getting to sleep, we were awakened by a sergeant who came into the room cussing and kicking our feet. He made several remarks about, "Stateside bastards—why don't you get up there and fight?"

He walked over to where one of the men who had been wounded was sleeping and kicked his feet. It was more than I cared to see, and I jumped up from the floor and grabbed him. Someone yelled to leave him alone that he was drunk, but drunk or not, I wasn't going to watch him kicking someone around. He whirled and spat a mouthful of phlegm at me. As he did, I ducked and pushed him away. Before he had a chance to regain his balance, I hit him, full in the face. The solidness of his nose and mouth melted. Blood ran from both nostrils. If he was drunk, he sobered up almost instantly and began fighting back. We both rolled on the ground, through the door of the hunt out onto the path outside. In a few minutes, it was over and he left, wiping the blood on his sleeve. I felt better. If I couldn't get to the front to fight the Koreans, at least there was someone back here who needed it.

In a matter of a few hours we were back out again for roll call. By this time the Koreans had moved in and were trying to sell everything from souvenirs to pile caps. Many of the fellows were trying to trade jack-knives for women; the Koreans wanting two knives for a woman, and the GIs offering one. They couldn't get together.

About ten-thirty in the morning while a truck was being loaded to go north, I walked over and asked where they were going. "Second Division," a soldier answered. That was enough for me. I walked to the tail-gate and hopped on, just as the truck began to move.

Some men on the truck were returning to duty after being hospitalized. Others like myself, were fresh from the States. Most were nervous, especially the new ones. Someone began calling for the Koreans by the roadside to bring on the women. It wasn't long until we saw some of their rare beauties—relieving their bowels next to the road. Howls of delight went up from the truck. The women would wave back, continuing with their business. On each side of the road, refugees were making their way southward, the men for the most part, wearing white coats. I wondered how they kept from getting shot, in white clothing. It was no good for camouflage. Suddenly it occurred to me that I could not fight without weapons. Somehow, I had forgotten to bring my equipment when I jumped onto the truck.

One of the men who had been up on the lines before, told me that the Second Division was not far from a turn-off just ahead in the road. I asked to get off there, so when we came to the crossroad, I left the truck and started up the road.

A couple of the passengers waved as they disappeared from view. Then I began wondering, "Where in the hell am I, and what am I going to say to whom when I report in?" I shrugged it off and started down the road. I walked possibly two miles before stopping to rest.

I had a rifle now—picked up when I jumped off the truck. The man who was shorted wouldn't have to pay for it. You didn't have to pay for equipment lost in combat, I decided. *Combat.* It dawned on me that no one knew where I was or *who* I was. What if I got killed? Worse yet, what if they charged me with desertion? I dismissed it with a kick at a rock, and continued toward the Second Division.

At dusk, I came in sight of a camp and saw the numeral "2". Upon approaching the sign, I saw that it was the Second ROK Division! "This is really great," I said aloud. "Now I've really done it." At least it was the frontlines, maybe I could work in with them. I walked into the company area, waving at anyone who looked halfway friendly and making like the long-lost brother returning home.

Everyone stared at me, strangely. They must have wondered what an American was doing up there with them. I was referred to a Korean who spoke English and reported that I was a radio-repairman assigned to work with them. He looked blankly.

"A what?"

"Radio-repairman. I understand you've had some trouble with your equipment lately, and I came up to help."

He said something to an officer standing beside him and replied, "We no have radio. You sure you come Second Division?"

"This is the Second, isn't it?"

He nodded that indeed it was.

"Then it's the right place." I explained that I'd stay there until my unit picked me up, which probably would be the next day. I didn't want them to think I was new in Korea. I explained that the driver had left me off at the wrong place. They invited me over to a fire built nearby and handed me a wooden bowl half filled with rice. The others sat dumbly, their faces aglow in the firelight. It was getting very cold, and my field jacket was far too little to keep me warm.

I took a spoon carried in my pocket and began eating the rice. It was pasty, without seasoning. Then I lay near the fire and tried to sleep. The Koreans talked in their sing-song gibberish and pointed to the north. My interest waned. I turned my back to the fire and the front of me grew cold. I reversed it, and my after-portion froze. I tossed and turned all night, and watched them poke the fire half a dozen times.

Around dawn, the area was a beehive of activity. The North Koreans had attacked during the night and taken a hill a mile or so ahead. The South Koreans were moving up to take it back, the English-speaking officer informed me. I wanted to go, too.

As they grouped, I fell in behind. Half an hour later we were in sight of the men being pushed back, firing as they ran. It was hard to tell who was who—they all looked alike. Everyone was firing, so having two bandoliers of ammo, I joined in. Frankly, I didn't know what in the hell was going on or what I was doing there, but before long, when the retreaters were even with us, a line was established. It figured that since we were holding, the ones coming toward us must have been enemy. I fired constantly, not taking the luxury of aiming. I raised my rifle in the direction of a man who was charging and shot. He fell and rolled to his right, dropping over a ledge about ten feet high and lay motionless.

My *first* enemy, and there was no sense of repulsion or conquest, just complete indifference. It was get him or get killed myself. I liked it better the way it was. Ten minutes went by and my ammunition was gone. It was time for me to leave, so I helped a wounded man back to the battalion area.

Some Koreans carrying ammunition up the hill from the road running along the base of the hill showed me the route to Ascom City. While I was walking, a jeep with four Americans pulled up beside me.

"What are you doing up here?" the driver asked.

"I got separated from my outfit and tried to get to them but wound up with the Second ROKs instead."

"What outfit do you belong in?"

"23rd Regiment, Second Division."

"We can give you a lift back to Ascom City and you can get a ride up from there if you want to. C'mon, hop in."

Just what I didn't want! I naturally assumed that if I had said the 23rd, they'd have taken me to it, and since I had been with it in the States, I could stay with it. Now I was on my way back and worrying about whether I'd be court-martialed for desertion. The air was bitter cold and the others in the jeep were wearing pile-caps with the fur ear-tabs pulled down. I didn't have one, so I had to hold my ears with hands which by this time were blue with cold.

We stopped to eat and built a fire to heat "C" ration cans, but I wasn't as hungry as I was cold. I crowded closer to the fire. All of the men needed shaves. Their clothes were stinking, and stiff with dirt. They remarked that my uniform was comparatively clean, and asked where I had got clean clothes. I passed it off with the remark that I had traded with another man at the hospital, since he was going home. They wondered then if I had been wounded. I had to answer that I had been in for a check-up. I was ill at ease with them—they knew what the score was in Korea. I didn't.

I was offered some corned beef hash, and nearly vomited at the thought of eating. It had been too long, plus the fact that I couldn't stand corned beef hash. The smaller of the four men had a cold, and his nose was running. It had dried on the sleeve of his jacket where he'd wiped it. Another's trouser leg had a large dark spot where he'd repeatedly set ration cans on it, allowing the grease to soak in. I thought they could take more care with their appearance and at least keep clean. It was dark as we left to finish the trip.

Upon arriving there I went to the hut where Crosse and I had been, hoping he'd still be there. It was late, and he was asleep when I went in. I saw that my gear was still in the corner just as I had left it. I lit a candle and awakened Crosse.

"Where have you been?" he shouted. "They've been looking all over for you. You're in for it!"

I knew he wouldn't believe me if I told him I'd been up on the lines killing Koreans, so I said I had gone to Occo, a small town outside the camp and couldn't get back. He pointed out that it was four o'clock in the morning, and that I should be getting some sleep. I took his advice, but try as I may, I couldn't sleep. I lay there, digesting the sounds of trucks and artillery. At five o'clock I heard the call for chow, and for the first time in days, I was hungry.

The stringy stew we were served for breakfast and the stew and potatoes for lunch were impossible to eat. Word had it we were pushing north at the same time my name was called out to load onto a train going south. I was a little perturbed that nobody said anything further to me about being gone for two days. Is an individual so insignificant, I wondered?

* * *

Whenever I think of trains, I'll remember with disfavor, the ride from Inchon to Pusan. No coaches—only boxcars. Seventy men to each car with only the heat from our bodies to keep us warm. We were on a single track, and northbound trains had priority, so whenever one came through, we'd pull over on a siding to wait. Koreans clung to the train like baby opossums on their mother's back. Occasionally one of them would fall off to be crushed by the wheels. It scarcely made a bump.

It was colder than I thought it could ever get, and the snow falling on us in the open cars added to our misery. It was too crowded to lie down to sleep, so we assumed any position that was half-way comfortable.

There was very little sleep to be had. The temperature got down to zero, and for chow we had cold rations to eat.

Nine days later, we arrived in Pusan; cold, dirty and completely disgusted. Crosse was shipped further south and I reported to my outfit where I was assigned to a radio team, which coincidentally was ordered up to the lines with a sergeant in charge.

"What will we be doing up there?" I asked.

"Assisting the forward observers in different outfits. We'll furnish them radios and take care of the repair work."

"How close to the lines? Will we get into any fighting?"

"Yeah, we'll get into it," he growled.

"How close to the lines?"

"A mile or two, why are you so anxious?"

"I'm not anxious, just—," I paused, searching for the word, then discovered that I was anxious after all. "I guess I am at that. What outfit will we be with?"

"The Second Division," he replied. My heart skipped a beat. At last I would be back with them. I didn't have any idea who, if anybody, was left in the regiment I'd known before, but I was certain that I could get back with them by just telling that I'd been in the 23rd in the States, Eventually, we arrived on the flank of the Second and went to work.

We helped repair radios and tested circuits for several days, and as it became increasingly boring, another man and I decided we'd *really* get to the front lines to see what was happening. We went. The other man, who was as anxious as I to view something spectacular, was equally disappointed in the front's quietness. Not even a firefight to interrupt the lull. When we got back the next day, we found the rest of the radio unit had received orders to move. None of the men in other outfits around us knew where our group had gone. We elected to remain where we were.

My new found friend thought it over seriously before asking, "What do you think of going to the 23rd? You said you knew someone there. . . do you?"

"I don't suppose all of them are gone. There should be someone I know. Why, you wantta go up there with them?"

"The big poop has it that they're involved in some kind of a big fight. We might get caught in a trap or something. Whattya think?"

"Let's go," I exclaimed, simultaneously lunging for the jeep.

Two hours later we were with the regiment, at least what was left of it *and* several others. They were re-grouping and organizing for something big. Rumors were that it would be a push to the Yalu. MacArthur had promised we'd be home for Christmas. Activity was at a high peak. We all knew we'd merely have to get to the Yalu, and that would be it. Homeward bound. . .the Old Man had said so. Conversation about it was wholesale. Hopes were high.

"The 7th Division is already up there building a camp," one man said. "The ROKs have more men on the Yalu now than all of China's population. Hell. . .it's as good as over," his partner replied.

CHAPTER FIVE
November, 1950

THE TEMPERATURE dipped into the minus twenties, and more equipment was issued as we were worked into a spirit of conquest. Then the big attack came off—only it was from *north* of the Yalu. The Chinese hit us with thirty divisions, and our attacks turned to a new direction. They were made by UN troops all right; trying to break out of traps they were in, surrounded by enough enemy to tax anyone's imagination. The "cops" in the "Police Action," felt like rookies trying to round up the Al Capone gang with sling-shots. Somehow, I found myself with the 38th Regiment.

On the 28th of November, we were holding an area around Ku-ju-dong, and being hit by Chinese from virtually every angle. We were pushed back. All of the company officers were either killed or wounded in a couple of days. The entire division was retreating, and upon reaching Kuneri, the 1st Battalion had been assigned the mission of rear-guard for the remainder of the forces.

The 2nd Battalion went to help the 1st; and while we were being hit so many times, so fast and by so many, I envisioned MacArthur standing majestically in his class "A" uniform, gold-braid and all, viewing his troops from a huge bandstand. From the comer of his mouth, he said to me, *"You'll be home by Christmas, Herb."*

But abruptly he changed his mind, and his location. Instead of being on a review-stand, he was running across the Pacific Ocean, and I was pulling his rear-guard as millions of Chinese chased us. Mac turned to me while running, and said, *"See, I told you, Herb—home by Christmas."* The day-dream was disturbed by a sergeant who spoke to me.

"We've got to get some help up here, do you know where the Turks are?" he asked.

"Gawd, I don't know. Don't have any idea."

"I just wondered. I can tell you where they are; I'd hoped you'd know their location. I'd like to send you for them if you'll go. I don't have anyone to spare. How 'bout it?"

"Sure, I'll go. Cheezus, did you ever see so many Chinks?"

It took about an hour to get to the Turks who were straining like race horses at a starting gate. They wanted to get into the fight. An officer had them on their way in a matter of minutes. On the return trip, artillery and patches of Chinese prevented us from using the route I had travelled before. None of the Turks with me spoke English, but after arguing for some time, it was agreed through gestures, that another route would have to be taken. We arrived at a little town above Kuneri, hoping for still another route that would eventually bring us out to the 23rd.

There was no special formation during the march. It was cold, bitter cold, and approaching a village directly ahead of us, we saw Chinese troops leaving it, going north. We scattered, and lay in wait for more than an hour, trying to determine if they were returning or if the village had truly been abandoned. We chose the latter, and with our weapons at the ready, pressed on into the town, hugging close to the buildings. My comrades whispered to each other in Turkish. Since I had no one to talk with, I conversed with myself, receiving no intelligent answers in return.

The village was deathlike. There was absolute silence, except for the resonance of far-off artillery. Silvery moonlight spilled a glow that appeared heavy enough to be cut, almost like thick fog. *A sound startled me!* I leaped through the doorway of a hut, and something struck me in the back of my neck! I whirled, ready to fire, but the bullets would have struck nothing except the mud walls of the hut. In the dimness of the room, my vision began to clear. I shook my head as though it would hasten the process. The object which had cuffed me was the foot of a man's body, hanging by the wrists from a rafter. His arms were stretched out and over his head so that he formed a "Y". He looked like Christ on the Cross; head bent down, helpless. I reeled at the sight. The body was moving, but only slightly. I had disturbed it.

Most of the Turks arrived by this time, and spoke excitedly to each other. Soon the entire group was assembled in and around the hut. The shouts of some of the men outside, promised still more victims in other buildings. The man I'd found was dead. Not long though—his body was still warm.

Dashing into the night air to see what the Turks had discovered, I was guided by one of them to an opening between two buildings where many others had been strung up in the same fashion. Some were obviously dead, their heads smashed and hair matted with blood. One of them was a captain. His bars had been removed from his jacket collar and the pin was thrust through the skin on his forehead, directly over his nose. His head was bent, and the two silver bars gleamed in the moonlight, dangling meaninglessly.

He labored to lift his head from his chest so he could speak. It required super-human strength, and his energy lay on the frozen ground in a pool of blood.

We did as much as we possibly could for them, cutting the living ones down, to make them comfortable before they died. In a matter of an hour, they were all dead. Twenty-one Americans, who but a few hours before had been defending the village against the Chinese. The area around their crucifixion was like a slaughter house, with blood spattered walls where they had fought, undoubtedly screaming against the torture of having their abdomens slashed open by bayonets. Some resisted until their intestines had whipped about under them as they hung suspended, creating bloody circles within which the organs were frozen. I was sick, and I was worried.

A hand rested on my shoulder and someone said, *"GI! GI!"*

I was snapped back to reality and looking into the grim face of a Turk. I had been lost in the thoughts of happenings long gone by. The youth who had reminded me of the unanswered questions all of us carry within ourselves, was still hanging before me. The Turk spoke again, "Gel GI, gideium!" From his actions, it was definite that he wanted me to move. Apparently the Turks were becoming concerned about the Chinese returning. From the looks in their eyes and the way they fondled their bayonets, I knew that the Chinese would not get more victims for the empty doorways of other buildings here.,

I asked for the radio. "Radyo? Orada," he said, pointing to his right. I moved to the radio set and endeavored to adjust the frequency setting. The radioman took my hand away from the dial. It was already tuned in to the 23rd. Ten minutes later I made contact with the battalion's radioman who advised that they were surrounded and to try getting to Kuneri by using an escape route. I mentioned the name, *"Kuneri"* a couple of times to the Turks, drew a line showing the escape route, as it was told to me, and we moved out.

Glancing back at the men who had been killed by the Chinks, I said a silent Rosary for them.

The trip to *Kuneri* at best would consume about four hours, and by then it would be daylight. I hadn't realized I was so tired, until we began moving. My muscles were stiff and sore from the walking and the cold which seemed to pierce my body like a million bullets.

Our column stretched out for what suggested to be miles; up hills and down, across valleys, to another hill, then climb again. Up and down. The sounds of small arms fire were growing nearer. Dawn was fast approaching. Suddenly the front of the column was hit by burp-guns from both the left and right. We scattered and set up positions. Then the point of attack shifted to the rear. Both ends of the column were fighting, like a two-headed snake.

Almost as unexpectedly as we had been hit by bullets, the Chinese launched a bayonet attack We continued firing on them until they got within bayonet range. The sounds of steel and cries of pain became entangled. The Turks were slashing and slicing the Chinese to pieces. At my side, one of them was fighting three Chinks. With the perfection of an expert, he made one sweep from the left to the right. The blade passed across the faces of all three of them, opening a deep gash. They dropped their weapons and reached for their wounds and just as quickly all three of them were bayoneted. He grinned with his achievement.

Never had I witnessed such a spectacle of knife-play. The Chinese were falling by the score, and we were cracking their defenses simultaneously. The first yellow fingers of a new dawn were spreading when we broke through. We had fought to the Sin-nan-ju—Hungnam Road, our destination. Men have been heard to say that a bayonet is good only for opening C ration cans. A good secondary use for it was found this night.

One more hill separated us from the position the 23rd had said they were holding. From the sounds in that valley, someone was catching hell. My blood froze as I realized that it was possible we had fought our way into Chinese positions. The hill overlooking the valley was reached. The sight was hard to stomach. On the serpentine road below were *thousands* of men and vehicles, bumper to bumper, moving slower than a snail's pace. Countless Chinese were on the hills across the valley. We were no longer a unit, scattered through the hills, so we drifted down to the valley to join the endless columns of the wounded, and the fighting. At least I thought they were fighting. Many were astride artillery pieces being towed by tractors. Others were half walking, half stumbling behind trucks that were barely moving. They looked more dead than alive.

I became annoyed. I recalled movie scenes where people had been condemned to death. They had stood blindfolded against a wall, making no effort to break away. What made the difference? They were certainly going to die and they might as well get killed fighting. These men were the same way. No fight left in them, just acquiescence to the inevitable. There was very little gun-firing at the moment.

From the head of the column, a tank was heard returning fire at a machine gun. A few of us went up to investigate, but before we had travelled fifty yards, we were caught in a mortar barrage. Shells burst in a walking pattern toward us. Men were standing up or crawling to get back a bit farther, only to be hit more seriously. A man next to me suggested that we relocate. He stood up, and at the same time a machine-gun fluttered on a distant hill. Bullets struck his body with a dull, sickening thud, passed through it and continued on. He coughed convulsively.

Small trucklets of blood were oozing out of his mouth between coughs, then gushing forth as each spasm hit him.

I called for the medic, but my plea was gulped down by gunfire and screams for aidmen from everywhere. Two of them would attempt to carry a wounded man out and suddenly they would all be gone. A direct hit would catch them. I turned back to see if I could assist the machine-gunned man. It was too late for anyone to help him. He was dead. The blood was not gushing now, only dripping from his cheek onto the ground. It froze almost the same instant it touched the ice.

Word came back that we were going to attempt piercing a fourteen mile road block. Before it had a chance to begin, however, a banzai attack hit. There were nearly a thousand screaming Chinese bent against destroying the measly hundred or so defending the hill and pass behind us. Gradually, the reaction of the events and the death of the man next to me made its way from my stomach to my brain. I argued that his death couldn't have happened so suddenly—then deduced that it wouldn't have, if he'd kept down.

The trucks stopped again. Drivers were deserting to scurry under their vehicles each time mortars began falling. "You stupid bastards, that's just what they want you to do, hold the column up!" someone cried out. "Get back in there and keep goin'!"

The drivers must have believed it was officers calling orders to them, for they got into the cabs of their trucks and started the procession again. Then the Chinese broke through our defenses. Once more we were fighting with bayonets. The sensation of my blade plunging into their bodies didn't at all compare with the sawdust dummies I'd practiced on so many times. In fact, the method wasn't the same. There were no parries or feints; just slash and slice, about the same as it had been to get to *Kuneri* with the Turks. Gradually we were pushed back from the pass. When we reached the road, vehicles and personnel were lined up as far as the eye could see. The Chinese commanded all the high ground and we were in a valley that was completely surrounded. Chinks stood on the ridgelines, like buzzards in a tree.

The few foxholes that existed were utilized. There was no barbed-wire, nothing to stop the onslaught. It was almost dark, and that meant there would be no air-drop for supplies. An entire day had all but vanished. Ammunition was desperately low. Whenever a man was hit, we'd grab his weapon and ammo. He wouldn't need it anyway.

A truck passed, loaded with wounded men. I fell in behind it, and was walking with my head down from fatigue when I slipped and fell to the ice. I scrambled to my feet, and found that my hands were covered with blood. The road's surface was coveted with streaks of fresh, liquid blood. I traced the trail, and with horror, saw that it was coming from a truck. Blood was sluicing from under the tail-gate, spilling onto the road. In my mind's eye I envisioned the many times I'd followed my brother on an ice route in the summertime, and how the water from melting ice would drip from the truck. I had always thought it was a tremendous waste of water. What a tremendous waste of men's blood.

Two men came my direction half crawling, half walking. One was missing his left arm. The other had lost both arms. They asked to get aboard one of the trucks. But there were already too many wounded on them. They lay intertwined, some unconscious, others writhing in pain. Many had stomach or chest wounds, and were bleeding profusely. It was impossible for anyone else to get into the truck. Another man helped me sort through the wounded. We found three dead ones, and removed them. The two armless men climbed on. From that time on we checked the trucks regularly to remove the dead. Then more living casualties could be carried. Corpses have never won a war yet. The wounded had priority.

This was our final stand in Kuneri Pass. Help could not be expected before morning. It was stay and fight, or stay and die—maybe both. Banzai attacks and mortar barrages sprung up more often after dark. We managed to stay down and survive most of them, but the vehicles in the valley were sitting ducks.

An enemy flare would go off in the sky, and everything assumed a ghastly red appearance. The wounded were screaming in the trucks. They were just lying there waiting for mortars to drop in on them.

There was very little medical aid. Under the conditions, it was impossible to get any. A truck would receive a direct hit and some of the screams would fall silent. Arms and legs would be blown off, whipping and spinning through the air to land several yards from the bodies of which they were once a part. The vehicles made good targets, bumper-to-bumper. All the Chinks had to do was lob mortars into the valley. They couldn't miss.

Apparently deciding mortars were too quick, too final, they switched to white phosphorous. Some of the wounded were unconscious and felt no pain, but the phosphorous burned deep holes through their flesh. It sizzled. Others were not so fortunate to be unconscious. Terrified, they were trying to raise themselves off the bottom of the trucks, and if successful, they were cut down by machine guns. Now and then one of the Chinese would infiltrate and run up to one of the trucks and toss a hand grenade in, screaming with laughter at the explosion. He'd be shot as soon as he was noticed, but by then, the damage had been done.

An artillery shell landed nearby, jarring the earth into my face. I was sick—sick of this enemy you couldn't fight on even terms. It was too impersonal. An artillery crew would go into action somewhere behind the hills and the next minute men were dead. How could you fight them if you couldn't see them, couldn't touch them?

Holes were appearing in the road increasingly, and trucks were abandoned as many drivers were killed. We were gradually breaking through the roadblock by a series of pull back and fight—pull back and fight. Men were crushed between trucks as they'd try to cross the road. The drivers were unable to stop in such a split second. Tanks began coming up to assist. Someone running across the road would get shot, and fall onto the roadway. The tankers, unable to see, would run over them. The sounds of battle and powerful roar of tanks drowned out the sounds of bones being crushed. I saw a man's face fill with horror as he realized that he was about to die. Thankfully, his screams were drowned under the churning treads of the tank. His face froze with an unexplainable expression—then nothing more. In a brief second he was dead, knowing only for a moment, what was happening. In the confusion it was unavoidable, but ghastly.

Three men lying in a ditch at the side of the road were screaming to be shot. I was knocked into a hole when a mortar came in. Almost at the same time, a flare hit the sky. An American soldier lay in the hole with me, his flesh seared by white phosphorous. His face was twisted in an agonized sneer. It was a mass of phosphorous burns.

"Go ahead you yellow bastard, shoot me!" he screamed.

"I'm not going to shoot you, I'm a GI myself," I replied.

"I don't believe you!"

"Well, look at me!"

"I'd like to be able to see you, I'd like to see anything."

With a horrible repulsion, I saw that he was blind. Both eyes had been burned out by WP. Helping him out of the hole, I got him on a truck with other wounded. It hadn't traveled fifty feet when it got a direct hit, killing all of them. He was better off anyway.

Walking and fighting, clammering for holes during barrages and helping the wounded was exhausting. My throat was parched from gunpowder smoke. I was thirsty. Unconsciously I broke an icicle from the bed of a truck and began sucking on it. The liquid relieved the dryness, but tasted dirty and salty. Thinking it was merely dirt that was frozen in the water, I tried downing it more hurriedly. In the moonlight it appeared to be black. My hands looked black, too. They were wet with blood. The icicle was frozen blood! I couldn't vomit, much as I wanted to. My stomach refused to cooperate. I could only remember once in my life that I had ever vomited, and that was when I had tried to drink a glass of seltzer. I wanted a seltzer.

We were emerging from the fourteen mile perimeter, and coming across men who had been in what was once a rear echelon. They were lying at the sides of the road and everything showed that they had suffered before they finally were blessed with death. The Chinese had jumped on their stomachs so they would burst and then strewn their guts on the rocks beside the body. Maybe the Chinks would cut their legs off before killing them, and after the disemboweling, would wrap intestines around their necks or drape them across the faces of the dead and dying.

A lieutenant came asking for help. His leg had been blown away, but others were even worse off. I wanted to help everyone of them, but it was humanly impossible. I would assist one and then fire at the Chinese some more, then get someone else on the overloaded trucks. A tank carrying wounded was passing through, so the lieutenant got on it. Ahead of it was a truck, also loaded with men. It came to a curve in the road at the same time an M-26 medium tank came roaring toward it. The tank nudged the truck very lightly in passing, but it was enough, and the truck being the lighter of the two, went rolling over an embankment, spilling its human cargo across the mountainside. Bodies flailed into the air, some landing ahead of the truck, only to be crushed under it as it hit the ground and bounced up, rolling again and again.

Air support and more tankers came in the morning with replacements and firepower. I came across the lieutenant I had helped onto the tank. He was killed about five miles from where I had last seen him. A bullet hole between the eyes. There were two of the original group missing, so I guess they got back all right. All the others were with the lieutenant, dead.

Four days of holding action, four days of killing thousands of Chinese and seeing over six thousand American and UN troops killed, and we were out of the Kuneri Pass, back to a holding action. Then guerilla warfare started. We were harassed by rifle fire from the hills around us. In one skirmish, I felt my first wound of the war, a bullet hole in the right leg, but it was serious enough to be hospitalized. I began to cuss about the whole damn mess. Of all the mortar fire we had been subjected to and automatic weapons fired at us, I hadn't got a single scratch, then some damn guerilla had to plunk a bullet into me. You can't win.

I remembered that during the hottest of the battles, the only men I heard who even began to measure up to real morale, were some men in "Easy" Company of the 38th Regiment. That's the way I liked it.

If they could joke about the tough spot they were in and still keep fighting, that's the outfit I wanted to be in. I decided that when I got back to my own outfit, my transfer was going to be to the 38th. *Oh hell!* I remembered that I was actually *AWOL* from the air-ground liaison outfit in Pusan! It would be kind of hard to explain when I got back, but I wasn't going to stay there anyhow, so it didn't matter. I would have to apply for a transfer to the division through channels. Goddam Army channels, always a way to snarl things up. I felt like I'd been kicked in the groin by the Chinese. I wanted to get even with them for it. In the meantime the big retreat down the peninsula continued, almost running out of ground on which to fall back.

Upon arriving in Pusan, I requested the transfer. It bounced from one basket to another for ten days before I was notified that it had been disapproved. I didn't wait for the papers themselves to get back to me. The next morning I slung my rifle on my shoulder and hitch-hiked to *Taegu*. At the replacement depot, I reported in as a hospital returnee. There were so many returnees, that in the confusion, they accepted my word.

The first night there I met two men from Easy Company of the 38th, Corporal Sowers and a fellow named Irwin whom we learned to call "Self-Propelled" because he had been in a self-propelled outfit with the 82nd Airborne.

"You don't want to go back to the 23rd, Herbert," Sowers said, "there's probably nobody left there you knew anyway. Why not come to the 38th?"

The 38th was the regiment I'd seen with such high morale at Kuneri. I hadn't forgotten, either, how hard it is for a new man coming into an infantry outfit. The people are not hostile, by any means, but there is a certain lack of response until you've actually been in combat with them. In Sowers and "Self-Propelled," I at least had two friends from the start. I decided to go with them. They had just been returned to duty from being hospitalized, so as names were called off for the trucks, I pretended to be a wounded returnee. The bandages on my leg strengthened the deception, and since my records were someplace else, and all they knew at the loading area was our names, I merely got on a truck headed for the 38th.

"Our captain will be glad you came up, and we've got a good bunch of fellows in our outfit, too," Sowers said, as we pulled away from Taegu. I felt good.

CHAPTER SIX
December, 1950

Upon arriving at battalion, we were briefed and sent to company. I was singled out as a replacement and taken by Dave Birnstein, for zeroing in. It was at that moment that I became exposed to the humor, and the downright malarkey, that was his trademark. "You see that bridge we're going to cross up there?" he asked. "Yes."

"We've crossed it at least four times—just up and back. Things have been mighty rough. They'll probably shoot us back over it again tonight." He looked at his watch as he said it. "Usually about ten-thirty is when it hits. They start sending artillery in and follow it up with *taku-san* Chinese. *'Taku-san'* is a lot, in case you're not up your Oriental phrases."

"Birnstein, don't give me a lot of garbage, will you? I've been in combat before. In fact, I was up at Kuneri. I know what it's like."

"You were at Kuneri? What outfit?"

"All of them. There was no way of telling who was who," I replied, sensing that he didn't believe me. "I was in a radio outfit at the time."

"What a deal," he chuckled, "just sit and talk on a radio. How do you get a racket like that, I've often thought I'd like to get into it. Got a connection?"

"Cut it out, will you?" I was beginning to get a little sore at his ribbing. "I was a rifleman, just like I want to be here. I've got no connections and not looking for any. That answer your question?" He looked startled. "Sure, sure—don't get all shook up. Hell, we're all in this thing together. But you got nothin' to worry about; I'll teach you the ropes and you got nothing to worry about. I'm an old hand at this and'll teach all there is to know. Just stick with me."

"Just take care of yourself, will you? I'll handle me," I replied. We reached the bridge and crossed it, turning left toward a group of houses where small camp fires were burning. Birnstein introduced everyone there at the time and I settled down to listen to their conversations. Before they had talked for five minutes, Sowers came into the area. Everyone jumped up and grabbed him, shaking hands, ruffling his hair and slapping him on the back. He was welcomed home.

"Tate and I were telling the boys last night you were due back," the fellow named Dickson was saying, "How's it going back in the area?"

"Fine. How's it going up here?"

"Great. Cheez it's good to see you back, Sowers. The feet okay?" Tate questioned.

"They're alright. Been lost lately?" Everyone laughed when Sowers asked that.

"Did you hear how we got fouled up a while back?" Dickson directed toward everyone crowded around, "Sowers here got his feet frozen and wound up with a vacation. See any *real women* back there?" Then before Sowers could answer, Dickson began re-explaining their escapade. His buddy smiled tolerantly. "Six days we were lost," Dickson continued, "Six days behind the lines, not knowing which way was which."

"I knew," Tate said; "you two didn't, that's all."

"Whattya mean we didn't?" Sowers argued, "I know north from south—you guys couldn't make up your minds where the hell to go." Then all three laughed.

"That's the way it was, no one agreeing with anyone else," Tate replied. "Only trouble was, Sowers got frost-bit a little worse than we did and was able to go back for a short rest."

The story flowed out, little by little. I visualized it as they talked. It was old hat to the men who listened, but the three had been given up for dead, so we all heard the version when everyone was together for the first time in weeks.

The situation had not been unlike that at Kuneri. They had been surrounded and cut off from any escape, which left them wandering aimlessly for six days. The main trouble was, they had gotten mixed up in their directions, and gone north instead of south! They met a Korean kid, who, after getting a hat for a present, disclosed the right direction for escape. They had travelled by night and slept by day.

As the talk continued, bringing Sowers up to date on what had transpired during his absence, Birnstein motioned for me to go with him. We went to one of the huts being used for shelter. They were of the conventional mud-wall Korean variety, with four or five men sharing each of them. The men had covered most of the wall's surface with multi-colored blankets and silks they'd found when the town was captured. It suggested the inside of a Reno gambling club, in more ways than one. A poker game was going full blast, and someone kept calling, "Give me the bug."

"That's 'Bugs' Hoover," Birnstein explained. " 'He's always yelling for the 'bug'. Aces, straights and flushes, you know."

I met the men I was to live with for the rest of my time in Korea. Some of them got up and shook hands with me, while others just nodded acknowledgment of the introduction. After watching the game for awhile, we went outside.

"What's your first name? I hate to keep calling you by your last."

"Dave's the first name, but everyone calls me Birnstein."

"Mine's Tony. What's the scoop on them? Who and what are they?"

"Well, McPherson's platoon sergeant. Used to be in the 82nd Airborne. He's about twenty, I think. We kid him about the time he went AWOL. When he came back, the old man told him he'd never make a soldier. That was back in the States, but in the four months he's been over here, he's gone from PFC to master. The old man made him master, too. Mac's plenty strict, but a helluvva good guy. You'll like him. Lt. Sokolski is airborne, too. 11th, as I recall. Dickson's married and got three kids. He was in the Reserves and got called back in, even though he'd had four years on the line during World War II. And, let's see—"he said, trying to give me data on everyone, "You've got Sgt. Brinnon, also married and has one kid. He's a good guy, always getting mail from home. Probably gets more than all of us put together. His kid signs some of the letters, too. I don't think he goes to school, though. Brinnon's a draftee. Then there's Crandell, and Annus who used to be in the numbers racket, and Joe Buckholtz. You'll get to know all of them anyway, no sense worrying about that now."

"Who's got the squad?" I asked.

"King. Forgot to mention him. He's a good Joe, too. Hell, they all are," he said, flinging his hands away from his sides, "No sense trying to say who is and who isn't. The amazing thing is the age. We figured it out one time and it averaged less than 21 years. I'm glad to see them finally settling down to a game of poker. They've been pretty hard to get along with for a few days."

"Why, morale low?"

"No, it isn't exactly low, just lacking in altitude, so to speak. We've been getting hit pretty hard for a long time now and have lost a helluvva lot of good guys. It's rough sometimes. Take the rest of the guys. . . they get in a bad mood and the first thing you know, they're snapping at each other.

McPherson and Carboni, our medic, got in a fist fight yesterday. Last thing I ever expected to see, but it didn't last long. When it was over they shook hands, laughed about it and Carboni patched Mac up. Crazy bunch."

Mentally I evaluated the information he'd given me on all of them, and without hesitation, I felt accepted. It's a difficult thing to explain, but until you've got something in common with infantrymen, such as patrols or an attack, you're just not one of them. It seemed different with these fellows. Birnstein began talking again.

"Here's the situation as I understand it now, if anyone can. That's one of the things that keeps us all shook up, not knowing half the time what the hell's going on. We hold half of this town—the Commies the other half. We've got to keep that bridge you see there. We've been gettin' run back and comin' back for about a week. Right now we're understrength to beat hell. See that railroad?"

"Yeah."

"They're just across it. That's the other side of the tracks. Maybe they say we live on the wrong side, who knows?"

"Why is it so quiet?" I asked. Only the occasional 'whump' of artillery broke the stillness.

"Hard to tell. That's what's so damn hard up here. One minute it's like this, then wham!—you get the book thrown at you. You don't know what to look for, except the worst. It's a bitch, but like I say, I'll teach you the ropes, just stick with me."

"Get off that stuff will you, for cripes sake!" I clipped.

"Just trying to help. Forget it. Hungry?" he asked.

"Now that you mention it, yes I am. How soon's chow?"

"That's why I asked if you were hungry," Dave replied, "They just got here with it. We'll have to go over to that jeep trailer. That's the mess-hall." We began walking toward the jeep. "Man, what garbage they serve up here. You'll see what I mean."

He went to a duffel bag and rammed his arm down into it, pulling forth two mess gear, caked with cold grease. Dumping spare-rib bones out of them, he handed one to me.

"Where do you wash them?" I asked.

"Wash them?" he laughed, "I've got news for you, brother. You don't!"

"You mean you're supposed to eat out of them this way?"

"Either this way or not at all. We don't have enough water up here to brush our teeth, and you worry about dirty mess gear."

"Didn't they ever hear about sanitation regulations?"

"The regulations stayed with the sanitation back in Pusan."

"I'll be dipped in sheep dip." I muttered, and handed the gear to someone else. I dropped out of the line. Ours was the last platoon to eat. The jeep had been making the rounds all morning. It always seemed that for something good, like eating, your outfit was last. But when it came to patrols, naturally it was first.

I got hungry again, picked up one of the messkits and wiped it out with my hand. The grease left it greasy and clammy. When I got through the mess line, all they had left was one pancake. I elected to search through the village for rabbits or chickens, or cats, dogs—anything to eat. Birnstein went with me.

We looked in, under and around every building in our area, but couldn't find a thing. Dave beckoned me to the corner of a building. "Do you see what I see?" he asked, pointing to an ox. "Care for some beef?"

"Hell yes, why not?"

He walked up to the ox, very cautiously. It made no move. He ran his finger over its forehead, making an "X" in the hair. Then he stepped back and drew his .45. Taking careful aim at the disinterested bull, he fired. I blinked with the explosion. He missed. He raised it again and fired five more times. *Still* the bull stood looking at him.

"You couldn't hit a bull in the head with a .45." I exclaimed.

Dave began to grin, then changed his mind. The bull was snorting with anger, and was about to charge. He danced around in front of it, not knowing in which direction to go. The bull was moving toward him with his head down. Birnstein side-stepped and grabbed his adversary around the neck. They were going in circles, Dave wanting to let go, but not daring to. Then he fell in a hole with the beast of burden standing over him in a half-kneeling attitude.

As soon as the bull stood still, I began firing with my BAR. Bullets ripped a tattoo across his body and he crumpled, rolling over on Dave. Blood was pouring onto my new friend. He thought he'd been ripped to pieces, and was screaming like a mad-man. I could tell that he wasn't hurt; he was actually sheltered by the hole, and the bull was merely holding him in it, rather than lying on him. I began laughing, and the more he struggled, the harder I laughed. I went to help him up, but by then I was laughing so hard and the ox was so heavy, I couldn't move him. Dave was too scared to help himself. Some of the men who had heard the firing ran to find out what was happening. Together, we finally got our buddy out of the hole, a mess of blood from head to foot.

Someone asked, "Why don't we butcher him?"

"He looks like he's already been butchered. Besides, what could we tell his next of kin."

"I'm not talking about Birnstein, I mean the ox."

"Beg your pardon."

One of the men, who had been a butcher before he came into the Army, said you couldn't butcher until the body heat had left the animal's body. He said it was unethical. Unethical or not, the bull was without two legs even before his twitching stopped. We built a fire and had steak, but it was lousy. The ox must have been fifty years old. It was a lot better than pancakes, though.

CHAPTER SEVEN
December, 1950—January, 1951

LATE IN THE afternoon I was told I would go out on a patrol that night. They said they were sorry to send me out that quickly on my first day in the company, but everyone was exhausted. However, it would just be a listening post.

At six o'clock, Birnstein, Self-Propelled, Sowers, Crandell, Tate and I were being briefed by King, who was in charge.

"We're going out to LP 5 for the night," he was saying. "There shouldn't be any trouble, we'll just lie low and watch for other patrols and guerillas. With the exception of Herbert, we've all been on LP's before. All you'll have to do Herbert, is listen for unannounced company. Got it?" I nodded that I understood and we moved out.

The LP was about two miles from the company area, but in Korea, two miles can be a mighty long walk up one hill and down another, climbing until your lungs and legs give out on you. Only you can't stop to rest.

We set up on the hill we were to use as a vantage point. It was a good one, and was shaped almost like an ice-cream cone with a near-vertical face looking to the north. Crandell and I did not have sleeping bags, since most of the company's had been lost during the last retreat, abut he did have one blanket. I lay between Birnstein and King, with their sleeping bags touching me. It did not offer warmth, but psychologically, it had a purpose. We settled down for the long wait.

The silence became weighty and oppressive. If you listened, you heard your heart beat. I could hear Sowers breathing as he gazed intently into the night. Occasionally he'd whisper for us to quit stirring, to get comfortable and lie quiet. The night cold was creeping into my body, pinching and nipping. I dozed and was about as comfortable as I could get under the circumstances, when what we thought was the sound of a tank brought us all awake. All that is, except Birnstein. Even a tank couldn't wake him up.

"What is it, Sowers?" King called out.

"I don't know, I'm trying to figure out where it's coming from. Better wake Birnstein. He's the only one still sleeping."

I reached over to shake him and discovered that his helmet was gone. I asked, "Do you suppose we heard his helmet rolling down the hill?" There was a collective sigh of relief. Somebody said, "Hell yes, that's what it was. He does that kind of stuff all the time. Someday I'm gonna use him to zero my M-1 in."

It must not have taken more than five or ten minutes to drop off to sleep again. As a hush settled over the night, someone began screaming for help. His voice was muffled and terrified. Crandell jumped up, lunged over the edge of the hill and grasped the edge of a sleeping bag, about to begin a head-long flight down the hill's icy slope. It was Dave again, only this time he had gotten upside down inside the bag. In his sleep he had worked to the edge of the hill. He fought like a madman until we could get him awake and out of the bag.

"Well if they don't know we're here now, they never will," Sowers said. As if pondering the possible outcome of the disturbance, he asked, "Which way are we going to go, that's the question. Which way?" Possibly deciding to face that eventuality when it presented itself, he settled down to continue his watch. The rest of us went back to sleep after warning Birnstein against any more such outbursts.

I lay there for a long time, looking at the stars above me, and considered that they were the same stars that gleamed over home, too. The thought occurred to me that it was not night back home—in fact it was actually the day before. We were west of the international dateline. We'd gained a day coming across the ocean. I rolled over and propped my elbows under me, looking out toward the darkness that contained the enemy. I worried about whether the rest of the platoon would like me. I'd be in a helluvva shape if they didn't. Maybe they'd think I was a bit too independent. Where would I be if they did? I couldn't get anywhere. I was all too fully aware that in times like these, it took the utmost cooperation of everybody, myself included.

I believe that for about half an hour, every thought that enters the mind of a man on an outpost or on a line of resistance, found mine. War is a great deal like the operation of a railroad, with its engineers in the front and his crew behind him. Only in war it's reversed. . .the crew is up front and the engineer directs them from the rear. The directors wear stars, too. A lot different than a striped hat and red bandanna around the neck.

The idea impressed me, and I was about to search into it further when Crandell began shaking us awake, exclaiming in a hushed voice that he had heard something. In a matter of seconds, everyone was in a firing position, waiting for the unknown. We were a few feet from each other on the ridgeline. To my left was Tate—to my right Birnstein. The exciting promise of meeting up with the Commies again and the cold biting at me were too much. I began shivering.

"What's the shaking for, Herb? I told you I'd take care of you, didn't I?" Dave whispered.

"Good, you can have my rifle and then you'll have two. You can shoot 'em from the hip like Roy Rogers," I told him. He just grinned.

Birnstein was a man of about twenty-four, with dark brown hair and serious brown eyes. He looked as though he might have been a bit near-sighted, judging from the lenses in his glasses which made his eyes appear a trifle small. But when he smiled, it was with a great deal of warmth. It was this appearance which gave the impression of sincerity—someone you could depend on. At that particular time though, the only thing it seemed you could depend on him for was to louse you up. Maybe it was an attack coming off on the hill that they'd discovered was occupied by the incident with the helmet and the yelling he'd come out with, moments earlier.

The next hour or so was a series of hearing a sound and trying to determine what it was, where it came from and what it meant. It was six o'clock before King decided to take us in.

On the walk back I mentally digested the events as they'd been experienced since my arrival in Korea. My eyes searched the hills, lying like rolling waves on an ocean. They were endless. Never had I expected to see a country with such a complete absence of level land. Some of the rises lay invisible in the haze of early morning, a pale blue-gray that seemed to defy penetration. The taller hills near us projected their peaks into the mist that was crisp, but heavy. The morning was perfectly still, just as it always is in Korea—when the war is elsewhere. The air was cold, and although the sun was beginning to appear, it was without warmth. I stamped breath into my feet a few times as I walked. From behind the curtain of distance, light small arms fire cracked, like the burning wood of a campfire. It was detached from us. Another man's war.

The day was primarily spent by resting and getting acquainted with other men in the company. "Self-Propelled" had gotten the machine-gun he'd asked for and was treating it like you would a baby. Carboni had received a new thermometer from home. He was testing it. "Holy hell!" he exclaimed. "It's 17 below!"

"It's not a far flung from it!" someone called back.

"No, it actually is, now I'm really gonna be cold since I know the temperature." Carboni replied.

"You know what you are?" Dave asked.

The medic's head whipped around as if he were about to be insulted, then with a tinge of 'irritation in his voice, questioned. "No, suppose you tell me."

"Man, you ain't nothin'," was the reply.

"Whattya mean—nothin'?"

"You ain't nothin' but. Nothin' but right, that is." Birnstein laughed. "I'm colder already since you said it was 71 below."

"I didn't say 71, I said 17." Carboni replied, then added, "You can't hear for listenin'."

A few days passed with only routine patrols, some with contact, some without. The weather became more bitter. Our line, which extended northward on the right, cut sharply to the south on our left. It seemed to be stable enough, at least we didn't move much, up or back. Before we knew it, Christmas was upon us.

A new man who had been assigned to the company the day after I came, seemed to spend most of his time with papers on his lap. He was hard at work trying to decipher something. That evening he called out, "Hey you guys, listen to this, someone's a poet!" Proudly sorting the papers he'd discovered, he began:

"Twas the night before Christmas and all through the tent
Was the odor of fuel oil (the stove pipe was bent);
The shoe paks were hung by the oil stove with care
In the hope that they'd issue each man a new pair!
The weary GI's were sacked out in their beds,
And visions of sugar babes danced through their heads,
When up on the ridge line there rose such a clatter. . .
(A Chinese machine gun had started to chatter.)
I rushed to my rifle and threw back the bolt,
The rest of my tent-mates woke up with a jolt;
Outside we could hear our platoon Sgt. Kelly,
A hard little man with a little pot belly!

Come Yancey, come Clancey, come Connors and Watson,
Up Miller, and Schiller, up Baker and Dodson!
We tumbled outside in a swirl of confusion.
So cold that each man could have used a transfusion.
Get up on that hill-top and silence that Red.
And don't come back till you're sure that he's dead!"
Then putting his thumb up in front of his nose
Sgt. Kelly took leave of us shivering Joes;
But we all heard him say in a voice soft and light:
MERRY CHRISTMAS TO ALL, MAY YOU
LIVE THROUGH THE NIGHT!"

Everyone was quiet, except for a casual remark that it was a damn good poem. Almost as quickly as it was upon us, Christmas was gone, without fanfare. The luxury of the holiday was gilded only by a chaplain's services and Mass. December gave up the ghost, and a new year whispered in. A week later we lost Wonju.

I was on a patrol when the attack came. We'd been given a mission to make contact, which we did—with about two thousand Commies. Air-liaison had spotted a formation moving into what they thought was attack position and we had to know what their intentions were. At sundown the order came to send a squad patrol beyond the outpost we'd been on before.

It was a long hike over frozen trails, slipping, falling and cutting our hands on the ice, and after a half hour of it, we rested. It was no easy job at that, with the weariness of climbing so deeply imbedded in our bodies. I had my canteen to my lips when Chinks hit us from every side with every kind of weapon; rifles from our front and front right, grenades from left and left rear with mortars from every damn place. There was no use trying to fight so many with so little. We radioed back to company what was happening and began falling to the rear. A few7 hours after the attack had begun, Birnstein crossed the bridge headed south, one more time. The next day the company was regrouped to take the town back.

Artillery came in support of the attack just as requested, forming a screaming wall of steel in front of us until ammunition ran out, which was far from uncommon. I felt naked, running across the bridge with no artillery protection. Finally, we had forced the Gooks back far enough to establish a perimeter, and we dug in on top of a hill, waiting for the counter-attack. Carboni's thermometer registered 32 below zero that night.

We all figured we'd have to retreat again and booby-trapped all the foxholes we were occupying. McPherson was directing operations.

Easy Company was spread out evenly in a continuous perimeter about one hundred yards in diameter around the knob of the hill. We had very little protection, but if anyone was going to take this hill, it would cost him plenty to do it.

Mac ran a check on the booby traps. "Make sure they're all set right," he said, "I don't want any of us to get caught in our own traps. When you get them rigged, climb out of your holes and lie on the ground, then if we fall back—you've got a straight shoot down the valley." We were busy for the next thirty to forty-five minutes getting the holes booby-trapped and when it was finished, Mac called Sokolski to tell him we were ready to fall back if it became necessary.

"You are so wrong, Sarge," the lieutenant replied, "You're not going to fall back. You've got to hold that hill. The best thing you can do is get the traps *out* of the holes and get the men *in* them."

"Lieutenant, it's blacker than a whore's heart up here now, it'll be suicide to try to take those traps out by feel." Mac almost shouted his answer.

"You should have checked with me before you put them in—get 'em out!"

Disgustedly, the sergeant told us to de-mine the holes. It was a nerve-wracking job, feeling for the invisible trip wires and following them to the trap. Occasionally a twig would snap as we brushed against it while searching for a wire. Hearts would stop beating, thinking it was the release trigger. We had set these damn things up for the Commies, and now we were trying to open the road for them to come through. After the job had been done in pitch blackness, the moon as if pushed to its zenith by some hydraulic force, shined through the night, wiping away much of the darkness. The hills were sharp in outline, gleaming like fine silver in the vivid glow.

A trip-flare went off down along the base of the hill. It exposed a column of the enemy about fifty yards out. Nobody fired, as that would have disclosed our position. They didn't know we were there, or so we thought. The flare hung in the air for a few minutes, then died out. Coincidentally, a call came from the Chinks at the foot of the hill.

"Hey, Easy Company—why don't you go on home?"

Somebody jumped up and yelled back, "We'd like to go home but there's no rotation. You're the bastards that are keeping us up here!"

The Chinks replied, *"Well come on down and fight then!"*

"Bugs" challenged. "If you want to fight, why don't you come up here? Or are you too yellow?"

They required but a few seconds to think it over, and after deciding they weren't too yellow, they blew bugles to start the charge. *"Sounds like Harry James, huh, Americans?"*

"Sound like Harry James, hell! It's more like Spike Jones!"

They must have considered the Spike Jones reference an insult, for their bugles sounded again and the charge up the hill was underway. The night was becoming very bright in the moonlight and we were able to see their maneuvering, but decided to wait until they were in point-blank range before firing. They worked around, trying to flank us, then suddenly unleashed a banzai charge. Screams of, *"Banzai! Die, Yankee pigs!"* and the sounds of their rifle-fire were garbled. The hills echoed.

We drew them into our sights and as they were about to break over the ridgeline, we squeezed the triggers. Nothing happened. About one out of twenty of our rifles would fire. . . Chinks stormed up the slope toward us. Carboni had said his thermometer read 32 below zero, but we hadn't considered that our rifles would freeze on us. As the Gooks came into our positions, we left the holes and battled hand-to-hand. Evidently they had decided to send a light wave in the first time to test our strength, and send in the full scale attack when the first one found out how many of us there were and what we had. After the initial contact, they pulled back. We heard them jabbering at the base of the hill. They'd hit us with everything they had now—knowing that we didn't have firepower.

MacPherson got on the phone and called the lieutenant again.

"Our weapons won't fire, Lieutenant—they're frozen up! What are we gonna do? They'll be back in a minute and there must be seventeen or eighteen hundred of them."

"Your rifles won't fire?"

"Right. Maybe one of fifteen or twenty is working."

"Piss on 'em!"

"That's alright for you to say. Lieutenant, you're back in the rear, but they're right on top of us. Dammit Ski, *don't kid with me!"*

"I'm not kidding you—*piss on 'em, piss on 'em!* They'll work!"

Mac recognized the truth in it. Others had pulled themselves out of just such jackpots by urinating on their weapons. The warmth of it frees the mechanisms to the point that they'll fire and then the firing itself warms them further. It's a good lubricant, too. He ordered us to do it. I strained for a lifetime to oblige the powers that be, but even though my existence depended on it, and that was more than a statement, I couldn't urinate. With chagrin, I thought of the hundreds of times I'd gone cross-eyed trying to hold back when a toilet was not available. Here I was, actually *trying* until I turned blue, and couldn't. I was not alone in my desperation. Others were having the same trouble. It was quite a spectacle, seeing these grown men, maliciously wetting on their weapons.

When it was learned that some of us were having difficulty, McPherson called to us, telling that if we had any left over to distribute it. One man in the company apparently had been hoarding for days. He was servicing about ten rifles. We were just holding them out to him and he'd ration the amount he thought was necessary before moving on to the next man. In the semi-darkness, his hasty aim was not too good. It became advisable to hold the weapon at arm's length to avoid getting urine in your eyes. He plied his organ like a fireman's hose, running the stream from our shoulders down to the rifle itself. Later, our fountain of salvation was awarded a Bronze Star for his valorous action.

The new attack would break momentarily, that we knew. My fox-hole buddy was a fellow whom I didn't know by name and knew nothing about. He was a dispirited lad, who said very little as we dug in deeper. The ground was frozen so hard that two entrenching tools broke in the process of digging. He had merely asked if I were Herbert when he came into the hole, and when I said I was, he replied that we'd be together.

In a hole to the right, were Birnstein and a BAR man. I hadn't met his partner. Before the next assault had a chance to come off, the man with Dave got up to leave. A blanket was wrapped around his shoulders. Mac asked where he thought he was going.

"I'm going back to battalion aid-station. I've got the chills, maybe pneumonia."

"Are you kidding?" Mac croaked, "We've all got the chills. Why in the hell shouldn't we have as cold as it is? Get back in your hole!"

"Go to hell."

"Say again? You're comin' in garbled."

"I'm going back to battalion, I'm about to freeze to death," the kid whined.

Mac left his hole and walked up to him, holding a bayonet in his hand. Placing it against the kid's stomach, he put a little pressure on the handle. "If you don't get back in that hole, I'll run this clear through you," he said. We all knew the sergeant wasn't kidding. So did the subject of his wrath. He got back into the hole.

"That damn guy is crazy," he whimpered, "I'm gonna report him when we get back. He's crazy." His teeth chattered and he tried to hold his mouth closed with his hand. Over and over again he muttered that he was going to report the crazy sergeant.

In the same breath that mortars and fire-arms were dumped on us, the banzai attacks broke loose. We were firing down the slopes of the hill at them as they advanced. Bodies piled-up, but the Chinese romped over their own dead. The air was so sharp that it was painful just to breathe. Not only painful, but unpleasant, as well. My BAR was heating up from the firing. The odor of fried urine burned my eyes. Ah, sweet essence of Korea!

One thing that had always bewildered me was from where the enemy came in such fabulous numbers. Looking into a valley, you could see nothing, then as quickly as you looked away, there would be a thousand or more right in your face.

They were attacking in battalion waves. The first wave was designed to destroy the resisting elements and the second wave was to take the objective. A heavy curtain of mortars was being dropped to keep us down, but the Chinks were marching through their own fire, dropping like flies from the shrapnel. Some got through though, and those who did were inflicting casualties. Once again they pulled back to reorganize. We took care of our own wounded during the lull.

I was re-loading my rifle, and crouched in a hole when I saw my foxhole buddy slumped in the comer, his head bent till his chin was resting on his chest. I reached over to see if he was hit, and saw a little blue mark over his left temple. He evidently had been hit during one of the firefights. He had died instantly, and so quietly that I hadn't even known he'd been hit. I placed his rifle beside me and took the ammo.

As soon as they both were reloaded, I was again in position at the edge of the hole, waiting for the next attack. My feet were so cold I could not move my toes. I felt that my brain itself was freezing. I caught a glimpse of the guy in the comer of the hole. Just a matter of minutes before, he'd been firing down the hillside. Now, his war was over. Before he was completely cold in death, many of the rest of us would join him. A cryptic thought entered my mind. I lay my rifle on the ground and maneuvered his body around to my feet, in front of me. I opened his jacket and put my feet inside, so that the warmth of his body would be of some benefit. Almost immediately they tingled with the promise of heat.

I was ashamed of what I was doing, and visualized the folks back home, if they knew of this, referring to me as sadistic or unscrupulous. It was a case of necessity, my feet were freezing. I asked God to forgive me for the thing I was doing, and placed the helmet over the kid's face. At least he wouldn't be staring at me every time I glanced down or while I was reloading.

In the sub-zero temperature, the body grew stiff and cold in a matter of minutes, and the chill returned to my own. I became increasingly nervous and crawled to Birnstein's hole so I could have someone to talk to. Someone that would answer.

Attack after attack came and each one was repelled. During the breaks in the attacks, Birnstein kept reaching under him, trying to fish something from the bottom of his hole, feeling in the dark. Occasionally he'd do it during an attack itself. Finally it got the best of me and I asked him what he was doing.

"I lost a spring from this pistol."

"What kind is it?" The pistol looked strange.

"A Russian. I got it from someone before we came up here. I was trying to work on it when one of the "banzais" came and I left the spring pop out of my hand. I've got to find it. I can't give it back to him like this."

"Hell, don't worry about what you're gonna tell him. You'd better worry about getting back to where you can tell him." I replied.

About four in the morning they hit us with the fifth wave. This time it was with the bugles sounding first. We figured it would be "the" one. In that, we were not mistaken, only they did it without their artillery support. We'd long since given up on getting our own artillery to help us. Something about a shortage of ammunition. No faltering light from flares, either. Too expensive to the taxpayers. We had to depend on the moonlight and good eyes. They hit us with bodies and burp-guns for a few minutes then a whistle sounded. They pulled back to lick their wounds. We still held.

We had had so many casualties, that when they hit us with the sixth wave, we were so greatly outnumbered and ammo was so low, we had no choice but to leave our holes and fall back. Dave's blanket-clad foxhole buddy was hit as we started down the hill. He was captured by the Chinks. We stayed as long as we could, tossing grenades and falling down the hill, firing as we went. It's impractical to fight bullets with bayonets.

When we arrived at the road some three or four hundred yards from the base of the hill, the Chinks had stopped. They were content to occupy our holes. On the way to battalion, some red-hcaded kid was constantly singing something about a "grizzly-fuzzy bear." He had entered the second chorus when the battalion CO drove up in his jeep.

"Where are you men going?"

"Retreating, sir," Red answered.

The colonel replied, "Aren't you in Easy Company?"

"Yessir."

"Well, Easy Company is in my battalion, and my battalion never retreats! Get back up on that hill! I want every man to take back his own hole."

"Some of them are holding the holes now, sir, but they're dead," Red shot back.

"Those of you who are alive have holes up there don't you? Take them back!"

"Can't do it, Colonel. There are too many of them."

"The *hell* you can't! I'll go with you myself." He told his driver to take the jeep back a little ways and bring his weapon.

I was surprised as hell, but being a colonel, he got artillery to come in and soften them up. In a matter of hours, we had the hill back. We had to clean it up though. Artillery had hit our dead. Their bodies were torn to shreds and strewn around the foxholes. It didn't do our morale any good to see the mutilated bodies of men we once knew, sipped and torn, mute testimony of the war. We gathered the pieces together and waited for Graves Registration to take them away. Sowers and Tate were carried out, in mattress covers.

CHAPTER EIGHT
January, 1951

THE WORD "RESERVE" according to the dictionary, means, *"That which is kept back or withheld, as for future use."* That's what it says in the dictionary, but to a man on the front lines, it means more days to live without constant fear, more time to sleep and a chance to catch up on the news. Strange as it may seem, the war is so close to you in a foxhole, that you lose all concept of its vastness. You know you're part of a big picture, but are lost in its magnification.

We were pulled off the line into reserve, and for some unknown reason, the weather cooperated. The sun broke through. Almost immediately the frozen earth relinquished its frozen state and turned into a giant quagmire. Discipline stiffened, and training became all-important. Replacements flooded in, and long-overdue mail began catching up to us. Back of it all was the roll of artillery, like soft thunder sneaking into your sleep. Occasionally we'd be called on for a patrol, but that was not often.

All of this gave Brinnon a chance to write his wife and son; McPherson the opportunity to catch up on his correspondence, and Birnstein the not to be ignored hours to spread his witticisms throughout. He was having a hey-day with new replacements.

"Such a nice bunch of guys to get into the war. Isn't that a shame, Herb?"

"Knock it off, Dave. They're going to have a rough enough time as it is, without scaring them half to death."

"Don't you think this one looks like Kelly? He'd make a good replacement for him. Ever use a BAR?" he asked, turning back to the new man. "I think we've still got his."

The replacement observed Birnstein with a combination of bitterness and amusement. "I've used one, yes. Whose did you say it is?"

"*Was,* son, not *is. Was* Kelly's."

"What happened to him?"

"Cashed in his rations. Gook got him last week. Such a nice guy. too. I think you'll like his weapon, he took good care of it. Only trouble is, it wouldn't fire when he needed it. We haven't had a chance to clean it up, it's a little bloody, but you can take care of that alright." The scapegoat eyed him casually. "You've sure got a line of crap, haven't you?"

Birnstein looked injured. "It's the dyin' trut', son." Then as if letting the kid in on a great secret, he walked closer to him, and looking around to see that no one was overhearing the conversation, said, "Get that '*trut?* I'm from Brooklyn."

"So what do you want me to do, stand on my head and spit nickles?"

"You can talk plainer than that, can't you? I can tell by looking at you that you won't last twenty minutes in combat. Not a snowball's chance in hell."

"What are you, the company's indoctrination specialist?"

"Hey, you guys, listen to this one throw his education around, will you?" Dave called out, as if directing everyone's attention to his newest enterprise of harassment. Turning back to him, he said, "Son, take if from me, you'll be sniffin' the roots of roses inside two weeks."

"Promise or threat?"

"You haven't been clued in yet have you? I'll blouse your eyeballs."

"Birnstein!" Brinnon called out. "You're transmitting again when you should be receiving. Knock it off."

"You tryin' to start a riot or something, Brinnon?" Dave replied. "No, but I will if you don't mind your own business."

"Are you for real?"

"Keep it up and you'll find out."

"Gentlemen," he addressed the replacements, who by this time, realized the levity involved in his statements, "You are to disregard my previous warnings. You'll probably draw your rations for at least a. month. By then we'll probably run out of mattress covers to put your body in." Then he ducked, anticipating a flying object from Renner's direction. His timing was uncanny. A pebble passed over his shoulder, missing him by inches. He moved away from his subjects of amusement, resigned to something less intriguing.

Bayonet practice in the mud; cleaning weapons to falling out for more bayonet practice, consumed many hours. Rice-paddies fertilized with "night soil" was our practice field. Lieutenant Sokolski was giving the instruction.

"This is a bayonet," he began, a smile on his face, "It is used to stick on the end of your rifle. If necessary, it can kill a man. Need I explain how?"

"Who's gonna get close enough to kill a man with it, sir?" someone asked.

"You are.. .who else?"

"The only thing I'll use that for," MacPherson remarked, "is to tie white handkerchiefs on it and let them wave in the breeze."

"You'll use it when the time comes, just like you've used it before. The only trouble is, Mac, you've been killing all those Gooks the wrong way. While we're here, we'll learn to do it by the book. Remember how you got two of them with a slash and smash of the butt?" Mac grinned remembrance. "Well, you did it wrong," Ski continued. "According to the latest poop I've been given, you should have had your light leg a little more forward. You could have been caught off balance the way you were."

"I made out okay, didn't I?"

"You're fighting the problem, Mac." Ski smiled, "We want to do it according to the book, remember. I'll show you what I mean. How about you, Brinnon?"

Brinnon got to his feet and sloshed through the mud to Ski, who handed him a rifle with a bayonet on it. They stood facing each other. Brinnon was invited to charge his opponent, and Ski side-stepped him like a matador at a bull-fight. 'That was only a half-assed attempt, Brinnon. Do your best to get me," he invited.

Brinnon made a mad charge, and there was a slight 'swish' as he left his feet and went flying over Ski's shoulder. He landed with a loud splash, half-embedded in mud. "Let's try it again," the lieutenant called out.

The maneuver was repeated several times, and Ski proved that he knew what he was talking about. Then we practiced it for a couple of hours, and broke off only after we were so completely covered with slush and mud that we couldn't even move around.

Chow time rolled around. It took about as long to eat chow as it takes to eat a pancake. As a matter of fact, that *was* chow. One pancake in the morning, and if we were so fortunate, an egg in the afternoon. Our supplies were coming in to us by air-drop. Sometimes the weather would clog up and there was no air traffic. Rations were scarce, but one day, a mail sack was included in the drop, and it was enough to make the entire war stop. Everyone read, read again and re-read the letters they'd received. Birnstein was practically rolling on the ground laughing at the one he got from home.

"Listen to this," he yelled. "My mother writes: 'I was so mad the other day, I couldn't see straight, listening to the news. The man on the radio was saying something about the war in Korea. He said that action was heaviest on the west-central front where the Chinese captured *one Jew*. I was so mad, I turned the radio off. I always knew those Chinese were prejudiced! Your dad turned it back on, and told me the man had said *Won-ju*. Wasn't that silly?' I'll be go to hell." Dave exclaimed.

"What kind of business are your mom and dad in?" I asked. "You said they were in business, didn't you?"

"Yeah," he answered unconsciously, engrossed in reading the rest of the letter.

"Yeah, what? What kind?"

"Iron and steel."

"What kind of iron and steel?"

"My mother irons clothes and my father steals food," he replied, turning the page without even looking up.

Ski beckoned for me.

"Herbert, your transfer's been approved."

"Transfer? I didn't ask for a transfer."

"Didn't you request a transfer when you were at Pusan?"

"Yessir." It dawned on me that technically, I was still AWOL from there.

"The papers finally got through to us. It's been approved. You can join the Second Division now," he laughed. "It just takes a little patience with these things. By the way, in case you're interested, you're a sergeant now."

The weather veered away from melting the snow and ice. It froze again. We found ourselves with head-colds and sore chests from coughing. A fast change in our future operations was rumored, using the stepped-up artillery we could hear as a means of proving the assertions. Some said it was a big push, while others insisted it was merely the artillery outfits expending their remaining rounds so they could call the war to a halt. Rumors were cheap, and multiplied faster than a dose of crabs.

Birnstein somehow had learned that a woman had a hut in a nearby village. One night he went over to her, determined to engage her services. Somebody had remarked that she could be had for a twenty-five cent piece. "Got two hundred, eleven dollars," he remarked, as he was leaving. An hour later he returned, looking as dejected as a man could.

"How'd you make out?" Carboni asked, tossing him a pro-kit. Dave threw it back. "Couldn't make out."

"Why? I thought you said it was cinched for a quarter."

"That's what they told me, but she wouldn't do anything for two-bits. I even offered her half a buck."

"Still no good?"

"No good, then I told her I'd give her two bucks. She just looked at me. I asked her what the hell the scoop was, she'd been accommodating everyone else for a quarter and wouldn't with me for two bucks? Do you know what she had the guts to tell me?"

"I give up—what?"

"She just looked like some Park Avenue debutante and said, '*I do have pride, you know.*' Did you ever hear anything like that in your whole damn life? A two-bit whore with *pride!*"

CHAPTER NINE
February, 1951, Hill 570

THE TRANQUILITY of reserve was broken. Lieutenant Sokolski excitedly called us together and said we were moving out immediately to assist the 1st and 3rd Battalions in pulling out of a trap they had gotten into. In less than twenty minutes, we were moving toward the line.

"This time we'll ride, though. Trucks are waiting for us now," he said.

We were happy that we were finally getting to ride into one of these deals instead of hoofing it all the way. Some humor was furnished by a sign which read, *"Drive Carefully—the pedestrian you kill maybe your replacement."* But as we rode, our joy turned to objection to getting there so rapidly. Other outfits were walking along the road and we were getting there faster than they, but the roads were lined with dead bodies. They were on every side of us, and it seemed we were merely moving up so that we might take our places beside them. It was incredible that the action had been that wicked, so close to us, and yet so far from us. We arrived at a point where the trucks could go no further. As we dismounted, Ski called Annus and me out for a recon patrol.

"Just want a two man reconnaissance. Get the dope on what they have and where they are, the usual stuff, then report back to me. Play it cool, though. Things are rough up there "

Hooking a couple of grenades onto our belts and a bandolier of ammo around our necks, Annus and I were ready. We left the road where digging in had begun. A colonel had come along exclaiming, *"You've got twenty minutes to dig in!"* Hell, the ground was so hard you couldn't have dug in twenty *hours*. It was a solid chunk of ice.

"How close should we stay together?" Annus asked.

"Spread out and surround them!" I replied. "If we see anything we'll just play it close to the chest and report back. I'm not about to get involved in any firefights."

As we moved parallel to the road, trucks were moving in the opposite direction. Behind them were men who were beaten to the point of absolute submission from lack of sleep and food. We broke away from it, and followed a stream toward a depression between the hills. Dropping to our stomachs, we crawled and inched our way forward. Annus held his hand up.

The brush made scraping sounds on my pants legs as I crawled to where he had stopped. The ice froze to us.

"Spot something?"

"I'm not sure," he whispered, "but I think those are Gooks over to the right of that knocked-out tank."

I moved around a bit to the left of a large clump of brush and peered out toward the area Annus had pointed to. There were possibly three hundred Chinese moving about. Only they appeared to be pulling back, instead of advancing. Where were the 1st and 3rd if these were Chinese?

"They're Chinks alright. Better get a coordinate on them and get back to the company. Sokolski'll want to know about this," I said. We noted the location on a piece of paper, and reported to the lieutenant.

"You didn't see any white troops at all then?" Ski asked.

"Not a one, they must be surrounded. It's the only thing I can figure out."

"Well, we can't move up until we get the order to. I'll shoot this info back to battalion and let them say the word. Better stick around close, you might have another patrol to run."

"Where in the hell would I go?" I asked. "I'm Regular Army with two years to go on this hitch. If this isn't something besides a "Police Action," it's a helluva long beat in a mighty tough neighborhood. Lot of cops getting killed."

He didn't hear me. He was already on his way to call in the information about our patrol. We expected only a short break, but it was morning before the word to move out came from battalion. From then on, it was a long walk, and we seldom stopped. The sounds of battle were still far away from us, but growing closer with each step.

On the next break, we could hear tanks up ahead and the sporadic stuttering of machine-guns. Black smoke from a firing 57 mm recoilless rose in the air, hanging as if suspended by unseen strands of silk.

"Suppose anyone knows where they're going?" Birnstein asked.

"I doubt it to beat hell, Dave. It would sure knock the crap out of the pattern if they did. Let's go over by that burning building to get warm."

"Sounds good to me, let's go."

We walked without talking and once we had become a bit warmer, decided to heat our rations in the coals of what was left of the building. Dave nicked his hand on the edge of the can's lid and cussed about the can opener slipping off, cussed about the rations, the weather, the Chinks, and the world in general.

"Swap you corned beef hash for hamburgers and gravy." he offered.

"Are you kidding, you wouldn't catch me eating that stuff if I was dead."

"Don't talk that way, Herb. You might be."

"What, eating that stuff!?"

"No, dead. Could happen, you know." he grinned.

"What a sense of humor. Someday I'm gonna knock the livin' crap out of you, Dave."

"Ah, Herb, you wouldn't wantta do that. There wouldn't be anyone to put you in for your decorations if I left."

Dave and I had developed a terrific comradeship by this time. Especially in combat. More than once we'd been out on patrols and had run into trouble. Without giving any signals, I'd move to another spot, and within a matter of seconds, Dave would be there. He'd anticipate what I was going to do even before I knew. It's a reassuring thing to have in a pinch.

"You've gone too far, Birnstein. Choose your weapons!" I challenged.

"Dirty words, Herb—dirty words."

An officer from another platoon came running in our direction, shouting, "Disperse, disperse! The mortars'll get you!"

Dave laughed, "The boogie-man'll get you if you don't watch out, Lieutenant."

"What's that?" the lieutenant called out.

"Nothing." Dave answered, "we'll disperse." He looked at me. "Whattya think about that? The guy just got into the company yesterday and already he's trying to tell us that a lousy couple of rounds of mortar are gonna get us."

"One would do it, you know." We continued heating our rations. "Well, aren't you gonna move?" Dave asked.

"Me? Hell no, why should I? You move."

"Better move, Herb. You heard what the lieutenant said, didn't you? Disperse or the mortars'll get you."

"He didn't say which of us had to, did he?" I noticed with aggravation that I had opened a can of corned beef hash by mistake. The lieutenant repeatedly yelled for us to move.

"Persistent cuss, isn't he?" Dave remarked. Then in his doleful tone said, "If you don't move, Herb, and we get killed together, you'd better make damn sure you hang onto your dog-tags, 'cause if Saint Peter gets our souls mixed, you'll wind up in Jewish Heaven, and confidentially, gefulte fish tastes like hell. Better move, Herb."

In the face of an almost steady diet of corned beef hash, gefulte fish would have tasted like bread pudding. An incoming round helped us decide to move. We stumbled down a draw to a small group of houses not burning, and approached one.

"You go in first, Herb," Dave said, "You've got a way with people. I don't."

"You cover me?"

"Got you."

I walked to the edge of one of the four houses in the group and kicked the door open. Someone jumped up from a small fire in the middle of the room. I rushed toward him. It was not a 'him' but a girl about fourteen years old, cooking rice balls for supper. Dave called from outside, "What's in there, Herb, are you okay?"

"I'm okay—just some chick in here?"

"A chick? You mean a *woman*?"

The kid stood petrified in her tracks. She must have been frightened to death when I jumped in the door toward her. Dave bounded into the room.

"Well whattya know," he exclaimed, "A real live girl...*a livin' doll!*"

"Lay off, Birnstein. Can't you see she's afraid? Let's ask her for something to eat."

"You're always thinking of your stomach."

We walked toward her, smiling and trying to convey that we were friends. Someone else at one time or another had had different ideas. She ran out another door.

"Must've thought we wanted to rape her," I said.

"Smart girl. Would you care to sup on some Korean rice-balls for supper?" He selected one of them and smelled it. "Not too bad. Quite edible, I'd say."

We thought hash would be a good swap, and left her the cans we'd been heating at the time one of her neighbors to the north had decided to send their calling card in on us. Taking the rice balls, we went back to our company.

In the morning at 6:30 we moved out for Hill 570, with Sokolski leading the first platoon in the route of march. We almost reached the top of a small hill when his platoon rounded a curve. Suddenly Ski tripped on a wire. To the man, we hit the dirt. I buried my nose in the ground and held my breath. No explosion came, though. There sat Ski in the middle of the road with a comic as hell look on his face as a flare shot into the air. It scared hell out of us, but the tension was broken and we were more alert for booby traps.

Birnstein worked his way up behind me. "Skinned up your nose, didn't you, Herb?"

"Yes, why, is it bleeding?"

"No, just a little skinned up. What happened, did Mac forget you were behind him and fail to signal he was making a turn?"

"Are you inferring I'm brown-nosing?"

"Certainly not, sir!" What ever gave you that idea?"

"Just checkin'. What the hell did you ever do before you came to Korea, Dave?"

"You mean the first time, or this trip?"

"Were you here before?"

"I was here on occupation duty before I got discharged."

"How long were you out?"

"Just a year."

"What kind of work did you do?"

"Who me?" He looked insulted. "*Work?*"

"I drew my 52-20 until it ran out, spent my savings and came back in the Army."

"Dammit Dave, you're nothin' but a bum—do you know that?"

"My, aren't we patriotic," he replied, "Sure I am—aren't we all? The only difference is, I admit it. How about the rest of you?"

His reply caught me off-guard. I had no answer for it. We were moving down a valley when mortar fire started again. One came especially close, and before its muffled explosion cleared away, Annus yelled that he was hit.

Three more rounds landed between us—hitting in the road. We all thought there would be nothing left by the time we could get to him. As the concentration let up, we called for the medic. Birnstein was talking in a real nice tone—comforting Annus until medical help arrived.

"Where'd it get you, fella?" Dave was asking.

"In the back—take it easy, will you?" He flinched as we tried to move him into a more comfortable position.

"Want a cigarette?" Dave asked.

Yeah, but I'm out. You got one?" Annus groaned. Dave fished one from the pack in his pocket, and after lighting it, placed it between

Annus's lips, muttering, "My last cigarette, too."

"What'd you say?" Annus asked.

"Nothin'. Just lie still, Doc will be here in a minute."

We crouched in the ditch, waiting for the medic who arrived and began taking off the upper clothing so he could examine the wound. I was thinking, "Poor Annus, and we haven't even started to attack yet." Birnstein and Carboni were piling up the pile jacket, OD shirt, sweater and winter undershirt beside him. A piece of shrapnel about half the size of a baseball dropped from the winter undershirt. "Goddam you Annus," Dave exclaimed, "there's nothin' wrong with you—that steel didn't even cut your stinkin' skin!"

Annus grabbed the fragment from Birnstein's hand, examined it carefully and said, "Birnstein, you should be a doctor. You're terrific! No pain, nothin'—just fix 'em up like that!" He snapped his fingers at Dave, blew a puff of smoke in his face and dressed.

"And you smoked my last cigarette—you phony bastard!" Dave shouted.

"Don't think I'm ungrateful." Jim Annus replied, "Thanks for the back rub." He climbed back to the road, leaving us laughing and Birnstein fuming.

An hour later and further up the trail we encountered a pile of trees which formed a road block. Sweeping to the left, we went around them, skirting the edge of a rice paddy. About 400 yards across the paddy lay Hill 570. It was smoking like an erupting volcano. Napalm smoldered from its base to the ridgeline.

"Welcome to the gates of hell," Annus remarked. Ski came back advising us of the plan of attack. He ordered my squad to establish the left flank with another squad supporting mine on the right.

"Better keep them down now. Our mortar preparation is due in three minutes," he said, leaving to go forward of our position.

The artillery was right on time and began pounding the hill, forming a rhythmic march ahead of us we advanced toward our objective. The other squad leader called to his men to spread out more as Chink counterfire mortars started. Again and again he called for dispersement.

One of his men yelled that the lousy bastards couldn't hit something even as big as a valley with mortars. A few seconds later the whole squad was knocked out by four rounds that *happened* to hit the gulley they were in. The heckler got a piece of shrapnel in the stomach and matter-of-factly stated, "Well I'll be damned." They hauled him off to the medics.

A machine-gun cut loose to our left, kicking up dirt in a skipping line across the road in front of us. The ground was so frozen that the bullets ricocheted off into the sky, to become lost in a fading whine. Sokolski thought I was hurt and asked if I was okay.

"Hell yes, I'm okay. You forget it would be against the Geneva Convention rules if they shot me? I've still got a safe conduct pass from the Chinese Volunteers."

Ski ran across the mouth of the draw where the machine-gun was set up. He drew its fire while Birnstein knocked the gun out with a rifle-grenade.

Crandell spotted a Gook to our left, but instead of shooting him, he got all excited, saying repeatedly, "What to do—what to do!"

Bugs said, "Give him a safe conduct pass." At the same time he emptied his automatic carbine into the Commie, cutting him to pieces with thirty slugs. Then he looked at Crandell and said, "There, he had thirty passes and now he's safe, the bastard."

Supporting artillery petered out, and Ski gave the signal to move forward. We just reached the base of the hill when someone tripped, discharging his carbine. It hit King in the arm just above the elbow. It could not have been helped and King didn't say a word about it. Sokolski dressed the wound and he himself was called to battalion. King caught up with us. The hill was smoking from napalm to the extent that you couldn't tell GI from Gook. We were close enough to fire point-blank at them, and they at us. Grenades were flying through the smoke in both directions. Annus got a piece of shrapnel in his right leg and went to battalion aid to have it removed. He'd be back.

I had just emptied a magazine when a Commie appeared about six feet to my right. I was reloading the AR on the run, and when he saw that I was carrying an automatic rifle, he turned chicken, smiled and dropped his burp-gun. Upon seeing that I was trying to reload the gun, his guts returned. He dived for his burp-gun, but it was the wrong thing to do. He might as well have dived into a meat grinder, because even though it was out of ammo, the rifle was still an effective weapon. I was so scared that I drew it back like a baseball bat and swung hard enough to have made Kiner ashamed of his homers. The stock of the gun and the Chink's head met with a resounding 'crack,' as teeth, blood and bones flew in all directions.

Rumors were passed around that the 1st and 3rd Battalions were just over the hill and we'd join them there. We had climbed the hill far enough that the dead, in their abundance, were being trampled everywhere. Artillery and napalm were really taking care of the hill for us. Some of the Gooks were still alive, but burning. Their screams came from all sides.

Frequently one would come to the edge of the smoke, firing, only to be chopped down by one of us. Birnstein got shot in the leg.

Bugs, a little to the right, crooked his arm to hurry us up. Things weren't going quite as rapidly as he wanted, so he called out, "Goddam it, get the hell up here! What're you doin' back there?"

Thinking he was referring to me, I blasted him with, "Well, what the hell are you, some kind of a hero or something? I'm just as far up front as you are."

"I'm not talking to you, dammit, it's those jerks behind you." "Self-Propelled" was having a hard time, wrestling the machine-gun over the ice, slipping and falling about every three feet. He was skinned and bleeding from the gun falling on top of his hands, digging them into the frozen ground. King, moving over to lend a hand, had moved about ten yards when grenades came rolling down the hill out of the smoke. We tossed a couple of them back, but others exploded before we had a chance to get rid of them. King dropped with a hole torn in his shoulder. Brinnon was next to get hit. "Doc" Carboni was in business, as one by one, the platoon was being knocked out.

The crest of the hill was reached, inch by inch. Someone stepped on a Gook grenade, just as it exploded. He did a somersault about four feet into the air, toppling in a twisted heap. In a second, he jumped up running around screaming, "I'm hit, I'm hit!"

Doc rushed to check him over. Not a scratch, but four men who had been around him were peppered with fragments. They were sent to the rear. The man who had stepped on the grenade had a sheepish grin on his face.

Commies burst out of the smoke holding grenades or burp-guns, and we found that a round or two wasn't enough to stop them. We were shooting them five or ten times before they'd drop.

Upon reaching the top, we began holing in. It was perhaps the most difficult, the hardest task of all, because the ground was frozen solid to a depth of almost three feet. Entrenching tools were as useless as a tablespoon. McPherson asked how I was making out.

"Fine," I answered. "What's real-estate worth on this knoll overlooking the vast expanses of North Korea?"

"It's too damned expensive, whatever it is." His expression froze. *"Herb, don't move!"* he said softly. He got up, and was moving toward me, looking over my shoulder. He walked a little to the left and just as he got past me he turned ,and stomped on the arms of a body which suddenly came to life. A Gook had been crawling up to get my weapon when Mac spotted him. For a supposed dead man, he raised a lot of hell. I swung my entrenching tool simultaneously with Mac's barking carbine. Brinnon, who had not yet gone back to the rear for treatment, fired at the same time. Joe Chink didn't have a chance.

Brush was burning clear across the ridgeline. We tried to keep warm by it, but it was useless. The only way to keep warm was to dig our holes. This accomplished, we settled in. The sweat froze stiff in our jackets. It was dusk when Mac asked for volunteers to get our sleeping bags and bring them up. There wasn't a man who had enough strength to walk that far. We stayed without them. It was too much effort to think about anything but rest. But, there was to be none.

CHAPTER TEN
February, 1951, Hill 570

As DARKNESS FELL, the wind in recognizing its cue, began to howl fiercely. Bugs Hoover crawled to my hole. Through chattering teeth, he asked, "Think it'll get cold?"

"It's gonna miss a good chance to if it doesn't."

The bleakness crowded out conversation, but the icy winds persisted. I wondered if the summers were as hot as the winters were cold. Bugs had been in Korea the summer before, and probably would know. "Bugs?"

"Yeah?"

"What're the summers like over here? I was just thinking about these long nights. I'll be glad when the days are^ longer. There's too much darkness in the wintertime."

"That's where you're wrong, the nights aren't short anytime. When we think of summer, we think of our own summers at home. Long days followed by brief, starry nights. But in Korea, the days are short and nights are long—any season of the year."

He fingered the sound-power phone he had taken in his hand. At his side was an automatic rifle, a light machine gun and several carbines. Stacked around him were ammunition boxes. The sound power phone he had brought with him when he came to the hole, but I'd gathered the other weapons from men who had been hit while we were taking this position.

The conversation drifted around, filtered through a minor point or two, then fell off. In the gloom, listening to the ice crack and fall to the ground from scrub brush, it was difficult to think of anything but home, and how long we'd be in Korea. Before us lay endless chains of hills and valleys, each to be conquered or surrendered in turn. Each collecting its toll in the currency of war. There was much time I to think. Bugs had a wistful expression, one that I'd seen many times before. His chin rested on the stock of the AR lying on the edge of the hole, pointed out toward the valley.

"Bugs?"

He stirred slightly, and hesitated before answering. "Wait a minute, I think that's someone moving around out there."

"Where?"

"See the light just left of that hollow spot in the sky?"

I squinted my eyes. The light appeared to be moving. "What is it, do you know?"

"I just wouldn't rightly know. I've been watching it for a long time out there. It moves, but I think it moves too fast to be a man walking. Apparently it's some kind of a burning light. You can see it flicker. It's probably back a lot farther than it looks, though. I guess there's not a great deal to worry about. It seems to disappear and then come back again. Could be a road a convoy is moving on. It might be that there's one point where the trucks head directly toward us and show their black-out lights." He thought deeply, seriously before asking, "Have you ever been out in South Dakota or some other place where it's real flat?"

"Not South Dakota, but I've seen Texas. The part I saw was pretty flat. Why?"

"You know how you can see for miles and the lights seem to be within walking distance?" I nodded understanding, and he went on, "That's what I was thinking of while I was watching that light. Not about South Dakota, but my own home in West Virginia. My home sets on just about the highest hill in our whole county. There's a farmhouse about thirty five miles from my place, and I used to sit out on the front porch at night and look at the lights in that house. They looked like stars, in a way. The only difference was that they were so far away, they globbed together and made one big light instead of a lot of little ones."

"Is that what you think about mostly when you're out on an outpost or holding a hill like this?"

"Most always I do think about home. I don't suppose I'm any different from anyone else. Most of us think about home. Generally I find myself wondering about my wife and baby. I'm well over half my way to going home, I think. According to the way the other men are leaving, I should be going home soon, one way or the other. Rotation will be starting before long, and then it might only be a month or two. Less, I hope.

"Usually I consider the sounds I hear, listening for everything, that's going on. You can tell whether things are important or whether it's just some animal in the night," he reflected.

"Do you wonder very often about what your wife and baby are doing back there in West Virginia?"

"Yes, I try to figure that out, too," he said evenly, "but I understand it's actually daytime back there. There're a lot of things she could be doing. She's there on the farm, and she's got many opportunities—things of various choice to do."

"I've got a great wife back home. She's a very trustworthy woman—a Christian woman, and I know, even now that she's praying for me. She's very interested in me. She writes me nice letters, but I can tell that she's somewhat worried about me. I try to encourage her and tell her that I'm really not afraid, and that nothing will happen. Everything will be alright and I'll get back home safe. It's not that she doesn't trust me, but she has some dread for war—which we all certainly do.

"We've got a great little baby who seems to be doing alright. My wife writes me that already she's beginning to say. 'Daddy.' We have great hopes for the future. Sometimes when I was back home, the wife and I used to anticipate what kind of a person our little girl, or our little boy, might turn out to be. That's before she was born." he added, grinningly. "We finally decided we wanted our little girl to turn out to be the nicest, most friendly woman in the community."

"Do you have a picture of them?" I asked.

"Yes, but it isn't a very good one. It got all wet when we crossed a river last summer and it's faded and cracked. Like to see it?" I answered that I would. He let the AR stay in its spot at the edge of the hole. Reaching into his pocket, he withdrew his billfold and handed the snapshot to me. I ducked low into the hole and blocking a corner, struck a match. In the flickering light, the photo appeared intimate and lifelike. His wife, an attractive woman, was holding the baby in her arms and standing in what appeared to be a farmyard. Behind them was a dark-painted barn with the numerals, "1909" over the main door. The picture itself was in poor shape, but her features were still distinguishable. The baby was possibly two months old.

"It must have been pretty hard to get used to being away from them, wasn't it?" I asked.

"I still haven't gotten used to being away from them. Until I was drafted in the Army, I'd never had what you'd call a *real* stay away from home. It hit me pretty hard for awhile. Of course I don't ever expect to get used to the Army, actually. Usually I intend to get through and get out just as quick as I can. Then I change my mind and think about staying in.

"Everything seems to go pretty smooth with me while I'm in the Army. I don't have any trouble with people, and everyone treats me nice and friendly. I feel personally, that it's a privilege to be here and fight for the things that we hold to be true, and brave and honest. I think it's a pretty sorry fellow who wouldn't."

"Think you'll stay in?"

"I really don't know right now," he sounded almost resigned, "One time yes, and the next time, no. I don't even want to think about being separated from my family any longer than is absolutely | necessary, and I know if I do stay in, it's going to be a series of separations and being together. That's no way to raise a family. Then, and this might sound funny to you, I begin thinking about our country and how people are trying to change it around to become theirs.

Communism, for example. As long as I have a drop of blood in my body, that'll never happen. I'm patriotic, Tony, there's nothing else to call it. I don't talk about that to other people, in fact, I think you're the only one I've really talked to like this. But I really mean it.

"I wasn't old enough to get in the last war, but I did what I could. I stayed on my dad's farm and helped, and I had a victory garden, too. I was happier working on that little garden than I was working in the fields with Dad, because the garden was mine and I was contributing something to it."

"Don't you ever get scared and think you won't make it back?"

"Not any more than you do, I guess. We all have that certain feeling of apprehension, but you know, when something does happen it happens so quick you don't have an opportunity to get scared. You don't know what to expect. I might be stretching it a bit, but I don't think we have time to be scared.

"I'd rather it would stay just like it is at this minute, with nothing doing. But a firefight, I think, is something to look forward to. It's something that gives you a lot of experience, and since we're going to be over here for a while yet, the more experience we get, the better off we'll be. Then in case an even bigger offensive comes off, we'll know more about what to do. Whether that happens or not, I expect to return." He turned back to his vigilance, leaving the more coherent world behind him. A detached world.

The thunder of artillery continued. The soft, whoosh-whoosh of outgoing stuff was beating a steady vibrato. Some of it was hitting out of sight moments later, while others struck the hill directly ahead of us in a matter of seconds. I relieved Bugs for the next tour of watch. The urge to build a fire was becoming overwhelming. Bugs attempted to sleep, but was twisting and turning, trying to get comfortable. He was turning blue with cold. Later, Brinnon was taken to the rear, but not without arguing that he wanted to stay with us. Mac had to border him back, threatening court-martial if he didn't go. Birnstein went to have his leg looked at, too. There was no sleep to be had, and Mac came around to make sure we were all okay. "Better get the men to check their feet, Herb. No sense just sitting here. Most of them probably are beginning to get frostbite. It might take their minds off just sitting around. Do you mind?"

"No, not at all. How many of us are there, anyway? I hadn't thought much about it, till you mentioned their feet."

"Thirty-two. Boy, it's really dwindled down, hasn't it? I'm gonna try knocking out a letter for home while you're checking them."

"Good idea." I got up and he took my place in the hole. Writing letters was getting to be a thing of the past with most of us, but every chance he got, McPherson jotted a note to his family. A lot of times it was a week before we stopped long enough for a mail clerk to even get them, but when he did, Mac had almost one to go out for every two days since he'd mailed the last ones. He took a message-form from his pocket and began scribbling on the reverse side of it. He didn't have enough light to really do a good job, but his intentions were good.

I went around advising the men to take their shoes off and massage their feet, leaving those who were sleeping for last. There were few sleeping, though. Most of them grumbled and griped, but they knew it was necessary. The only honorable way to go to the rear was on a stretcher or in a mattress cover. Frostbite was taking almost as many casualties as bullets, but they raised hell about it in the rear.

The artillery began dying away as we finished checking feet. Two men had black toes. They had to go back, probably losing their toes, if not the whole foot.

Mac was asleep, with his hand holding down the stack of message-forms. He'd had a lot to write, judging from the number of slips of paper. I waited at the edge of the hole for several minutes until he stirred and sat up. He moved his hand and some of the paper began blowing around. We scrambled them all back together. He said it would soon be time to move out again.

"We've got to take the next hill by noon, Herb. As soon as we get on it, they're supposed to send relief up for us. As long as we've gotten by without sleeping bags this long, we might as well go without them now, don't you think?"

If McPherson got knocked out, it would leave me in charge of the platoon, so lately he had wanted me to be in on as many of the decisions as was practical. The possibilities of his getting hit were so remote that I had never even thought about it. He was indestructible. I replied that it was a good idea to travel as light as possible. The idea of resting was too much to consider.

Night was reluctantly surrendering to sunrise when our platoon was gathered for briefing. Daybreak—always the eternal daybreak that signals attack or be attacked. The whole timetable of war seems to center around darkness and light, as an ally or an enemy. There was always the senseless urgency of going forward. For what? To take another hill, call GRO, have the dead hauled away; hold against the counter-attack, fall back, hold and call GRO to haul the dead away? lit was following the same pattern, without variation. Slivers of light were breaking through the darkness as Mac briefed us.

"Our route of departure is along this ridgeline to that finger over there. We'll be leading all three of the platoons in the sector, but I don't have a map to show you how it looks on paper. We'll be in the lead with the other two platoons taggin' along. Tank support is supposed to be here by 0630. They'll lend support when we need it." I was studying the terrain carefully. Every nook and cranny meant shelter. There was practically no cover, only slight depressions here and there, but none were big enough for a man's body. As usual, the enemy was more stable—he was dug in. With no trees for us to hide behind, or to jump to from one to another, it was just naturally going to be a case of being there with a little more power than the Chinks had. I was thankful for the tanks. They could hit the spots we couldn't get to.

Mac continued, "We'll attack at 0700, using a marching-lire order after artillery has softened them up. It's supposed to begin at 0630, the same time the tanks get here. If we get into any jackpots, we'll just have to tighten down and do the best we can. Any questions?" Of course there were questions—always—but they could not be answered until the enemy was searched out. The advance was going to be murderous, we accepted that. If the Chinks had gotten reinforcements and we didn't get ours, it could very well develop into slaughter for all of us. Looking around, I counted the number of men for this operation. There were thirty, since the two with frostbite had left. Thirty against how many Chinks? The two platoons behind us were being committed for this operation, but too many times before that had been the case, and when we'd get hit with more than we'd expected, our support was becoming involved in its own private fight, leaving us ours.

We made a final check of our weapons, slamming a clip into them and sliding the bolt forward. Somebody muttered a curse about suicide mission. Then a welled up fear took place—the fear that invariably worms its way into you before an attack. It grips like a fist, with icy fingers touching each vertebra in turn, finally lodging in your brain. Guts are but a tangled, coagulated mass—tight inside—like concrete, and just as heavy.

We lined up, moving away from the hill onto the finger leading over to the next one. The tanks were jockeying around to the northeast base of the finger, into firing position.

Artillery came on schedule, and our objective was pounded by the big stuff. Each puff of smoke and crash of shells seemed larger than the one preceding it. We reached the halfway point across the finger and halted, lying in wait for the barrage to lift.

Suddenly, as if repelled by a gigantic wall, the outgoing artillery turned in its flight and began falling on our position. It seemed incredible that the Chinks had spotted us and called in counter-fire, but the Chinks were always doing the incredible, and the murmur of outgoing artillery turned to screams and crashes of incoming stuff. It was a veritable million bolts of lightning and thunder clapping about us. Ahead, the hill was still getting hit by artillery and so were we. Mac was writhing in pain on the ground.

"*Good Lord—not McPherson!*" I said aloud. As soon as the barrage let up, I crawled to him.

"Don't those bastards know the score?" he grimaced.

"What'd you expect them to do—invite us in for rice? How bad are you hit?"

"Feels like my leg's blown off—right one. Those were our own men in those tanks blasting us. Dammit, they should know we'd be out here. They must have thought we were Chinks. *Sonofabitch!* Did you ever see anything so stupid?"

I checked his leg. A piece of shrapnel had passed behind the kneecap. An ugly blue mark bulged out the opposite side where it was attempting to break free of the skin. No use trying to walk with the shrapnel in it. Mac handed me his knife and told me to cut it out. It must have been numb, because he didn't feel the pain of the knife's cutting. I handed him the shrapnel which was about the size of a quarter and he put it in his pocket, saying someday he'd show it to his son and tell him a big war story. We bandaged it, but when the time came to attack the hill, Mac wouldn't go back. Instead, he hobbled on one leg, wincing with each step.

About three-fourths of way across the finger, the true Chink stuff started in on us. The earth was rocking and rolling like a ship caught in a hurricane. I buried my head in the frozen ground for protection against the explosions. Ice scraped and cut my face. The earth is the only stable thing man has, and as it tossed us about a crazy dizziness that could not be shaken away was the climax. My head pounded. Hearing was a missing non-existent power. Shells were falling to the rear, preventing us from falling back and small arms fire from ahead had us pinned to the finger.

When it receded for a split second, a soldier from one of the other platoons crouched over and hurried to a wounded man. He was bandaging his leg when another round came in. The soldier's head snapped back as if struck by a giant club. He pitched forward over the body of the man he had been treating. He was nearly decapitated. In a moment a direct hit got both of them. A leg was severed, and went spinning through the air unobjectively, landing on the side of the hill, rolling and tumbling down the incline. The bandage was caught in the breeze, blowing away.

We were exhausting our ammunition, and as the artillery let up, Mac signaled for us to move back onto Hill 570. At some time during the encounter, the two platoons which had been behind us were run off the hill. They'd probably been caught in the artillery barrage and were forced back. We were alone. The breath was freezing in my nostrils, forming icicles and clogging my nose until I breathed through my mouth almost entirely.

We had escaped from the finger and were in our holes when we noticed that McPherson was still out on the finger, trying to crawl in. There were two of them trying to get back, but because of his wounded leg, Mac was having a rougher time of it. I left my position to bring him in.

"You lousy mercenary," he said as soon as we were in relative safety, "you really wanted that watch, didn't you?"

I remembered then that I had loaned Mac my watch for a patrol two days before. He thought I had brought him in so I would be sure not to lose it.

"That's a helluvva way to talk," I replied, "Keep it so you'll know what time to knock off work and go home."

"That's not the way to tell time over here, you know that. Thanks for bringing me in, fella, I was only kidding about the watch." Artillery tore into the hill and finger almost all day. We called on the power phone for rations and sleeping bags, explaining that we had some wounded men. The reply was that rations would be sent up, but for our medic to take care of the wounded until they could send someone to remove them. Doc was at it again, and at dusk, the rations still hadn't arrived. Our number was now down to twenty-one, nine of whom were wounded. We had no blankets to cover them and could not build a fire, since that would show the Chinese where we were. The twelve of us who were on our feet volunteered to carry the wounded ones out. McPherson was in bad shape. I was put in command.

"Take care of the platoon, will you?" Mac asked when he called me to him. "There aren't many left, but you'll make it, no sweat."

"Don't worry about me making it, fella. You worry about getting back yourself. Did you ever see a guy so lucky, Bugs? Mac gets hit in the leg and first thing you know he'll be back in a hospital with nurses cooing over him, adjusting his pillow and taking his temperature. Wow, what a life!"

"Better watch those nurses," Bugs added, "I knew one once in the States who worked in the station hospital at this post, and she lost her job in the men's ward. Didn't know how to handle a bed-pan. Instead of slipping her hand under the buttocks and *sliding* the pan in, she'd grab you by the handle, lift you up and sock you down on the pan. Painful as hell."

"This guy has more crap than the whole country of Korea could use for fertilizer. You've got it made, Mac. Cake, then a trip to the States, parades for you at home."

"Just to get home and see the family will be enough. You've got my address—be sure to look me up. Don't forget, will you?"

We agreed that we wouldn't forget and four men began picking up two of the stretchers to move down the reverse slope of the hill. They'd reached about half-way down a different route than we'd used coming up when they got into a mine field. Explosions rocked the hill. It wasn't long until McPherson and the other man who had been in the movement, came crawling up the hill.

"These damned Gooks are attacking," Mac shouted, "get in your holes!"

He didn't know it was a mine-field they'd been in, but when the explosions went off, he had jumped from the litter and climbed the hill, in spite of his bad leg.

The other man made it in a few minutes, minus his left arm.

We put them in a hole and tried to shelter them with our own bodies. It began to snow, and the wind whipped it around us, onto them. A call for the medics brought the answer that they couldn't get through the minefield we told them about. The four volunteers never got back. They died on the slope where they were hit. The Gooks had quietly by-passed our hill and at sunrise we were surrounded. Our phone lines had been cut. We had no communication. Time crept by.

The remaining rations were doled out about one spoonful to the man. The wounded came first. Mac became delirious with the cold and his wounds, but he was still living. Shortly after, a man with a belly wound died. Snow covered them.

Night crowded out the daylight. Once again we were alone in the darkness, forgotten; certain that a big push had come about and that there was no chance of ever getting back.

I sneaked to some of the Korean bodies on the hill. Surely on at least one of them would be some rations. It was pitch black and the bodies were stiff, frozen to the ground. Rolling them over for searching was next to impossible, but like an animal gnawing at a steel chain to gain freedom, I worked them around to go through their pockets.

Without warning, a series of flashes and deafening cracks hit my face. They stopped, with their echoes reverberating and becoming lost in the hills. I couldn't understand what had happened. My brain was playing games again. I continued to crawl, and when the flashes came this time, I saw that a Korean who had evidently been wounded in the fighting three days before, was lying on his back with his head pointed toward me. He was too weak to raise his burp-gun to fire it, but had it lying at his side, squeezing the trigger with his thumb. He was firing over his head, point-blank in my direction. Twenty rounds from my BAR crashed across his face and through his body. The bullets kicked him into the air and spun him around.

In his pockets was a can of chicken-noodle soup. American rations, covered with blood. Reasoning that the blood was not inside the can, I grabbed it. Like a child who had found his grandmother's lost spectacles, I rejoined the men on the hill. We gave our wounded the soup, explaining we had more. We tried to sleep so our stomachs would quit gnawing.

Mac's leg was frozen almost stiff, but he was conscious again and hanging on to life with the tenacity of a bulldog, out for a kill. An hour or two after eating his minute portion of the soup, he vomited without making an effort to rise and turn it away from himself. Almost as soon as it spilled onto his chest, it froze. We lifted him up so he wouldn't choke on the phlegm and turned him on his side. Within minutes, he passed out again. During the night, five men died.

Dawn heralded a new day, our third since coming to Hill 570. For breakfast we had snow. Ice for cereal; fluffy new snow for dessert, and to wash it down, snow melted by breathing into our helmets. We were in the midst of eating when an enemy patrol was observed at the base of the hill.

They must have heard the firing on the slope the night before and wanted to find out what had happened. Perhaps the patrol members themselves didn't like the job of going through their own dead. Their probing was limited to the valley below us. They were returning to their own lines.

"Three-hundred and sixty degrees of Chinks," Bugs mused. "The slimy slant-eyed bastards. Why don't they go the hell home?"

The strain was too much for one of the men. He jumped up, screaming insanely at the top of his voice, "You can't kill me—you can't kill me!"

Bugs and I hit him at the same time. We knocked him to the ground and held his mouth closed. He clawed like a tiger. We pounded his head on the ice until the struggling ceased, and he lay curled as a kitten would in front of an open fireplace on a cold night. The vigorous movements created heat in my body. Finally I was warm. Then just as quickly, I fell into an anguished shiver.

The patrol had heard the outcries. They stopped and surveyed the hill, searching for its cause. With shrugs of indifference, they resumed their journey.

The sun, shrouded in a haze, lifted to a point directly overhead. Several of us found ourselves completely at the mercy of nausea. We were vomiting spasmodically but nothing was in our stomachs to be lost. Only water. Our guts ached from the effort. I stared at the snow around me. If only there was something with substance that would quell the spasms. *Anything.* My eyes fell on red blood, frozen in the snow. I turned away. *It would be sacrilegious to eat the blood of your comrades.* I thought of a Polish family back home who used to have "duck" soup once or twice a week. It was nothing more than blood, cooked with potatoes. I had tried it once. It wasn't too bad. At least it had been cooked, but *frozen blood!* I shuddered with revulsion, remembering the icicle I'd eaten accidentally at Kuneri. It had made me sick then. I *couldn't* do it again.

As though guided by some unseen force, my hands reached out and encircled a piece as big as my fist. I was no longer a reasoning human being, only a starving animal who needed food. I broke off a chunk with my teeth and almost immediately spit it out. My hands were trembling. My eyes were merely two peepholes for something other than myself to peer out through.

I worked the matter in my hand until it became soft and pliable, taking on the appearance of raspberry jello whipped by a mixer. Then I closed my eyes, tossed it into my mouth and swallowed without chewing. My tongue became oily, like I had just finished a dose of mineral oil. There was no taste, save for the dirt from my hands that had changed the blood's consistency. Other men on the hill were observing my movements. *I was naked before the eyes of God.* I prayed forgiveness, then repeatedly replenished my empty stomach. The others, accepting that it was an absolute case of survival, joined me. They ate their fill, gratefully.

That afternoon a counter-attack came off and a heated artillery duel took place. Tucking our heads into our shoulders, we cringed in the holes. Mac was shocked into consciousness. He was in good spirits, now that the chance of getting out awaited. Some of the Chinese were making a play to come back up on the hill and became engaged in a firefight with what was left of Easy Company, pushing the attacks. The little ammunition we had was being used on them as they backed toward us. They had no idea we were firing at them. The cross-fire was eliminating them. Others flanked the hill and disappeared. Our own men came rushing to the summit to help us.

Medics checked the remaining wounded, loaded them onto litters and started the trip to the aid station. Mac extended my watch before they took him away. It had run down and stopped, but Mac had not. He feebly grasped my hand and told me to take it easy. The remnants of his platoon, ten strong, watched him leaving us. The six medics and three wounded were almost at the bottom of the hill and the joy of their finally getting treatment, was almost overpowering. From behind an opposite hill, six tanks came lumbering in.

Like giant robots, they rounded a curve in the road and stopped. The turrets moved about, searching aimlessly like the tentacles of an octopus, then stopped, pointing toward us. That they were mistaking us for Chinks was unthinkable, but the absurd was occurring. They began firing on the group struggling to make it to the valley. Rounds were landing all around them. Miraculously, at that point they hadn't been hit, but in a moment the tankers got the correct range. They poured in the heavy stuff, supported by machine-gun fire.

We stood on the hill, shouting at the top of our lungs to cease fire. It was too late. As quickly as it began, it stopped, either through the tankers' satisfaction with the job, or the realization that we were friendly troops. The nine men were scattered about the hillside. I ran and tumbled down to McPherson. He wasn't even breathing. The litter had been torn to shreds. His body was twisted grotesquely, completely shattered. A tense silence enveloped me. *Killed by his own men.* Vowing I'd kill the tankers with my bare hands, I ran across the valley. A colored boy who was in the lead tank which sent in the initial fire climbed down as I came toward them.

"I knowed they was 'Merican troops and told the man so," he apologized. "Only, he said they wasn't, and to fire on you. Anyone hurt?"

"Nine men dead is all. Where's your officer?"

"In the next tank back. Better watch him, he's a bear-cat."

"The stupid bastard."

I walked to the tank and told the gunner sitting on top someone wanted to see the ranking officer. In a moment an officer stuck his head out of the turret and asked if there was something he could do for me.

"You know you just blew hell out of a bunch of men on that hill you blasted?"

"Yes, that's what I just heard. Sorry about it—a helluvva mistake."

"You're goddam right it was a helluvva mistake. Is that how you got your commission, by killing off everyone around you?"

"*Sergeant! Who do you think you're talking to?*" he screamed.

"*Who?* Dammit your feet don't fit a limb! You—who in the hell do you think I'm talking to? *You!* I'd like to use as a ram-rod for a 155 and leave you stuck in it until a firing mission came in!"

"*I'll have you court-martialed. You can't talk to me like that!*"

"Oh can't I? Would you admit that you ordered your men to fire on American troops? Try explaining that, *you sonofabitch!*"

He turned white and ducked his head into the tank. I assumed he was calling back for someone to take me into custody and started back to see if I could help on the hill. Not far from the tanks, my knees buckled. I collapsed from sheer exhaustion.

CHAPTER ELEVEN
March, April, 1951

THE INTERVENING MONTH was absorbed by a succession of patrols and outposts. Replacements were arriving in ever growing numbers, and gradually the ice and snow gave way to slush, creating mud. The war for a brief space of time, was immobile. For many, the word that rotation of troops was about to begin, gave added hope, while others resigned themselves to a long wait. Some began worrying about living long enough to be rotated, but everyone became just a little more cautious than in the past. There was a reward at the end of the rainbow now, and summer warmth was nearing. Annus, Birnstein and King came back to the squad.

Replacements eyed us with envy of our short weeks yet to serve in Korea. To us, it was merely becoming their responsibility to take 011 a share of the war. Someone mentioned that you only live to die.

"Everyone lives to die." I recalled reading that in a book once, but I couldn't remember when.

I was lazily watching our jets going on a mission or returning for more napalm. The earth quivered as more tons of explosives rocked it, and a murky gray cloud hung over the hill being bombed. The whine of incoming mail warned that it was searching out a goal. Instinctively, I grabbed my helmet and lunged for a hole. Someone called out to get under cover, but his cries were drowned out in an ear-shattering crash. Shrapnel screamed vengeance.

A moment later a freckle-faced kid climbed into the hole with me. "Someone got hit then." he said, excitedly.

"Who was it, do you know?" I asked without the true interest

I should have had.

"I don't know, a corporal, I guess. How long have you been here?"

"Long enough, I suppose. Who are you?"

"Just got here today. I'm a replacement. Name's Jennings—I'm from Illinois."

I looked at the boy. A slight gust of wind caused him to stir fitfully under the sun shining feebly, out of a clear sky. He was fingering his M-1 and checking the clips to see that they were clean and would be able to function without jamming when he needed them. He'll learn, I thought to myself.

"How long have you been here in Korea, Jennings?"

"I got here ten days ago. That is I got to Inchon ten days ago. Just came to the company this afternoon. I took basic at Fort Knox. Third Armored Division. It had quite a record during the last war, you know."

He was eager to talk—most fellows are when they get to a new outfit. Makes them feel better.

"Regular Army?" he asked.

"You might call me that. How about you?"

"Not exactly regular, I guess, but I did volunteer in a way. I could've been deferred but told the draft board I wasn't asking any favors. Been in now about six months. Will be six months the twenty-third. Have you had much combat yet?"

I weighed the question in my mind with a cynical tolerance. I was unable to define the word, *much.*

"Not as much as we'll have before it's over. Things are going to get a little quieter than they are or have been for the past few weeks, though. Don't worry about it." I replied.

"I'm not worried about it," he bit back. "Don't get the idea I'm scared, either. My brother wasn't and I won't be."

There was a quality of tenderness and yet stubbornness about him. The set of his jaw may have disclosed something his eyes held back. He'd make a good soldier, if he didn't get it before he had a chance to become one.

"What about your brother?"

"He got killed in the Pusan Perimeter. He'd been on occupation duty in Japan and came over here with the first troops when the Commies came down from up north. When he got killed, I just, I had to take his place and finish his job. That's why I didn't ask the draft-board for a deferment. I wanted in."

"I think you'll like the outfit, Jennings. Good bunch of boys, and not a one that won't help you every bit he can."

"You're in charge of the platoon, aren't you?"

"Yes."

"I heard someone mentioning that, what was his name, McPherson, got killed? They said you took his place when he died."

"Nothing unusual about that. Someone gets killed and somebody else takes his place. Happens every day."

"Good way to get promoted."

"Yeah, and each stripe puts you closer to getting knocked off."

"Why?"

"Patrols and outposts for one thing, plus the fact that the only place a good non-com or officer can be, is leading. Don't you remember that from basic?"

"Yeah, I do, but I always considered it to be a lot of bunk."

"That's the trouble with a lot of us, we think basic's a lot of junk. I was the same way. Not that I thought all of it was, but since I've been over here, I can see that training is damn important, it really is."

"You mean just knowing how to fire a rifle?"

"Is that all you learned in basic?"

"No, I don't suppose, but it seemed like all they ever talked about was firing the basic weapon."

"How about patrolling?"

"We had that, too."

"Map reading?"

"Yeah."

"Field expedience?"

"Sure, we had all of it."

"Well there's a damn good bunch of examples."

"How important is patrolling over here?"

"Now look, Jennings, you were sent in here because you had finished basic and supposedly were ready for combat. Don't come in asking a bunch of silly questions about how important is patrolling and do you really have to clean your rifle for three days after you're fired it. Some of the stuff you got in training you can leave at the training center, but other things that by now should have become common sense, you never want to lose. It has to become an operational part of you, something you can use when you don't even think about what's going on around you. You can't stop and figure everything out before you do it."

"Will you show me how to do these things?"

"*Show you?* How in the hell can I show you? I just said it was part of you! I can show you one thing that might be right at the time, but the next time you'd do it, it would be all wrong. You can go out on an outpost with us tonight if you want to. It'll give someone else a chance to take a break, but you've got to remember, they're not 'aggressor' forces you're looking for. They play for keeps."

"You mean a listening post?"

"Right."

"Will there be Chinks up there?"

"Why, do you want to get some?"

"I sure do. How about putting me on a machine-gun?"

"Would you want to carry it up that far?"

"To get some Chinks? I sure would."

"Then talk to Self-Propelled. He's been trying to figure some way out of carrying it up there. In fact, if you go, he can stay back here. Have you fired a light MG yet?"

"Got expert' on firing at Knox."

"That's good enough for here."

It was about time to get the men ready for the outpost, so we left the hole and went to draw ammo and grenades. After introducing Jennings around; Birnstein, Carboni, Annus and I hauled him out to take over the night's work. It was past sundown. Upon reaching a small pass, we lay low, waiting for complete darkness. It began to rain, but that was alright, because we could expect the night to be really black in the rain. Although it meant we couldn't see Joe Chink, he couldn't see us, either.

Birnstein remarked to Jennings, "So you're gonna make like a prostitute?"

"A what?" Jennings asked.

"A prostitute."

"I don't follow you."

"You're going on an outpost, and that's just like being a prostitute, you're living with no visible means of support." Then he guffawed at his own witticism. He got little response from any of us, and his smile disappeared. He settled like a spanked pup.

Carboni said he had gotten a letter with a picture in it from his girl in Ireland that day. He wanted to have another look at it before we moved on up. Birnstein asked to see it. Carboni passed the picture over to him.

"Hmmm, white girl!" he jibed.

"What did you expect, Abey?"

"Knowing you, it's hard to tell."

"Man, don't talk that way, I'm gonna marry her."

"This gal?"

"Yeah, what's wrong with her?"

"On the whole, I can't tell. I've known her for but a short time, you know. Isn't she a little fat?"

"Hell no she's not fat! You're just looking at her from a fat head. That's why she looks that way."

"You say she's Irish?"

"Yes why?"

"Just wondered. Where did you ever meet her?"

"Pen-pal club."

"You mean you've never met her?"

"No, but I can tell she's a good girl."

"How, by the way she dots her 'Is' or crosses her 'Ts'?"

"Dammit Birnstein, you don't know anything, do you?"

"I know better than to believe in something like a pen-pal. She just wants to quit spending so much postage writing to you, and the only way she can do it is to marry you. What're you gonna live on when you get married? Postage stamp glue?"

"If that isn't a helluvva way to talk. Love, man. L-O-V-E, love. That's the menu."

"Go on, Carbonation, the minute you tried to kiss her, you'd stick together from the envelopes you've licked to each other. You're gonna look cute with her hanging from your lower lip."

"You make me so mad I could eat pork, Bean-brain."

"You a Ginsberg?"

"Are you kidding?"

"If you are, prove it by showing your circumcision; if you're not, go to church and get converted."

"Why in the hell should I get converted?"

"Then you can get three days off for Yom Kippur. Hey, come to think of it, I've got some days off coming pretty damn quick now. Or did I just have them? Can't remember when my days of religion are. Such a beastly war, you know.

"Reminds me of an uncle of mine once who went to church after a big poker session. Been out practically all night. His wife was so happy he finally got up enough guts to go to church, that she mentioned it to the minister, who called on him to sing a hymn. The old boy was snoozin,' and the wife had to shake him twice. Uncle had been dreaming of one of those big hands he'd had the night before and he sat bolt upright in his pew.

"The minister smiled down at him from the pulpit and said, 'Brother, would you lead please?' The old poker face dropped, and he looked at the reverend blankly, and replied, 'My lead? Hell, it can't be, I just dealt!' Never went to church after that."

"You said all that to say what?" Carboni asked.

"That you should never let a woman lead you into church, particularly when they're playing the 'Funeral March,' backwards."

"Backwards?"

"Backwards, yes. Didn't you ever know that that's the Wedding March?"

"I know that I'm talking to the biggest bull slinger in the Far East."

"Maybe in the Far East, but my uncle in Texas was the one. He had a big cattle ranch that shipped stock all over. I remember one time when he shipped five hundred head of bulls to the east; the next day two thousand head to the west, and the following week he sent five thousand bulls off to the north. He was the biggest *bull-shipper* in Texas."

"Oh, cheezus, deliver me from this guy," the medic groaned.

Jennings in the meantime had been watching them with curiosity, and unable to contain it any longer, asked me. "Do they get along alright?"

Birnstein was quick to answer, "Get along alright? Why Carboni would've been dead long ago if I hadn't saved his life. Didn't he ever tell you about the time he was so slow in keeping up with us that he got cut off? The Chinks started firing at him and he was in the middle of one helluvva firefight with them until I ran out into the rice paddy on his flank to draw their fire away from him."

"Did you get hit?" Jennings asked.

"No, they were using burp-guns and you can duck away from them at a hundred yards. Takes a little bit of footwork and you feel silly, like you were imitating an adagio dancer, but it works."

"Don't ever try it, Jennings." I said, giving the signal for everyone to get ready to move on up to the outpost.

We were to spend about two hours each on watch, but Jennings wouldn't go to sleep. He sat at the machine-gun all night gazing into the night. He wanted some Chinese to come around, but none came. It continued to rain, and when morning finally did arrive, it was not a sunrise, but daylight that just happened. The rains in Korea have always puzzled me, because usually it actually hangs in the air and gradually lowers itself to the ground. Then again it may drop like hail stones. No wind to blow it, no thunder and lighting, nothing but rain that turns the dust to mud, then the mud to dust. It's the only place in the world that has dusty mud.

We left the listening post. I was in the lead on the twisty, narrow trail. Staying on our feet was a problem, because the mud was as slick as ice, and the soft mist on top of it added to its treacherousness. We were feeling our way along, inches at a time when suddenly there came a loud tumbling, scraping sound as a steel helmet rolled past my side, bounding on down the hill. A split second behind it came a rifle, sliding and turning end over end, following the helmet. Then a pair of glasses came sailing through the air, The next object was Birnstein, who came to rest in a tangled heap at the bottom of the hill in a clump of weeds. Since the fall was a long, steep one, we felt certain that at best, he had broken a leg.

"Are you hurt, Dave?" I called. He just lay there groaning. "Are you okay?" I repeated.

"Yes, I'm okay." he gasped.

"Sure you're not hurt?"

"I'm okay, Herb."

Then seeing him in such a position brought out the humor of the accident. He had been quite a spectacle, falling as he did with his equipment preceding his own descent. I started chuckling at his ridiculous antics. He squirmed uncomfortably.

"Don't laugh, Herb." he pleaded.

I couldn't stop laughing, and the more I tried, the more I roared. Dave slowly arose and brushed himself off. He examined his glasses, which had broken, and put them in his pocket. Then he collected his helmet and rifle as I continued to snicker at his slow, methodical movements.

"Don't laugh at me, Herb, please." He asked heavily.

"Why, I thought you said you weren't hurt?"

"It's not the pain, Herb. . .it's the humility."

He volunteered to finish the trip back to the company in the lead, then if he fell again, he wouldn't foul any of us up in doing so. Not far from our destination, we sat down for a rest. The rain lessened and the sun looked as though it might break through. That, however, was something which could not be considered dependable. It looked that way many times, but it seldom kept promises.

Birnstein and Carboni began joshing each other again about the Irish girl.

"Let me see that picture again, will you?"

"You fall in love with her?" Carboni replied.

"No, I'm just trying to find out what she's got you're so interested in."

"You can't tell that from the picture."

"Well let me read the letter then."

"Like hell I will! It's personal."

"Does she have to write you through pen-pal office channels or do you have a connection and write her direct?"

Carboni didn't bother to answer. He longingly eyed the photo and handed it to Dave who glanced at it perfunctorily before passing it to

Jennings.

"See what can happen to you when you spend too much time in Korea?" he jeered, "Let it be an object lesson in, *'this can happen to you.'*"

Jennings took the picture, turned it around and looked at it with a stifled grin. You could tell what he was thinking, but he was courteous enough to keep it to himself. "Nice looking girl, Sarge." he said to Carboni who smiled his thanks.

"See, what'd I tell you, Rabbi?" he directed toward Dave. "Jennings appreciates good wholesomeness. Why aren't you more appreciative of feminine beauty?"

"You call that beauty? What the hell are you gonna do when she loses what she's got?"

"Hell, I'm not marrying her for beauty. She's a great gal."

"You're making a mistake."

"It's not yours. I'm the one making it, if anyone is." Carboni snapped.

"See what I told you? You admit it yourself."

"I didn't say I was making a mistake. You don't know your ass from third base." Doc was brusque. "Besides, it's none of your business."

"You tryin' to start a riot?" Dave grinned.

Doc didn't answer him, for at that moment, both of us caught the shadow, or the sound of *something* or *somebody* behind a nearby rock. It had appeared for a fleeting instant, then ducked back. We motioned for the others to be quiet and rose to our feet, moving slowly to the corner of the big boulder. Carboni, who was nearer the spot, was ahead of me.

"Better not go around there, Doc." Dave said, "it might be a Gook."

Carboni glanced back, saying, "I told you before, Rabbi, to mind your own business. I'm a sergeant, remember?" With that statement on his lips, he jumped around the boulder and the reaction on his face told us that he was startled at what he saw. Before I could get to his side to see what it was, a burp-gun cut loose. The slugs tore from his stomach, up through his chest and across his face, sending his body reeling backwards. He never knew what hit him.

Jumping back so that I could come around behind whoever it was, I sensed that he had anticipated that movement, and decided instead, to climb the rock and come out above him. I was convinced then, that he would be looking for me from above, and didn't know which way to go. It had to be one way or the other, I concluded, and selected the climb is the better of the two ways.

The rock was wet. I slipped off once, and tried again. The BAR I was holding in one hand wasn't helping much, either. Upon reaching the top of the boulder, I was looking down at a Chink with a burp-gun at his hip, trying to peer around the opposite end of the rock from where Carboni had been killed. If I'd gone around the end I'd started to, I'd have walked into the same thing the medic had.

A noise warned him, and he looked up and saw me. When he did, he whirled, but the gun barrel struck the rock and deflected it. Before he had a chance to step back and fire at me, I emptied my BAR into him. He spun half around and fell. Jumping off the rock, I hurried to Carboni.

Birnstein was beside himself, exclaiming apologies to Carboni.

"Dave, he can't hear you, you know that." I argued.

"Dammit Herb, he's got to understand I was only kidding him."

"He knew that. Don't you think he knew you that well? Cheezus, he really got hit, didn't he?" His face was nearly tom from his skull, and the rest of his body looked like he'd been under a huge sewing machine. The slugs were as close as the stitches from one. Annus and I dragged his body over to a pile of brush and laid him down. Dave went to it and placed the picture of the Irish girl in the jacket pocket. Then turned his back and moved away by himself.

"Come on, let's get back and have GRO come pick him up." I said.

We turned to Jennings. He sat staring blankly into space.

"Jennings."

No answer. We took him by the arm and pulled him to his feet. He groaned something incoherently and wouldn't focus his eyes on anything. He just stared.

"Jennings!"

Still no answer. Annus drew his hand back and slapped him across the face. That's what he needed to bring him back to his senses, but then he began babbling.

"Good God, I saw him killed! Right before my eyes he got killed!

I was sitting looking right at him when he got it. I saw every one of the bullets hit him. They started right here and went right up his body. *I saw them, I tell you!"* Tears streamed down his cheeks.

"Snap out of it Jennings!"

"He was standing right there and *I saw him get killed!* He didn't have a chance. I'll bet my brother didn't have a chance, either. He probably got killed the same way. I don't want to. I'm scared of dying." He broke down, sobbing uncontrollably, *"I don't wanna die!"*

"You're not gonna die if you remember to do things with a little common sense. Don't go jumping around rocks to see what's there. Come on, let's go." I urged.

He stumbled along blindly, looking back over his shoulder every now and then. He was still not sure of what he had seen. When we got back to the company, we turned him over to Lieutenant Sokolski and told him what had happened. Ski said he wouldn't send him out again for a few days. Birnstein went with Graves Registration to pick up Carboni's body.

*   *   *

While Dave was gone, a wire crew from signal arrived with surveying equipment to check our bivouac.

"What's with them?" I asked King.

"Beats the hell out of me. Maybe we're getting television."

"Cheezus, can't you hear those commercials now? '*Men...do you get up in the morning, feeling tired, dull, low and out of sorts? What you need is—*' "

Don't tell me, let me guess." King replied, holding his left hand over his eyes and extending his right for time to think. "A woman."

"Woman? What's that?"

"Some one to do your laundry for you, raise your kids—and of course the sundry other things expected of the weaker sex."

"She's gonna have to be a member of the stronger sex by the time I get back."

"Lot of laundry, huh?"

"Yeah—lot of laundry. Let's find out what they're doin' over here." I'd almost forgotten about the signal crew.

They were scanning a tree over from top to bottom. One man had climbed to the top of it, and with instruments, was sighting across the ridgeline of hills in front of our position. A man at the base of the tree was taking notes on whatever the one in the tree was doing.

"What's the scoop, friendo?" King asked.

"Heard you guys complaining about it being too dark up here and we're trying to fix you up with night lights." The corporal answered. "Night lights?"

"Night lights, moonlight, call it whatever you want to."

"What the hell are you talkin' about?"

"Artificial moonlight."

"I've heard of artificial insemination, but what the hell's artificial moonlight?" King asked, turning to me.

"I give up. What's this artificial masturbation you mentioned?"

"Insemination, not masturbation. That's when they take the sperm from a man, put it with a woman's and baby-san, hawa yes."

"Looks like it would take all the joy of livin', excuse me, lovin', out of—"

"Yes, we know, we know." He turned back to the corporal. "You mean you're putting lights in here?"

"Right."

'Oh, great. Nothin' like advertising where you are, is there? That'll draw more artillery than an American Legion convention gets prostitutes." The corporal looked at King. "You won't be here anyway, you guys are moving on up, so this will be behind the lines far enough it won't matter. Besides, the First Cav's had them for a couple of weeks, and they think they're terrific."

"You tellin' me?"

"You've heard about them then?"

"Not the moonlight, just the First Cav." Then slipping back into the radio announcer routine, King said, " *'The First Cavalry Division... You'll recognize these men by their distinctive shoulder patch. . .black and yellow. The line drawn diagonally through it is for the purpose of separating the horseshit from the chickenshit. First in Manila, First in Tokyo and First in Pyongyang'"* He gave me a wry grin, and remarked. "The truth of the matter is, the 'slogan should go—*'First in AWOL; First in VD, and First to paint everything mustard yellow!'* "

"Are your skirts clean?" the corporal asked.

"Are they clean? I don't get you." King replied.

"I just joined the outfit a couple of weeks ago, so I can't say, but back in the States, the Second was getting some pretty bad blasts in the press." He took out a cigarette, lit it and took a long drag and hesitated before exhaling, as though testing ice before walking on it. "Like I say, I don't know too much about it."

"Blasts like what?" I asked.

"Like leaving your dead behind. Now that I'm in the division, I guess, I should say, 'our' dead."

"Who's gripping about that?"

"It's in several papers."

"Who said it?"

"The First Marines."

King looked as though he was about to break the blood vessels in his temples. They stood out, large and blue. "You mean they accuse us of not taking our dead out when we leave?" he retorted.

"That's what they said."

"Never happen."

"Do you suppose they mean at Kuneri?" I asked.

He thought carefully, then answered, "It must be, Kuneri."

The corporal said, "That was the place. They said the division was so interested in getting out that they left their dead behind."

"Those lousy sonsofbitchin' sea-goin' bellhops!" King exclaimed.

Kuneri. . .Kuneri, where over six thousand Americans were killed in a matter of four days. Kuneri, where trucks were lined up bumper to bumper for fourteen miles while the Chinks dumped mortars and white phosphorous on them; where the blood ran from under the tailgates, spilling onto the ground. I remembered the two men, one missing an arm, the other both arms, asking to be taken aboard one of the trucks. But the trucks were already filled with wounded, squirming in pain like worms crawling in a can. There were some dead ones too, and we took them from the trucks to make room for the wounded. Certainly we had left some dead behind. What other choice was there? Should we have left the wounded and taken the dead out?

The signal corporal changed the subject, but fast.

"You asked about the lights. Have you ever seen those big spotlights they use at fairs and parades? Recruiting uses a lot of them." We nodded agreement and he continued, "These are about like them. They're 200 million candle power and work like the lamphouse in a 35 mm movie projector. Double carbon. They're about five feet in diameter, and the beams will be bounced off the clouds."

"What'll that do?"

"It'll light things up like the brightest moon you ever saw."

"How about that?" King yipped.

"Good for night baseball, but it'd be mighty rough on patrols, wouldn't it? I mean you'd be right out there where they could see you." The corporal interrupted. "They wouldn't be on all the time. Just whenever you called for them. As far as patrols are concerned, the lights can be on and still not illuminate everything. They could be fired into the ground and wouldn't bounce. Then you can find your way back by just heading for the beam. It's really great for outpost duty, 'cause when they're on, you can see Joe Chink."

"I'll buy that." Then as if to really substantiate the fact that they actually worked, King asked, "How do they know exactly which way to shine them?"

"Artillery coordinates." The corporal said, busily making notes while his partner called data out to him. "They use the same method of firing these as they use for firing missions."

"When are you gonna start using them?"

"In a couple of days, as soon as you guys move out. They're gonna have them in George Company area tomorrow night."

King snapped his fingers in remembrance. "George Company, that reminds me. Do you know a sergeant named Jordan, Tony?"

"Jordan? Bill Jordan? Not yes, but hell yes!"

"He was over here this morning looking for you, but you were still out."

"*Sonofabitch,* the last I heard of that guy was when I was with the 23rd back in the States. What's he doin' over here."

King shrugged. "What's any of us doin' over here? Beats the hell out of me."

"How'd he find out I was with Easy Company?"

"I don't know that, either. All I know is, he asked if you were around and said he knew you. He wants you to look him up."

"George Company?"

"Right. He's a platoon sergeant."

"Sonofabitch, Jordan!"

Sure I knew him. I knew that George Company had a helluvva good soldier in him, too. A short man, bulging with muscles, he had more angles to do the things he wanted done the way he wanted, and still make the brass think they were the masterminds behind the operation, than anyone in our old outfit. He had a full, round face, and eyes that danced with impish delight. A firm jaw and. white, even teeth left little doubt that he was a man with determination.

Glancing at King, I realized that they looked a great deal alike, except that Jordan's hair was a little darker. In fact, it was almost black, whereas King's was dark brown.

"Wonder if I'll have a chance to see him today?"

"I doubt it, he mentioned something about going up on outpost for a week. That's why he came over this morning."

"How long's he been here?"

"I don't know. I told him you'd be over to see him, so didn't ask too many questions. Besides that, he was in a hurry."

"I've got to get over there soon. Sure would like to see him. It's been about two years now."

* * *

Dave returned with the GRO men, carrying a mattress cover that sagged in the middle. In it was Carboni's body. They loaded it on a truck and left. Dave dejectedly sat down with a long sigh. I went to him.

"Did you hear about the artificial moonlight we're getting?"

He just looked at me with a blank expression. I repeated my question. "Did you hear about the artificial moonlight?"

Possibly he decided it didn't do any good to stay glum, but whatever the reason, he snapped out of it and said, "No Herb, I didn't. Suppose you bring me up to date."

I explained what we'd been told by the signal corporal and mentioned the Marines' statement about Kuneri.

"Those damn Marines'll do anything to get their names in print, won't they?"

He didn't elaborate. The incident died there. By dusk when we -were sent out on another outpost for the night, he seemed to be his regular self again. Perhaps a little more serious, but still Birnstein.

CHAPTER TWELVE
April, 1951, "Operation Yo-Yo"

THE RAIN was falling in large drops that seemed to break into millions of particles as it made contact with the earth's surface. It made a slight ringing sound when our helmets interrupted its downward flight. Water was running off the front of Dave's helmet, onto his rifle sitting between his knees. Occasionally he'd free one of his feet from the soupy mud to watch the rain destroy a bit of the juicy stuff that had clung to the heel of his boot. Then he'd giggle at the ridiculous pastime and free the other foot from its prison.

"What a life without a wife." he remarked.

"What in the hell would you do with a wife up here?"

"Are you kidding?"

As if to ponder the consequences of a wife on the front lines, neither of us said anything further for a few minutes. Dave grinned every now and then as a secret thought crossed his mind. The mental spouse was taking a beating.

"Let her up, Dave. She'll get her butt scratched in the mud."

His eyes glowed. "Herb, you know what I'm gonna do when I get out?"

"52-20?"

"No, I already used that. This isn't a real war you know, so they probably won't have anything like that for this 'Police Action.' I mean about these so-called luxuries of life, like a bed and pillows and everything."

"I give up, Mr. Binglestein, what are you gonna do?"

"The name's Birnstein. First thing I'm gonna do is throw the bed away and get a box, fill it with rocks and everyday, add one until it gets soft. Then I'm gonna post my wife—forgot to tell you I'm gonna get a wife—gonna post her outside the door on guard and have her wake me up every two hours for a massage. If she goes to sleep on guard, I'll have her locked up and court-martialed."

"What kind of punishment?"

"Whatever a courts-martial shall direct."

"Any idea how much time she'll get?"

"Twenty years if she's lucky."

"In the bastille?"

"Nope, got a better place than that. My bedroom. She's not gonna have to be passionate, boy-san. . . just patient. Man, it's been a long time."

He extended his lower lip past his upper, and as you blow a fly from your nose, sent the rain dripping from his helmet out into a spray. His face lit up.

"Forgot to tell you, got a letter from home, and Mom wanted to know if there was some way she could send some chow over here to us, and would we like some corned beef hash."

He laughed in advance, anticipating my expression of disgust at the mere mention of corned beef hash.

"I was just kidding, but she did say she was gonna try sending some stew. I can almost taste it now. Mother Birnstein's good old-fashioned Irish stew."

"Birnstein's Irish stew?"

"I can see the sign out in front of a little restaurant." he dreamed, moving his hand slowly across his face as if making the vision appear. " 'Mother Birnstein's Tasty Irish Stew. Mmmmmmm, it's good!' "

"Reminds me of an Italian restaurant I went into out in Battle Mountain, Nevada. Big sign in the window says: 'Genuine Italian Spaghetti.' Went inside and the joint's owned by Chinese and they had colored cooks. You can imagine what the spaghetti tasted like."

"Yeah, but my mother is Irish. The old man's Jewish. Damn good stew."

He became engrossed in thought and looked at his feet, both in mud to the ankles. We'd brought empty ammo cans with us so we could at least keep our asses dry. That's a laugh, now that I think of it. We were wet from the dermis out. Completely drenched.

War always changes a man's way of living, his conception of values, and certainly his attitude toward others. Would Korea ever settle down into a land of peace and tranquility after the war? But, what was it like before the war broke out? I wondered about that, and asked Dave. I should have known better in the first place.

"Dave?"

"Yeah?"

"You were here before the war. What are the people really like?"

"Ugh!"

"Whattya mean, 'ugh'?"

"Just that. When I say this place is for the birds, don't hand me a lot of bread crumbs. That's not what I mean."

"I mean the people. Have they changed any since all this started?"

"Well...a little. I remember back in '48, I saw an old papa-san riding a donkey, and about fifteen yards behind him was an old woman carrying a pack on her back, trudging along. I asked him why, and he grunted, 'custom.' Right after I got back to Korea, I saw him again, riding that same donkey. Only this time the woman was fifteen yards in front of him. I asked why, custom? 'Nope,' the old man grunted, 'land mines.' Yep, Herb, Korea's changed."

"You simple bastard, you never had a concrete thought in your head in your life."

"Short life."

"Think you'll make it?"

"Whattya mean?"

"Think we'll get above the 38th this time before you get killed?"

"Hell yes! Haven't you heard? Why, I'm the main string in this 'Operation Yo-Yo'!"

"You're an absolute half-wit, do you know that?"

"Thank you."

"Welcome."

"I had a teacher once who was a half-wit. Real cute gal, too. Remember one time I was in school and she was all shook up about something in the room, and said for each child who thought he was a half-wit to stand up. Nobody moved, so finally I got to my feet. 'Dave Birnstein, do you feel you're the only half-wit in the class?' she asked. I replied, 'No, teacher, I just hated to see you standing there by yourself.' I don't think she ever liked me after that."

"You're wonderin' why?"

"She wasn't my type anyway."

"I doubt if you have a type."

"Are you kiddin'?"

"You couldn't get a girl if you were the last man on earth."

"The hell I couldn't!"

"How about that chick you tried to make back down the line and couldn't, even with two bucks?"

"Doesn't mean a thing. She was too skinny, anyhow."

"Skinny? How fat do you want them? She was all wrinkles."

"That was nothin.' You should have seen the one I went with back home."

"I'll bet."

"She was so fat she used innertubes for garters. Went to a party one night and really had a blowout."

"Quit it, you're killing me."

"I don't wantta do that, Herb. I'll leave it for the Chinks. The way I figure it, you have about three more days. I'm gonna miss you, Herb, but when your time comes, I guess there's nothin' you can do about it. I just hope when you get it, it'll be fast and you won't suffer muck I'd hate to see you get a gut wound and suffer. You deserve to die quick."

"Go to hell."

"Hah! So whattya think Korea is already?"

CHAPTER THIRTEEN
A *"Chicken" Named Pickens*

'OPERATION YO-YO' continued. We'd run the Chinks north and they'd run us back twice as far to the south, until May, when the action increased. So did the casualties. Because of them, I became platoon leader.

Reports came in that placed Chinese troop masses about two thousand yards from our own positions. We were sending a patrol out for reconnaissance, and one of my squads was selected. Jennings, who had been anxious to get some Chinese, and yet careful not to; Annus who had been irritating Birnstein in the more recent days, with Dave and me, made up the patrol. We hadn't gone very far when Annus lost a heel from his boot. He was bitching about it.

"Shut up, Annus?" Dave snapped, "Your chances of survival went up a hundred percent when you lost it."

"Why?" Annus asked.

"Because now you're a lower silhouette, you stupid bastard."

"Knock it off you guys." I was brusque in my statement. "If you want to fight, just wait, you'll get all the fighting you want before long." I had no sooner said that when rifle-fire began cracking around us. Then it stopped except for one that seemed to be a sniper. His aim wasn't so good, for he wasn't hitting a thing. Thinking I had him spotted, I started to raise my M-1 to take a shot at him and it dropped from my hand. I picked it up again and it slipped out of my hand for the second time. Looking at my sleeve, I saw that the sniper's aim had been better than I had thought it was. Blood was running down my arm onto my hand. It wasn't too bad, and since we were in a position that we could see what was going on, we got the dope on the few hundred troops, damn near as many vehicles as troops and the firepower that was being massed in the valley below. Then we went back, turned in the report and I went to the aid station to have the slug removed. It was a big open wound, because the bullet had flattened out when it hit the flesh, and stopped, wrapped around a bone. I was anxious to get back to the company because if what we had seen in the valley was any indication of what was in the offing, things were going to happen fast and furiously. I didn't want to miss anything.

It was two days before I did finally return, and activities were growing. More replacements had arrived. Our new medic named Ryan was among them. One of the group was a master sergeant who had been put in command of my old platoon. But there was compensation for me, I had been promoted again. So had Dickson.

"How do the boys like this new guy, Dick?"

"Not worth a damn. He's lot of big talk and big stripes, but not a man in the platoon likes him. I don't think it'll be long before you're back as platoon leader. Sokolski put him in his place yesterday and told him to take his stripes off. Pickens, that's the sergeant's name, didn't want to and Ski had to give him an order to. Told him we didn't wear rank up here, that everyone in the outfit knows who we are and what we are. He hasn't done it yet, though."

"Has he taken any patrols out?"

"No, he was called out for one but said he had a cold or something. If you ask me, he's as yellow as baby shit."

"Then he won't last long anyhow."

"Just long enough to foul everything up. We're behind you, so for get him."

"If McPherson knew someone like him had his platoon, he'd not only turn over in his grave, he'd spin like a top."

"Forget it, Herb. What the hell, let this guy hang himself. You know how long he'll last with Sokolski. He'll chew this sergeant up and spit him at the Chinks."

"How've the patrols been going?"

"They're gettin' clobbered."

"What's happened?"

"Twelve man patrols, usually. Four or five get back. Some get hit, and some get caught. Hope to hell we don't get one today, something's gonna break. I think we're gonna mount an offensive."

"Yalu again?"

"Probably."

"Anything cookin' today?"

"Not as far as I know. There's a patrol going tonight, but we've got to get some booby traps put out. I think if we do that instead, we won't be called on for patrol. Would you rather do that?"

"Hell yes." I answered, thinking about my arm which was still pretty sore from the bullet I'd gotten two days before. "How soon do we leave?"

"I don't know, better check with the new sergeant."

"Where is he?"

"Beats the hell out of me, probably trying to build a new bunker for his CP. WHat a bastard."

"What does he look like?"

"About five ten or eleven, weighs in the neighborhood of 190. Clean shaven, wearing fluorescent stripes. You can't miss him."

"I'd rather you go with me."

"Okay, come on."

We finally found him, inspecting rifles. He was holding one up toward the sky, looking down the barrel. Then he handed it back to the owner who happened to be Jennings, with the remark, "It'll have to be cleaner than that."

Jennings just looked at him. "Cleaner than that for what?"

"To pass my inspections."

"It's always been alright in the past, what's wrong with it now?" Jennings grated.

"Whether it's been alright in the past or not is immaterial. I'm platoon sergeant now, and I say it's dirty."

Jennings looked over Pickens' shoulder and saw Dickson and me walking up to them. He began smiling. Completely ignoring the sergeant, he called out. "Hey Tony, straighten this guy out, will you?" Pickens turned around and there was little doubt who he was. Six of the biggest stripes I've seen and his name embroidered on the pocket of his jacket. "Who are you, a replacement?" he asked.

"Kind of." I answered.

"This is Tony Herbert, Sarge. He had the platoon till he got shot the other day."

"Oh, yeah, I heard about you. Got yourself hit, didn't you?"

"Just a scratch."

"Why did it take you so long to get back then?"

"I fell in love with a nurse, and couldn't leave."

"Really?"

"No, not really, her name was O'Reilly." I quivered slightly at the old, much used pun. It stank.

"I think the platoon is beginning to shape up pretty well. I've got most of them familiar with what is expected of them. It'll work out in due time," he said.

"I suppose," I groaned. I felt like hell seeing the men kicked around as he was doing, or would before it was over. "Want me to go with Dickson to set the booby traps out?"

"Are you familiar with how it's done?"

"Reasonably."

"Okay but keep in contact with me, I might want you to run a patrol." Then he turned back to Jennings and began explaining that a speck of dirt, if neglected, can result in a pit in the barrel, and over a period of time can render the rifle inadequate.

"Why didn't you tell him to blow it out his homesick ass?" Dick commented when we were out of earshot.

"Cheezus what a jerk. Who in the hell does he think he is anyway?"

"He just came from a training center, and you know how those characters are."

"Piss on him, let's booby trap the joint."

Going to the ammo trailer, we picked up about twenty-five charges and traps and left the company area.

"Are you sure you've got the right area where these are to go, Dick?"

"Yeah, Pickens said earlier this morning that this is the place. Why don't we set these with a hair trigger? The Chinks have been cutting around them recently and maybe a hair trigger would stop some of that."

"Alright with me. How hairy do yon want 'em?"

"So they'll go off if you breathe on them."

It took us about three hours to get them in, and our nerves were practically shot when the job was finished. Pickens had other ideas about the booby traps.

"Take them out." He hissed, belligerently.

Dick glowered at him. "Take them out?"

"Uh-huh."

"Ferchrissake, we just put 'em in!"

"Well just take them out."

"What the hell is this," Dick argued, "a game or something?"

"No game, soldier, I told you to put them in and now for the last time, I'm telling you to take them out!" he shouted.

"Why?"

"Why what?"

"Why take then out?"

"Goddammit, don't ask why, just do it!"

"You mean you aren't even going to say why?"

"I don't have to tell you what causes me to decide something. As long as you're in my platoon, you'll do as I say, and no lip from either of you."

I just looked at him, but the look on my face told what I was thinking.

"And," he continued, "you can wipe that smirk off your face, Herbert."

"Who, me?" I asked. "I didn't say a thing."

"You don't have to, but I don't intend to take any guff from anybody here, do you understand that?"

That was more than I cared to hear. "Who in the hell do you think you are, Sergeant?" I demanded.

"I'm the platoon sergeant, that's who."

"I saw this platoon before you even know where in the hell Korea was."

"Look, you might as well get this straight right now. You may have been the honcho before I got over here, but I've been assigned to straighten it out, and by gawd, I'm gonna do it."

"Straighten it out? Sonofabitch, the only thing that needs straightening out is the casualty reports." Dick bellowed.

"Yes, and that's the first thing I intend to take care of. There've been too many casualties. We've got to cut down on them."

"How are you gonna do that?" asked Dick.

"I don't really know yet, but I'll get the answer. These patrols are getting hit too hard. You're taking too many chances."

"What the hell are we supposed to do? They say, 'make contact.' We make it."

"I'm not going to argue with you, I don't have to. You two are taking a patrol out tonight, so get busy on those booby traps."

"Is that the way we're going out?" I asked.

"That's the route."

"Did you know that this morning?"

"I found it out about noon."

"Then why in the hell didn't you say something?"

"You were already out there putting them in."

"What's wrong with sending a runner out?"

"Dammit to hell, Dickson," Pickens shouted, "I'm not going to tell you again, I don't have to answer to you. Count your stripes and look at mine. That's your answer."

"Well, I'll be goddammed." I muttered.

"And that goes for you, too!" Pickens smiled triumphantly when he said that.

"How about you going out on this patrol with us so you can show us how it's done?" I replied.

"Masters don't go on patrols."

Dickson gave him a dirty laugh before saying, "The hell they don't! Tell us more. McPherson was a master, the same as you, and he didn't think he was too good to go on patrols with his men."

"Where's McPherson today?"

"He's dead."

"That's right, and I'm not going to make the same mistake he did."

My blood was boiling, thinking of the way Mac had struggled the days before he got killed, trying to keep his men together and get them out. The way he hobbled on one leg after I cut the shrapnel out of his knee, so he could stay with us on the attack against Hill 570, and this lousy bastard had the guts to stand there belittling him.

"Dick" I interjected, "let's get the hell out of here before this zebra gets his head knocked off.

"Are you threatening me?" Pickens shot back.

"I'm not threatening anybody, I'm just saying right here and now, stay the hell out of my way."

I half-shoved Dickson and we left, but as we did, I noticed two men who were standing behind him about fifteen yards who had been listening to everything that had been said. Dick told me they were new men in the outfit, named Greer and Valdez. One of the two looked familiar. I remarked about it.

"I think it's Greer you've seen before. Remember the wise guy who gave Birnstein such a hard time when we were in reserve a couple of months ago?"

"Yeah."

"Same guy."

"Where's he been?"

"I don't know, he wound up in battalion for awhile, but they probably couldn't stand him and shanghaied him up here to us."

"Kindda nosey, isn't he?"

"You mean the way he hung around listening to us with Pickens?"

"Uh-huh."

"He and Valdez both have their noses so far up his ass, that if he ever stops suddenly, it'll take a major operation to separate 'em."

"That bad, huh?"

"Hell, it's worse than that. Greer took basic under Pickens and was an acting-gadget, now he thinks he's gonna get promoted right and left."

"If he's anything like that sonofabitch, he probably will be."

We walked without talking. It started to rain. Dick held his hand out and remarked, "Feels like lead pellets." Then he stopped dead in his tracks. "Cheezus, we've got those traps set with hair triggers. These rain drops will set them off, bigger than hell!"

"They're not that loose, are they?"

"Are you kiddin'? The breeze will blow 'em all to hell."

We didn't press the conversation further, instead, began to honestly wonder and worry about the possibilities. Dick was grumbling inaudibly. I asked him to speak more clearly.

"I didn't say anything, just griping about why I ever joined the Reserves. Wife and three kids waiting for me at home, and what am I doin'? Making a fool, maybe a mess of myself."

"You'd bitch if you were hanged with a new rope."

"How in the hell do you take things so calmly?"

"Not much more I can do, is there? He'll hang himself."

"I'd like to help him."

"Wouldn't we all?"

Upon approaching the spot where we were to remove the booby traps we'd placed earlier, we took a break. Neither of us was anxious to begin the job. I looked at Dickson, puffing on a cigarette which was held inside his cupped hands to keep it dry. He looked like some movie star, but I couldn't for the life of me recall who it was. I'd often wondered about it, and finally my curiosity got the best of me. "You know Dick, you remind me of some movie star. Who is it?"

"John Garfield," he snapped.

"Well cheezus, you didn't have to bite my head off! Don't you like the idea?"

"No."

"What the hell's with you?"

"I'm just beat, Tony. So dammed tired of this whole mess I don't know whether I'm comin' or goin'. Some lousy bastard like Pickens has to come along, and if things aren't rough enough we have to get some stripe-silly moron in the outfit. I've been told for a long time that I should go to Hollywood to try to get a job as a double for Garfield, but instead I join the Reserves and get called back in."

"How much longer do you have to go?"

"You mean in the Reserves?"

"Yeah."

"Six more months, then they can jam it."

"You say it but you don't mean it. You'll probably re-up the minute you get back home."

"I'll be damned if I'm even gonna join the church for fear they'll mobilize all Christians. C'mon, let's go, what the hell, you only die once."

We began mapping out the best way to remove the traps. The rain was falling steadily. We stood looking at the gimmicks, some with little flat trips extending from the end. As each drop of rain hit and splattered on them, we held our breath. Slowly, warily, we moved in to disarm one after the other. Water poured down our faces, but it was nothing but pure perspiration. It seemed a lifetime, but actually was only about half an hour before the last one was neutralized. We breathed a sigh of relief, and it stopped raining.

"Well, that was nothing at all, was it?" Dick said, and set on the wet ground, fanning himself with his helmet.

"No sweat. Wow!"

"Let's go tell 'Stripes' we're finished."

"Hell no, stay here. Soon as we get back we'll have to get ready for a patrol. We might as well goof off for awhile."

"I'll go along with that."

I dozed and dreamed of hot baths, clean sheets, a football game, hunting, chocolate cake, milk, the works. Then I shivered and thought of coffee. I liked milk better, but I was wet clear through and coffee would warm me up. Coffee and cake, gawd, would that taste good! What the hell, I'm not at home. Where would I get them? Is that the only place I could find coffee and cake, at home? If it is, I've got to go there. How? Get wounded, that's how. I might get killed doing it though. Not if I did it myself. How? With a shot through the foot. Hell, I couldn't shoot myself. Why not, then go home. Coffee and cake. If I shot myself I wouldn't be able to look at my face in a mirror when I shaved. To hell with it, I'll grow a beard. What the hell's the matter with you, Herbert, snap out of it! You're yellow, that's what you are. The hell I am, I'm just tired and cold, and hungry. How long has it been since you've had a bath? What's a bath? You're crawling with bugs. So who in the hell isn't?

I'm at home. Liberty Avenue hasn't changed a bit. Looks good. Something's different though. Hell yes, I'm wearing civvies. Pass a sign, saying, "Join the Army—learn a trade." Just got out of the Army. Got my trade. Looking for a job. Turn into a big office and sit outside the wooden rail watching the women working. Millions of them, typing away. The paper said they had an opening for a man. What a racket, a man with all these dolls! They're all college graduates, too, I can tell. Notre Dame, Washington and Lee, Texas A & M. How in the hell did they go there? Connections. Lot of other men are waiting for a job, too. They're college graduates, no doubt about that. They look like it. They went to school while I was in the Army. Oh well, what the hell?

The door to the office marked, "Private," opens. A tall, luscious blonde walks out. Immediately the room smells better. Perfume, probably. She's wearing a knit dress. Wow, does it fit!! She slinks over to the rail and places her hands on it and leans toward us. What's she going to ask for? College diplomas, business experience, weight, size? What would she want with a man? I know what a man would want with her. She looks each of us full in the face, lingering on each one. Then her moist, full lips part. She speaks. "Any of you gentlemen know how to field-strip a BAR?" The others shrug their shoulders. Poor bastards been in school studin', leading a sheltered life. The Army's great! Where else could I have learned such a trade? "Yes ma'am, I do." I grin with exploitation when I say it. She smiles encouragingly and takes my arm, leading me down the rail to a gate, swinging it open so that I might enter. She has not taken her eyes from mine. We go into her office and close the door. She leans against it. Bedroom eyes, wow! "You didn't think I really have to have a man who knows how to field-strip a BAR, do you?" What a knit dress! "I just wanted to know that I was hiring a real man." She moves closer. Her mouth is warm and soft. She trembles in my arms and her lips search mine. She steers me to a waiting divan and disrobes. She wears no underthings. Her naked body is alive; hot, and sensual in my arms. Every muscle in her back strains forward to unite with mine. Sweat rolls down my face. I wipe it away. It comes back, with increasing intensity. I feel like I'm drowning.

Dickson woke up about the same instant I did. The rain had started again and was coming down by the bucketsful. Under it all, I knew that I was perspiring, too.

"How long were we asleep?" He asked.

"I don't know, but it wasn't long enough, I'll clue you."

"We'd better go, don't you think?"

"Wait a minute."

"We're getting wetter than hell here. C'mon."

"I can't go now, wait a minute."

"What's wrong?"

"If I started back now, I'd pole-vault all the way."

"What the hell are you talkin' about?"

"Nothin'," I replied, fearing she might never return if I told about her. "I was just kidding. C'mon."

CHAPTER FOURTEEN
"Old Soldiers Never Die..."

PICKENS was not in the company area when we arrived, but was at battalion being briefed for the patrols that were going out that night. Crandell got a box of cigars in the mail, and looked as though he wanted to smoke all of them at that moment in case he lost the box, yet determined to save them for later. He had a problem.

We didn't wait long before Pickens came back with the news that I didn't have to go on a patrol and that MacArthur had been relieved his command and sent back to the States. That's the order of importance we placed on the two items.

Mac had made an address to Congress when he got back to the States. Something about, "Old soldiers never die—they just fade away." Birnstein, as usual, had some wisecrack to make. He took his place a pile of ammo cans, and with a long expression, extolled, "Old soldiers never die—they just *smell* that way." Then he went into a eat oratory on how he would end the war if it was up to him. Pickens interrupted to tell us that we'd have to put barbed-wire entanglements up in front of our positions. Word had come through that something was brewing.

It was nearly dark when we finished, and coming from nowhere, our planes passed over our holes and began strafing the valley on the side of the hill in front of us. We thought they were nuts, and firing on our own troops, but a few minutes later the radios cracked out a message that Chinks were gathering in that valley for an attack. We got into our holes, ready for the onslaught. I was happy. You can shoot a million of them from a hole. It's a helluvva lot better than shooting them out of their own.

. .1e first attack came under the illumination of artificial moonlight. I was beginning to like the stuff. You could see them all right, but sometimes their shadows would get us all mixed up. It didn't take long to get it straight which was which, though.

The Chinks were changing signals on us. Instead of attacking with a whistle and retreating with a bugle, they were coming in on the bugles and falling back on whistles. Something new had been added, too. Each bayonet charge was accompanied with cries of, "Chin-chilly-lye-lye-lum!" Then when they'd regroup, the call was, "Ho-lahndo, ho-lahndo!"

The first, second, third and fourth waves were beaten back, then the fifth which was by far the heaviest, formed.

King asked, "How are the grenades holding out?"

Jennings checked what he had, and found one. A quick reply from the other men indicated there were damn few. King was goofed off.

"This is great. How're we supposed to hold them off, with spit-balls?"

"Aren't there more coming up?" I questioned.

"You know what they said back in company?"

"No."

"Wait until you need them."

"We need them. Why don't you call back and ask them to send some up?"

"I tried a little while ago. Better let Pickens do it."

"I don't know where he is. To hell with Pickens, I'll do it myself." I cranked the handle on the phone. Nothing happened. I gave it a more vigorous turn. Still no response.

"We've had it," I groaned, turning to King. "No communications. The phone's dead. What the hell we gonna do now?"

"The phone out?"

"Bigger'n hell."

"Cheezus, how 'bout you and Bugs checking it?"

"The wires?"

"Yeah, that's probably where the trouble is. Be careful though, some of the Chinks may have gone around us. They might have cut them."

Bugs crawled over, and together we began tracing the wire. We were fumbling, stumbling down the hill without finding anything wrong, when all hell broke loose up on the ridgeline we had just left. Artillery and small arms were tearing up something.

"We'd better get back up there, those guys need help." Bugs said, hastily.

We had gotten approximately halfway to the top when we saw what we thought was Birnstein walking down the hill toward us. The artillery had let up and it was a bit quieter, so I called out, "Hey, Birnstein!" No answer. In stage whisper, I called out again, "Hey, Birnstein!"

Instantly, somebody opened up with automatic fire. They weren't our BARs though, it was burp-gun fire. Like weeds growing out of a swamp, the hill came to life. It looked like a piece of candy swarming with ants. The Gooks had overrun our positions. The hill was crawling with them.

"Let's get the hell out of here!" Bugs screamed, running down the hill.

"Just don't get in my way!" I yelled back. I lost my balance and passed Bugs on the way, rolling end over end over end like a football. I wound up lying against a log. A second or two later, Bugs joined me. The Gooks were still coming down the hill, but carefully.

The two of us crouched behind the log, trying to regain our breath, trying to figure out what the hell to do next. Fear infiltrated into every bone. The joints in my body seemed to be drained and scraped clean of all lubricant. They ground, one against the other until they cried out in pain. The situation was not an illusion. It was real, almost to the point of being unreal. Behind us lay fog, in the valley a few feet further down. Protection. But protection for how long? If our own troops were there, they'd be trigger happy as hell. It's a cinch the Chinks were. It was also a damn sure cinch we couldn't stand off the whole Chinese Army.

My own voice startled me when I spoke. "Where's the rest of the platoon, Bugs? What's happened to them?"

"They've either gotten out of there or been caught. Which ever way it is, there's nothin' we can do lying here. Let's get the hell going!"

Another long stare into the night brought nothing. Before, we had seen the Chinks coming down the hill toward us. Now they were gone. That in itself was bad. It wasn't like those bastards to stop when they were rooting us out. Then again, maybe they were holding up for a bigger drive. At the same time, they could have been behind us. Too many doubts whirred around in my mind. I tried to straighten them out, and in the process, dismissed the fear. In the interests of self-preservation, we headed for the protective cloak of fog.

The loss of a buddy in war is one of the most miserable, tormenting experiences a soldier can confront. On the hill we were leaving, were many of the men who had grown to become an integral part of my life. Birnstein, King, Dickson. I hoped it was sudden.

We came across other men who were dug-in in foxholes and warned them about the attack that was coming off. They didn't appear especially interested in making a grandstand display of their might, and joined us. Before we had reached the bottom of the third hill we'd climbed, it looked like the Pied Piper and his followers. In the darkness and confusion, the problem was trying to determine who was to lead. We were all trying for it, but falling over each other in the attempt to gain it.

"Halt!" It was the voice of an American, but we had no especially outstanding features that would identify us as such. At least not in the dark.

"Okay, we've halted."

"Who goes there?"

"Friends."

"Who?"

"Americans trying to get behind you."

"Just a minute." He called for a lieutenant. The lieutenant came forward.

"Who are all of you?" he asked.

"What's left of the first platoon. Who are you?"

"Part of the First Bat. How in the hell are we gonna get out of here?"

"You new in Korea, Lieutenant?"

"Yes. Why?"

"Just wondered. I don't know about you, but I'm going down that draw to your right."

"You can't make it down that way."

"Why not?"

"I sent some men back that way after a new radio and they didn't come back. That was earlier this evening."

"So?"

"They probably got caught."

"Are you surrounded?"

"I guess, the communications went out earlier."

"We'll take a chance on it. Got to get back to our company."

"I'm against it."

"I'm sorry."

"That's an order. Can't afford to lose any more men."

"These are not your men, Lieutenant. They belong to Easy Company."

"I said, 'That's an order.' "

I moved restlessly. My hand fell on my arm. I wore no stripes. What the hell, this guy didn't know me. What should I make myself, five star general? No, we had one of them over here and he got fired. Field-grade? Not enough of them. I looked too old to be a lieutenant. "Lieutenant," I prodded.

"What?"

"Do you know who I am?"

"No, and I'm not going to argue about it."

"Lieutenant, do you know who the commander of Easy Company is?"

"No, can't say that I do."

"As a matter of information to you, he is a captain named Herbert. I am that Captain Herbert. Now will you get the hell out of our way and let us through? And you can retract that order you gave me." I smiled friendly. "I realize you couldn't tell who I was in the dark. Plus the fact that I'm not wearing any rank."

"Yessir. I'm sorry sir, I didn't know. I hope the Captain and his men get through okay. Can I help you with anything, sir?"

"No, I don't believe so, we've been here too long already. Gotta go." We left.

The hands on my watch pointed to three-fifteen. We still had a few hours before daylight. Occasionally a machine-gun would open up on something. We wondered if the distant gun was firing at one of nature's tricks on tired men or if the Chinks were actually that far back. The terrain was beginning to look a little more familiar. By four-thirty we had found part of our company. It was a mass of confusion.

"These guys are running around like a pregnant fox in a forest fire." Bugs remarked.

"Not any more than we are, I guess."

We checked on who was there, what was happening, and found that the CO had been hit and evacuated. Lieutenant Sokolski had assumed command of the outfit. He sent for me.

"What happened up there?" he asked.

"Beats the hell out of me, sir. Bugs Hoover and I went down to check our commo lines, and before we could find out what happened, the hill was Joe Chink's. They got every one of our men."

"I don't think so. What time was that?"

"About two-thirty."

"Good. I've been in touch with them since then. Did you start to check the lines *before* or *after* the attack?"

"That's what we were doing when it came off. We started *before*. Why?"

"I've talked to them since it started. That means they might still make it."

"They weren't trying to hold there, were they?"

"No, no. I ordered them off the hill. With luck...well. I want you to take a patrol out. Get about ten men. You know the old man got hit, didn't you?"

"I heard about it. Bad?"

"Not too bad. At least he's out of it."

"Who do you want me to take on this patrol?"

"Whoever you want. Swing around our left flank toward George Company. The LP's been giving us half a dozen different reports. If we go by what they've been sending in here, there are at least five million troops with ten thousand tanks over there. Got to have something more accurate than wild guesses."

"Yessir."

"You can take Greer and Valdez. Hoover might want to go with you. He's good man. I don't know, just ask for volunteers."

"I've never had Greer or Valdez on a patrol."

"Doesn't matter. You'll have to sooner or later. Might as well be now."

"You say George Company is to our left?"

"Yes. Why?"

"I just wondered. Do we make any contact with them?"

"No, and don't make any contact with the Chinese. We can't lose any more men. You'd better get going now."

I turned to leave and wondered about Pickens. I hadn't seen him since we got back. "Where's Pickens, Lieutenant?"

"A damn good question. Wish I knew. Said he was gonna check on something a couple of hours ago. That's the last I saw of him," he replied, busying himself with sorting ammo. "He's probably around somewhere. Doesn't seem to me like the kind of man to take undue chances."

"That's for damn sure."

"I know what you mean," Sokolski smiled, "take care of yourself, Herb. I'm gonna need someone I can count on."

Bugs said he would go with the patrol. Valdez and Greer had no choice.

Twelve of us, eight from the group of replacements with whom I had never worked, drew more ammo and grenades for the job. I issued instructions and we were ready. But there was a delay. Dickson returned. He looked beat.

"What in the hell's happened to you?" I asked, making no effort to conceal the happiness of seeing him again. "What about King and Jennings and Birnstein? How about the others?"

"I think they're all okay. Birnstein might have got hit. What happened to you? The first thing I know, you've bugged out on us."

"You cheap bastard, I didn't bug out."

"I know it. Sonofabitch that was close. I don't know where the others are, but they'll be along. Where you goin'?"

"Patrol. Wanna go along?"

"Bullshit!"

"Yellow?"

"Yellow hell! Who you got with you?"

"Your two buddies." I tantalized.

"Who, Greer and Valdez?" he asked, excitedly.

"Better believe it."

"Yeah, I'll go along. I'd like to see how these pupils of the great Pickens are. Be right with you."

He went to Sokolski and got an okay. We were almost clear of the company when we came across Pickens. He didn't appear to be tired from anything. Raring to go.

"Where are you men going?" Sarcasm dripped from his voice. "Patrolling."

"Who told you to take Greer and Valdez?"

"Lieutenant Sokolski, and we're already late."

"Where've you been?"

"Trying to find the company. Where have you been? Sokolski's been looking for you." I was interested in his answer.

"Over on the left flank."

"Anything over there?"

"No."

"That's what I figured."

"What do you mean by that?"

"Nothing, only I haven't heard anything over that way. Thought it was quiet."

"Oh."

"You look worried, Sarge."

"I think it's my ulcers again. Got stomach trouble. I think I'll go back to battalion aid this morning."

Bugs jabbed me in the ribs. "C'mon Herb. Let's move."

When we were out of earshot of Pickens, Dick said, "He's got stomach trouble alright. No guts."

"The biggest seven-stripe sergeant the Army has," Bugs said, "Six on his sleeve and one down his back."

"I don't know," I replied, "I suppose all of us get cold feet now and then."

"You sure as hell do." Bugs joked.

"Why do you say that?"

"How about what you said when we were lying behind that log on the hill?"

"Last night, you mean?"

"Yeah."

"Why, what'd I say?"

"You don't know?"

"All I know is I wanted to get out of there."

"Hey, Dick!"

Dickson stopped an,d let the other men pass. We caught up with him. "Did I tell you what Tony was saying when we got run off that hill last night?" Bugs asked.

"Huh-uh"

"Here he is with Chinks all around, bullets zipping around his ears, and he's saying, 'Oh Lord, I know I'm gonna die. I know all my life I've been bad, but please, God, please... if I'm gonna die now, please...give me a running start?'"

"Well whattya know?" Dick said.

"You got your running start. Didn't you, *Captain?*" Bugs laughed.

The patrol didn't show us much. We found no Chinks and when daylight came, we headed back for the company. I had been interested in how Greer and Valdez would perform. I was surprised. They pretended to get into the spirit of the thing. No gripes, nothing. In fact, they seemed to be pretty sharp soldiers. I judged that I had been mistaken. They were not cut from the same cloth as Pickens.

CHAPTER FIFTEEN
The Kid Whips A Problem

THE RAIN, more of a fine white mist than the stinging downpour that had so often presented itself in the past few days, continued relentlessly. It clung to the scrub brush, to the trails and to our clothes. The uniforms hung on our bodies like dishrags draped over a picket fence. Mud never had a chance to dry and flake off. But it didn't matter. We were past the point of super-saturation, and the dirt was synonymous with our very existence. Bugs, Dickson and I hurried to report to Sokolski and find out if any of the others had gotten back from the hill. They had.

Jennings, King, Buckholtz, Ryan, Annus, Brinnon, Crandell and the whole bunch was there. All except Birnstein!

"Where's Dave?" I inquired.

"He got hit." Jennings answered.

"Where is he?"

"In that litter jeep over there."

"How bad?"

"I don't know. I wanna tell you something, Tony."

"Can it wait?"

"Yes."

"Good, I want to see Birnstein before he leaves."

I hurried to the jeep. Dave was lying on his stomach with his arms crossed under his chin. He looked comfortable enough.

"Dave?" I half-whispered.

He jumped.

"Were you asleep?" I asked.

'No, not exactly. I was just lying here thinking."

"About what?"

"Wondering if I'd get sent home."

"Where'd you get hit?"

"Up on that hill."

"I know that."

"Then why ask?"

"I mean where on your body?"

"Promise you won't laugh?"

"Promise."

"I got hit in the ass." He looked a little ashamed.

"I always did say you were half-assed."

"It's not funny Herb. It hurts more when I laugh. How am I gonna pursue my trade when I get back?"

"Did you peddle it?"

"No, dammit, I mean sitting on it."

"So they shot you out of the saddle. Couldn't happen to a nicer guy."

"And now I'm goin' home."

"Quitter."

"Shit! I'm lucky, I got hit. You'll get killed. You RA men are nothing but cannon fodder. You're here to bear the brunt of the war until us ER's can make the world safe for democracy again."

"Okay, you're smart, Dave, how much longer will I be here?"

He squinted his eyes and pondered, as though consulting a crystal ball. His answer was just what I expected. "Til you die, son. 'Til you die."

I shifted the belt around my waist and lined the canteen up a little more. It was already okay. Neither of us spoke. It wasn't what Dave had said. We both got a boot out of harassing each other, so what we quipped didn't matter. It was what was being left unsaid. But when someone left, you had to tell them goodbye, didn't you? Dave started it. "Tony?"

"Yeah."

"I sure hate like hell to leave all you guys, you know it?"

"I suppose, but be damned glad you are."

"I was kidding about your getting it."

"Don't be foolish. It's probably the surest thing in Korea."

"Not as long as you keep fooling them like you have."

"The Chinks?"

"Both sides. The old man thinks you're braver than hell pulling rear-guard action all the time when we're retreating. I won't tell them your secret."

"Secret?"

"That you're not brave and holding rear-guard. You're just too damn slow to keep up with the rest of us." He looked like he was not quite certain about what to say next. "I guess I should say the rest of them. I'm gone now."

"Ain't you the lucky one?"

"Think I'll see if I can come back here."

"You'd better have the psychiatrist make a check while you're back there. I think you've got more trouble than lead in your ass. You've got rocks in your head."

He looked at me swiftly. The jeep driver was getting ready to pull out.

"Tony, you know, I'm luckier than hell."

"You said that before."

"I don't mean just getting a million dollar wound. I mean I'm lucky I was walking south instead of north."

If the laugh wrinkles around his eyes became more pronounced. It was difficult to determine whether it was from pain or stifled mirth. I wasn't going to bite.

"I suppose." I replied.

"Would've been a terrible waste of shrapnel. I'm already circumcised."

The jeep roared and the driver slammed it in gear.

"Take care, Herb."

"You do the same, and if you come across any women back there, you know. . . ?"

"You kiddin'? Ever tell you about the WAC who went out for a knick-knack and came back with a *tit-bit?*"

The jeep zoomed away, sliding and turning on the twisting road. In a moment it disappeared from view around a curve. He was gone. Just like that.

Birnstein's leaving the squad put King in the position of assistant squad leader. Until this moment, it hadn't occurred to me that through men getting hit, being out of action for prolonged periods of time, and the casualties we'd sustained, I had been made squad leader over the others. The same men who had been in the outfit when I joined it. It didn't matter to them, but I remembered how concerned I was about whether they'd like me when I came here. Taking over a squad they had been in before they ever heard of me was not the way to win friends and influence people. Pickens and his platoon leadership was a good example of that. With the CO knocked out, Sokolski wasn't in the platoon anymore. He had his hands full with the company. Pickens was platoon leader. I wondered how long it would be before we went into the attack with him. When it came to patrols, it didn't matter much because he was always going to be where the action wasn't, like last night. If things were popping on the left flank, he'd be on the right. He was yellow. Not very much to build confidence on. I didn't want to go into the attack under his command. Neither did anyone else. Why did someone like him have to come along when there were so many good men who could do the job so much better?

Bugs Hoover, for example. Guts from the letter "g." King, although never in much of a position to show command authority, was a terror with a BAR. Now he'd be my ASL. It was a toss-up on which was the best man in the squad. They both could think plenty fast when it counted. More importantly, they could think together under fire. They had coordination, and there were a lot of dead Chinks to back that up. In retrospect, I began to appreciate how much Birnstein had contributed to the squad without any of us realizing it. He would lead you to believe he was the worst soldier in the whole United States Army.

Nothing was more in error.

Things within the company were in an absolute stage of disorder. The CO, with whom most of us never worked in direct contact, was gone. That removed our officer from the platoon. Pickens had taken his place, without the confidence of anyone, including Sokolski. Everybody was as nervous as a prostitute in church, and the weather itself was depressing, plus getting the hell knocked out of us the past few days. I wondered what Joe Chink would do, right this minute, if he were aware of the psychological advantage he held over us? I closed my eyes and hoped, very hard, that he didn't know. This was a stupid war.

Then there was Jennings whom I had not had much time to worry about lately, but nonetheless, still a problem.

Although Jennings wasn't the smallest member of the squad, he gave you that impression. You'd have thought he was the youngest, but he wasn't that, either. It might have been his slight build, or his boyish personality. I hadn't had much occasion to work with him since the Carboni incident, and wondered how he was making out.

The rest of the platoon seemed to like him all right, although he kept to himself quite a bit. He was not a demanding person, but then again, what the hell could you demand in Korea? His first few weeks in the platoon had been unending torture for him. The thought of his brother getting killed the way Carboni got it was always with him. Maybe he was afraid, actually afraid. If he was, that was bad. He might crack under pressure. That could be disastrous, not only to him, but to everyone else. I hoped that his withdrawal from others around him was nothing more than an adjustment. An adjustment that was being accomplished. He had to forget about his brother, or rather, if he was going to think about him, it had to *create* his courage, not *destroy* it.

Jennings possessed all the inherent qualities he needed. It was just a problem of cultivating them until they prospered. Before I had gone to see Dave off, Jennings had wanted to tell me something. Maybe it was right in line with this period of cultivation. Maybe it. wasn't, but in either case, I had to give him a chance to say it. He was eating a candy bar when I found him. His face no longer sported freckles.

They were hidden behind several weeks of dirt and hurried washings in mud puddles. At least he didn't have a beard as most of us did. He didn't have to shave yet. He scooted over so I could sit down beside him.

"How's it going?"

"Not bad." he smiled.

He finished the candy and folded the wrapper, several times, pressing it carefully on each crease.

"Was there something you wanted to tell me awhile ago? I'm sorry I rushed away from you, but I wanted to see Dave before he left."

"Sure, that's alright," he stated gently. "I understand."

A silence followed which indicated he didn't want to press the subject further. That was the dangerous thing. Maybe it was something he wanted to, *had* to get off his chest.

"Don't you want to tell me about it?" I encouraged.

"Yeah, I'd like to, but after you left and went over to Birnstein it somehow lost its importance."

"Don't say that, Jennings, if it's something that will affect you, it is important. How does the old saying go, 'We're in this together'?"

His eyes shone with internal triumph when I said that. Suddenly he was eager to talk.

"That's just what I meant."

"What did you mean?"

"I think I've found myself." He coughed a nervous, embarrassed laugh to cover up the statement that had identified his past performances as inadequate. "I think I've got the straight of it now."

"When did this happen?"

"Last night when we got run back here. Something happened last night."

"What was it?"

Tears pushed their way to the surface of his eyes.

"I killed a man."

Had the occasion itself been less important, I would have told him to forget it. But it *was* important. This was the very thing I'd wanted to happen. Now we had the benefit of a few minutes to talk it over after it had happened. A few minutes that could mold him for the rest of his stint in Korea.

"Don't cry about it, fella. Be happy you got him instead of you getting it yourself."

"I know it, and I don't know why I'm crying. I think maybe it's because I've finally blown the cork off whatever it was inside me. I feel better."

"Good."

"I can't remember what happened, isn't that funny? I remember being in the hole and King telling me to get out and start back here. The Chinks came from all around us. I just fired into a bunch of them. I know I got some of them then, but when we got on down the hill I picked up an AR from a body and we held up there for awhile. Before I knew what was coming off, there was a Chink right on top of me with a bayonet. I fired that BAR until it was ready to melt. I got him alright. The awful thing was that I could see his face as plain as day from the muzzle-blast."

He trembled with excitement, not nervousness. He had reached the core of his trouble and had penetrated it.

"It wasn't so hard at that, was it?" I asked carefully.

"Lord no, it was do that or get killed."

"That's exactly what it is over here, Jennings. *Do it* or *get it*. That's why we're all here. That's why some of us won't get back, because we're *getting* while they're *doing*."

"I know it, and after I killed—that's an awful word, isn't it?"

I nodded and he continued, "after I got this one, and he's the one I think about because he was so plain in the light of the flashing gunpowder, I felt great. Not because I had gotten my first one, but because. . .well, *maybe* I got the Chink who got my brother at Pusan. It's the only way I can live with myself, by telling me I *did*."

"Maybe you did at that."

"I hope so." He paused. "You know what, Tony?"

"What?"

"I'm not afraid to fight now."

"Of course you're not. Whoever told you you were in the first place?"

"I did."

"Right. You were your own worst enemy."

"I know it, and I've got that whipped now."

"Good boy." I patted him on the shoulder. "Welcome to the squad, soldier."

He smiled encouragingly, and I left. I left before the illusion of killing the Chink that got his brother, was destroyed. It could plunge him into the category of a mere killer instead of a valorous kid who had avenged his brother's death. He had avenged it by getting one of them. Let him think it.

Only, the *Chinese* did not fight in the Pusan Perimeter.

CHAPTER SIXTEEN

GEORGE COMPANY moved in close to our left the next day and I got Pickens' okay to run over to see Jordan. It had been darned near a lifetime since I'd seen him. There would be a lot to talk over. Chances are, he'd have a woman stashed away somewhere. He wouldn't be Jordan if he didn't.

I thumbed back, through the pages of memory, to Seattle. Jordan and I took our first week-end pass from the division together and headed for town. It wasn't long until he singled out a bar as a likely prospect. Prospect for what? Women, naturally. I insisted that I wasn't interested. He was. He plunked himself on the barstool and ordered a beer. I ordered the same. While the bartender was opening the bottles and pouring, Jordan searched the bar in the blue mirror which hung behind it. He spotted a blonde moving our way. He nudged me to move over. That placed the only empty stool next to him instead of me.

"You said you weren't interested, didn't you?" he had laughed.

The blonde put her purse on the counter and ordered a scotch and coke.

"Scotch and coke, did you hear that?" Jordan asked me out of the corner of his mouth, "Who the hell ever Heard of scotch and coke?"

She didn't hear him. Casually, he appraised her in the mirror. Her eye caught his occasionally and then shyly ducked back to her drink. It wasn't long until she asked him for a light. He lit her cigarette for her and asked if he could buy her a drink. While she was replying. "Yes," he was asking me to loan him a five-spot. She tossed them down so fast the bartender just left the cash register drawer open. Finally, Jordan raw that she was drinking up all the money with the drinks taking no visible effect. He leaned close to her.

"Pardon my asking, honey, but how much does it take to make you dizzy?" he inquired.

She looked at him hopefully. I saw the dollar signs reflecting in her eyes from the register behind the bar. She smiled.

"Five dollars, soldier, but the name's Daisy."

Jordan was deeply wounded. He muttered something about, "No conquest," and we left. I started in on him when we got to the sidewalk.

"Why the devil do you have to have a woman? Can't we just have a beer?"

"Sure, but if we're gonna have a beer, why not with a woman? The trouble with dames around an Army camp, is they make a man get rusty with his line. So back home a guy goes with a chick for a couple -of weeks before he goes to bed with her. That's okay, you've got plenty of time back there, but on pass you don't have. Out and out propositioning leaves me cold. Where's the conquest?"

He got wound up on a long sermon on the importance of conquest.

"Take that gal for instance. She didn't leave any room for my approach. That's important. A conquest is built just like a brick-layer builds a house. The woman keeps what she terms her self-respect. When she does go to bed with you, it's only because she wanted to and was going to all along, but she wanted you to think that she was falling for you. You both play the same game. You make a play, she sidesteps it. You make another and she parries. Finally when the bar is about to close and she figures you're about to vamoose, touche'. She leads you the way to her place or leaves the place of battle up to you. She has kept herself respect by not saying right out that it would be five dollars, and you feel a conquest. Chances are, you've been wondering what color pants she's wearing and it winds up that she doesn't believe in gilding the lily. Doesn't even own a pair of drawers."

He had made his conquest that night and it cost me another five dollars. I slept at the camp. Seattle didn't show me much.

First thing I'd do when I got to George Company would be to ask him for the ten bucks he owed me. I wondered if he would remember when he got it. My step quickened. I was real anxious to see him.

The company was busy digging in and setting up communications. I asked where Jordan was and was told to go over to the CP. At the command post they said he was out on an outpost and would not be back until the next day. I was disappointed. I found out which was his platoon and asked about him. One of his men said he was in Jordan's platoon and damn glad of it.

"Pretty good man?" I asked.

"Gung-ho as all hell." the soldier answered. "If they ever pinned it down to cases, two-thirds of the casualties the company slaps the Chinks with would go to Jordan."

"Pretty rough, huh?"

"Fightin' sonofabitch. He's got a carbine that the CO himself wouldn't dare touch. He's got the stock oiled down 'til it looks like black walnut. Cleanest gun I ever saw."

"That sounds like him."

"Know him?"

"We were together in the States."

"How long's it been since you've seen him."

" 'Bout two years."

"Oh, yeah? He'd be glad to see you. Why don't you go out to the OP?"

"I'd like to but I've got to get back to my own outfit. Tell him Herbert was here and ask him to look me up will you? If he doesn't get a chance to get over to Easy Company, I'll get back here as soon as I can. And tell him I want my ten bucks. He'll know what I mean." The soldier grinned, feeling that he knew something about his platoon sergeant that nobody else did. Maybe it would put him in better stead with Jordan. It was obvious that the sergeant was liked, and admired.

It was good that I didn't take time to go out to the OP to see Jordan, because when I got back to my own company, I was told to get ready to go to the battalion for a few days. We had a couple of hours before it would be dark, so if we hurried, we might make it through okay. Bugs, Jennings, King and I were sent together. We asked what our mission would be and were told that we'd be running battalion patrols for recon and intelligence.

"Why us?" I asked Pickens.

"They wanted four good men, and since you guys seem to be so thick, you should go together."

"What about the rest of the squad?"

"Who've you got now?"

"King,—" I began. He interrupted.

"I know you've got King, He's standing right there beside you. Do you think I'm blind? I mean who else is in your squad?"

'Dammit you should know, you're platoon sergeant, aren't you?"

"I'm asking you about your squad, you're not asking me about my platoon."

"Excuse me all to hell. If you'll shut up for a minute, I'll tell you."

"Don't get wise with me."

"Nobody's getting wise unless it's you. We've only got a little bit of daylight left. If you don't mind, I'd like to get there before dark."

"Who else do you have in your squad?" The words were measured, and overly pronounced.

"King," I began purposely, "Buckholtz, Annus, Hoover, Jennings, Crandell and Dickson."

"I've taken two of them away from you. I just wondered how well you kept informed."

"You what?"

"I've taken two of them away from you. You should know these things."

"How am I supposed to know if you don't say anything about it?"

"It's up to you to find out."

"What the hell are you, some kind of a tin god or something?"

"If you'd stay around here once in awhile you'd know who I am." It was obvious that he was stalling for time. Precious minutes of daylight were being lost. He wanted us to foul up in the darkness so he could point his finger and say, "See, I told you." I didn't argue. There was no time for that. *The bastard.*

"Crandell and Buckholtz are in the third squad now."

"Okay." I could argue that out later with Sokolski. "Can we go now?"

"You're not making much of a fuss about losing two of your men."

"You said you were the boss. Giving me anyone in their places?"

"Greer and Valdez."

Just what I figured. I could straighten that out when I got back, too.

"Can we go now?"

"Go ahead, and when you get to battalion, check in with the S-2. They'll take over from there and let you know what they want."

The more I thought about Pickens as we made our way to the battalion, the more involved his presence in the platoon became. True, we needed every man we could get, but not men like him. All of us were fighting to live, but he was fighting to keep from fighting. Each of us in our own way had passed that eccentric of illusion—of wondering if we'd make it and what it would be like. It was a normal course, to gamble with death, I gave up any pretense of liking Pickens. It was taking all the will power I could command to keep from beating hell out of him. Nobody mentioned him. It would have only added fuel to the violence. And now it was getting dark before we were even halfway to our objective.

I asked Bugs, King and Jennings if they had any idea where the trails were that led to the battalion. They didn't know. The night closed in like a photographic darkroom. Complete darkness. In a matter cf half an hour, our eyes would adjust themselves to the darkness, which in itself, weakens as the moon sprays a glow from the horizon. Right now though, it was murder. Everyone was gloomy about the prospects of continuing before we could see better. I was sure we were on the right trail, but there was no sense in trying to feel our way, inch by inch. We sat down to rest, and to wait.

Voices. Only mumbling, but definitely the voices of men approaching from a little to our right, and coming toward us. Koreans? GIs? Chinese? We split, with Jennings beside me on the left of the trail and Bugs and King opposite us. In a moment we recognized the voices of Americans, perhaps five or six or them. For their protection as well as our own, we challenged them. They identified themselves and asked which way they could go for medical help. They were wounded, trying to get back. In the group of six men were two with legs missing and one with a mangled arm. The other three were helping them. We directed them back down a trail we had come up They began the arduous trek, stumbling and falling.

Our sight was returning now, and we had to get to the battalion. Since the wounded had made it through the area we were going to, why couldn't we? It didn't take us long to make the decision. Not more than five minutes after the group had left us, there was a tremendous explosion from their direction. They had gotten into a mine field. There was no sound from them. It must have been fast.

Bugs discovered something. Communication wires.

"At least it leads in the direction we're going," he whispered, "Why not follow it? It's be the easiest way of getting there."

"Okay," I answered. "You trace it for a while and we can change around."

He got on his knees and took the wire in his hands. From time to time he'd grunt as he'd fall into a hole. "Watch it," he'd warn. "There's something here." We'd maneuver around the obstruction. It became my turn. It wasn't long before I bumped into barbed wire. A tin-can rattled. A startled soldier challenged us.

"Who's there?" he called out.

"Is this the Blue Battalion?" I replied.

"Who's there?" he repeated.

"Fella, I don't know who you are, but I hope to hell you're the Blue Battalion. Where are we?"

"You're sitting right under the sights of a machine-gun and you'd better say who you are and why you're here."

"We're from Easy Company, sent here for S-2."

"Don't move another foot." he cautioned.

"Don't tell me we have to go through that identification routine again?"

"No, but if you come much further there won't be enough left of you to identify. You're in the middle of a mine-field."

"My achin' back! How in the devil are we gonna get out of this?"

"You've only got a couple between you and us."

"One'd do it."

"Do you know how to feel for mines?"

"Yes, with the back of my hand."

"Better start feeling." He answered. I sensed that he ducked behind something in case my "feelers" were none too good.

"Bugs?" I opened my mouth, but that's all I could say.

"Yeah," came the reply, "we're ready. Go ahead."

"Did you call me a gourd-head?"

"No, but that's as good a name as I could think of."

"Yeah? Well, here goes nothin'. So long, it's been good to know you."

"Now just take it easy, we'll go up with you, you know."

"You wanna hunt for them?" I asked, hoping he did.

"Quit stalling."

I placed the back of my hand on the ground and raised it a little. Then I began the slow, methodical sweeping motion trying to find the mines and hoping beyond hope that I wouldn't. We advanced painstakingly, inch by inch. Abruptly, I made contact with something—something that made a helluvva noise. Sweat was pouring from my face. My eyes burned from its saltiness. The noise was caused by a ration can that someone had placed in a spot where anyone coming into the area could be sure to knock it over. I had humored them. It was no use. I was too nervous, and there was no sense in taking a chance on the lives of others. I called to the machine-gunner.

"We're gonna have to stop. Can't see anything."

"We called into battalion that you were here. They want you up there." came the reply.

"That's a damn shame what they want. Unless you give us some light, we don't move another foot."

"The Chinks would blow us to hell if they saw a light."

"We're gonna blow you sky high if you don't. Would you rather get blown up by mines or artillery? Take your choice."

He talked it over with battalion. In a moment, a flashlight beam stabbed the darkness. What a relief. We were guided on into the gun emplacement. There a guide waited to take us to the battalion S-2.

CHAPTER SEVENTEEN
Prelude To Hell

THE INTELLIGENCE SECTION of battalion was in a makeshift bunker, a log-roofed emplacement dug into the side of a hill. An orientation for men from various units within the battalion had just concluded. Ill-concealed excitement and concern reflected from the faces of those leaving the meeting. Their expressions and caustic remarks about "advances" and "opposition," meant that either we were going into the assault. . .or the Chinese were.

The last person from the meeting had cleared the doorway leaving the bunker. I pressed against the side of the passageway and wormed through the double blankets that prevented the light from spilling outside. A Coleman lantern hissed. Over in a comer, a captain was sleeping on the dirt floor with his battle jacket rolled under his head while a sergeant busily transferred figures from one sheet of | paper to several others. These were then being placed on a master sheet. I reported to a major standing before a map showing our positions and the Chinese defenses. A black line crossed the front indicating our location. Above its place on the map was the characteristic red line where the Communist line lay. Xs marked gun positions and units that were exposed to any attack that might come off. The acetate over the map showed that it had changed many times in recent days. In places, red and black smears almost obscured the map itself. The major was making alterations even now. His grease pencil was busy. I waited until he glanced my way.

"Excuse me, sir." I began.

"Yes, what is it?" he replied without stopping.

"I'm one of the four men sent here from Easy Company."

"Oh yes, be with you in just a minute." He surveyed his work and was satisfied with the new symbols and lines. He looked around. "You're Herbert, aren't you?" I nodded. "I remember you from when you were here before. Tell you what this is all about. Care for a cup of coffee?"

"Yessir, I'd like some, but the three men with me are still outside. How about them? I just wanted to find out what was what before telling them to come in or to wait."

"Bring them on in. We'll have to go on into the 2-3 shack in a minute, but they can wait here. Go ahead, get them." he directed.

The nauseous sweat of unclean bodies swelled from the hot coffee. The major began his briefing.

"We've been getting so many reports that conflict on who's got *what,* and *where,* that we have to get something more dependable. That's why I asked Sokolski for men with experience. We have a listening post I want you to man. There might be something breaking out that way. If it does come, I think it will be from that vicinity. Above all, for God's sake, be as accurate as you can. To hear the men who have been out there, all the Chinese on the whole front are in that one spot. We can't strengthen that side and weaken another unless it's absolutely necessary. Let's go on into the 2-3."

We followed him. Operations personnel were busily tabulating information as it came from intelligence. Four telephones were carrying the voices of as many outposts and patrols. Reports were pouring in from all directions. There would be a report of a flare being tripped in this area; artillery coordinates for a couple of rounds of mortar in that spot; estimations of troops masses observed here op there, until the whole report, consolidated, ended up as one great big hassle. I don't see how they were keeping anything straight in their minds or on the maps. Evidently they did, though.

The major explained to others who we were and why we were there and we were given a jeep driver who doubly served as a guide to take us to the LP. He said he had rations for us. We had almost passed through the doorway leading back into the first bunker room when the major called me off to the side.

"I talked to Lieutenant Sokolski and he wanted me to tell you not to worry about your men being shifted around. He said he's got the squad back the way it was, and that two or three more of them would be coming up tomorrow. Your company hangs in a blocking position right now, so you don't have to be concerned with anything happening to the others because you're gone."

"Thanks. Did he say who was coming up or anything?"

"No, but he did say you were going to have eight men for awhile."

"Good deal. Thanks a lot, Major."

"Okay. Good luck, and remember, try to give us the straight dope, will you?" Oh, by the way, the men you're relieving have been out there for some time. Send them back with this driver. They're probably pretty worn out."

The guys on the LP were happy to get relief. We endowed ourselves to a long watch. Since it was our first night on the post, and the words of the officers back at battalion were to say the least, foreboding, the remainder of the night would find the four of us on guard. The darkness was about shot anyway, so our decision, to stay awake was not difficult to arrive at.

Less than an hour after sunrise, Dickson arrived in the company of Greer and Valdez. Crandell and Buckholtz followed soon after. We worked out the shifts for the following night. The five who had just come in, had travelled in daylight and by vehicle, so they were the logical choices for the next go. They were given the afternoon and night to sleep until their shifts came up. Greer and Valdez were not interested in sleeping.

"You guys had better grab some sack time." I cautioned.

They grinned secretly at each other. "Do we have to now, *Mother?*" Greer asked.

I endured the remark. "You don't have to, but you're gonna have a hard time staying awake tonight if you don't."

"Never went to sleep on guard yet." Valdez answered.

"Well don't tonight, either."

"Don't worry about it."

"I'm not worried about it. It's your ass if you do."

Night closed in, and S-2 issued another word of concern. They were certain something would be coming off soon. Liaison planes had reported masses moving in our direction. They were not masses of clouds. They were Chinese. Dickson had completed his four hours watch at eight o'clock; Buckholtz was on until midnight, followed by Greer and Valdez from twelve until four. Crandell would take over as their relief. I heard the first shift change, and had just dozed off when Greer nudged me.

"What is it?" I asked, sleepily.

"I'm sleepy, Sarge."

"Who the hell isn't? I told you today to get some shut-eye. You wouldn't listen."

"I couldn't sleep then."

"Well you sure can't do it now."

"1 can't stay awake... I can't do it."

"Do you know what happens to men who go to sleep on guard up here?"

"I can't help it. I can't stay awake."

"Tell Valdez to whisper sweet nothings in your ear."

"Already tried that. He's sleepy, too."

"That's a damn shame. Get the hell back up there, and I'm tellin' you... if you go to sleep, I'll have your ass."

He went back, but very reluctantly. I dropped off again. Valdez' turn to gripe came next. *"Sarrrrge?"* His voice came loud enough to awaken me. "I'm going to sleep. I'm going to sleep."

Jennings sat up. "Let me take one of their places for awhile. I feel awake enough."

I could not buy that. "You took your shift last night. It's up to them to take theirs. If they can sit around playing cards all day, they can stay up all night. Damned if any of us are gonna do their work so they can goof off!"

I crawled to them. Neither of the two looked drowsy. I suspected that they just wanted to see how far they could go. If given the opportunity to bluff their ways through now, it would be a continuing thing. They weren't going to start it.

"Are you really sleepy?" I asked.

"Really, Sarge." Greer answered.

"Okay. Think company would help you any?"

"It might." said Valdez.

"Well, tell you that I'm gonna do. I'll give each of you five companions. How's that?"

They liked that. That meant the whole damn squad would be up, plus more men. I don't know where they thought I'd get them, even if I had intended to. Reaching into the box of hand grenades beside them, I took out two. Turning to Greer, I placed them in his armpits. He looked puzzled.

"Hold still!" I demanded.

"What're you gonna do now?" he asked, apprehensively.

"This answer your question?" I jerked the pins on both of them. "Now do you know what'll happen if you go to sleep?"

"I can take them out when you leave." Valdez grinned.

"Think so?" I grinned back, "Here's something for you, too."

After both had gotten grenades under their arms, I placed one in each hand and pulled the pins on them. "Just in case you think you can work a way to get rid of them, open your legs, Valdez." He hesitated. "Open them!" I gritted. He opened, and another grenade between the knees rounded out the operation quite well. I matched that on Greer, and put the pins into my pocket.

"Now, in exactly two hours, your shift will be up. I'll put the pins back in then. In the meantime, if you get sleepy again, I wish you'd go down over the forward slope of this hill to do it. No sense killing all of us."

"We can't stay like this for two hours."

"It's up to you, but the sooner you go to sleep the sooner you quit drawing your rations. You might as well learn right now that you've got to carry your own weight around here. People will help you, but I'll be *damned* if they'll do everything for you so you won't have anything to do. Now shut the hell up and take your watch!"

I went back to sleep. About every five minutes I'd hear one or the other complaining, "I'm dropping one of them Sarge. I'm dropping one!" But they didn't. In about an hour I went back and placed the pins in the grenades. If left long enough, one of the two would drop one. That would start a chain reaction and blow them all to hell. Sitting beside two boxes of grenades was enough to make them really hang on to what they had. After the pins had been returned and the suspense was over, I told them to put the grenades in the boxes. They just sat there.

"Put them away," I repeated, "why just sit there holding them?"

"We can't let go of them. Can't move." they said, passively.

I laughed, and took the explosives from under their arms and between their knees and returned them to the boxes. In order to get them out of the men's hands, it was necessary to pry their fingers open. They had sat there so long with them that their hands were numb. They couldn't have left the grenades drop if they had tried to. I took the shift until Crandell came on duty at four.

"How's it going?" he yawned.

"Okay so far, but there's something fishy going on over to the right and straight ahead."

"See something?"

"Can't see anything, but it seems *thick,* know what I mean? Like the sound is stopped by a lot of 'something.' I don't know how to explain it."

"Well, you've been out here," he replied, "and if it's something that's happened since you started listening, you'd notice it more than I could just starting."

There was no need to talk. Only look and listen. Would daylight never come? There was nothing in the night but dark, clumpy shadows that sometimes moved. No way to change the illusion except close your eyes, hard, and open them again. By the time the earth stopped dancing around and returned to normal, you had only dazzling stars busily scurrying through the darkness. The vision of shadows moving around would slowly return. Back from where you started.

Crandell yawned again and stretched his legs. He tried to get comfortable. "I ache all over." he said, not complaining, just remarking.

"Know what you mean. I haven't slept, what you'd really call sleep for so long I don't think I'd know how."

"Ain't it the truth?" he answered quietly.

"You know something?"

"What?"

"I'm getting punchier than hell."

"Why?"

"I keep thinking I see somebody moving out there."

"That wouldn't be too surprising, would it? That's why we're here."

"You take a look."

He wiggled around until he caught the direction I had reference to. I didn't have long to wait to get his reaction. *"Sweet mother of shit!"* he exclaimed, "They're there alright. Right at the foot of this hill! Must be *ten thousand of them!*"

"Better get the word back to battalion, quick."

"What are they doing?" he asked.

"Must be eating. At least that's what it looks like." I cranked the phones. No answer. "Sonofabitch, why in the name of hell do the damn communications go out every time we get in the middle of something? Now that damn thing was okay five minutes ago. I heard the static."

"I'm gonna get the rest of them awake. We've got to warn battalion." While he was arousing the other men, I got what it looked like in the terms of how many there were, and what they were going to do. It was big. Dawn had cracked by this time. It was getting light fast.

Jennings went ahead as a runner to battalion. The rest of us skirted around, endeavoring to determine the prospects a little more reliably. A few mortars dropped behind us. Maybe somebody had spotted Jennings. If that was the case, we could expect anything. The Chinks ahead were satisfied until now that they had not been seen. If Jennings was spotted by one of their snipers or lookouts, it would tip them off that we knew they were there.

The word of the Chinks' presence must have reached another outfit sooner than we had spotted them, for our jet fighters began strafing the valley behind us. We watched them drop napalm and machine-gun the Chink troops. It apparently was the match that lit the fuse, for before the fifth plane had made a second pass, the Chinks were up the hill on top of us. We bugged out, with them firing at our heels. Then we were really in for it, because they were so close that our planes couldn't tell Americans from Commies. The jets were strafing us, too. Crandell got hit in the shoulder by one of them. Dickson tried to help him but Crandell insisted he didn't need help. The Chinks held up and we made it to a road. Vehicles were making their way toward our company. We grabbed a ride on one of them.

A little way up the road we came across a hitch-hiker. It was Jennings, and he was limping badly. I jumped off the truck and helped him aboard.

"What happened to your leg?" we asked.

"I got smacked by a mortar right after I left you."

"Then you were in that barrage we heard?"

"Yeah. That was all in my honor, did you know that?" he seemed pleased.

"Somewhat dubious distinction, I'd say. How bad's the leg?" I wanted to take a look at it.

"It's alright. They wrapped it for me at battalion."

"Did they say anything about us coming back to battalion or for us to go on to the company?"

"No, but they were moving out and didn't seem to worry much about you."

"Then we're sure as hell not going to battalion. Let's get back to the company. Does anyone know you were hit?"

"Yes," Jennings answered, "they called the casualty report in to Lieutenant Sokolski." He looked proud. "This means I've got a Purple Heart, huh?"

"Sure does," I grinned, "just make sure you don't get anymore,"

"Herb?" Dick called out. "Don't you think we're about due for a rest period? We've been on the go for a long time here. Seems like we should have some kind of a rest break."

"I remember hearing something about a five days rest and relaxation behind the lines. Let's see if we can't get on something like that when we get to the company. We haven't had a break for damn near seven months now."

"We've got it coming to us." he winked convincingly. "We'll insist on it."

"What is it Dave would've said? 'You know what you are? You ain't nothin' boy. Nothin' but right that is.' *You're right.*"

CHAPTER EIGHTEEN
"Massacre Valley," May, 1951

IF WE HAD any ideas of recuperation leaves, they were shattered into
nothingness when we arrived in the company. Sokolski was almost frantic.

"Cheezus, am I glad to see you guys. I'm in one helluva spot. I don't
think we've got half the men left."

"Why, what's happened to them?" I asked.

"Pickens cracked up on me for one thing. He's gone."

"Cracked up? Where is he?"

"They took him away. You know that chintzy SOB had been hiding out
on us? Every time a patrol or something came up, he was where we
couldn't find him. Finally I caught up with him and sent him out on a
patrol and damned if he didn't come running back, screaming that they
were after him."

"What happened to the patrol?"

"Wiped out." he said dejectedly.

"And he made it? The only one?"

"Afraid so."

"Sonofabitch. Who did he take with him on patrol?"

"Luckily, nobody you knew. They were all replacements who came
into the company yesterday. First day in combat, first patrol."

"You gonna write a letter to their parents?"

"Sure, I want to, but what the hell could I say, that their son died in
battle? That it was for a just and reasonable cause? He did it valiantly and
bravely? I can't tell them that a psycho-neurotic master sergeant caused
it."

"Why don't you wait a couple of days? You look tired."

"I haven't slept for three nights."

"Why don't you take a break? You can't keep going like this forever."

"Break? What's that? I've got to have a count on the company. Will you get it for me? By the way, you're platoon leader for the second. And in case anyone asks you, you've been promoted. New you can fill Pickens' shoes."

"That's for damn sure."

He laughed. "I mean in stripes, not in the hospital."

"Maybe that's what you meant, but that's not what I was talkin' about." I joked. "You knew that Jennings got hit this morning, didn't you?"

"Yes, I got the word."

"Want me to check on the company?"

"Yes, and soon as you get finished, grab some sleep. I just want you to have the dope for me in case I want it."

"Lieutenant?"

"Yes?"

"Have you heard anything about rest and relaxation leaves?"

"Yeah. They're supposed to start in Juvember."

"Oh, one of those deals, huh?"

"Looks that way. Going somewhere?"

"Yessir, gonna check on your flock and see how many sheep y'all got left."

"That's a helluvva way of putting it."

"Helluvva war, too."

"You can say that again."

"Helluvva war, too."

"Get out of here." he said menacingly.

It was getting dark, but we hadn't had time to rest when Ski called for me. "What's the count on our company now, have you got it?" he asked.

"Yessir, I do. You're the only officer, but we have 94 men left. Jennings might have to turn in though; he's got a pretty bad leg."

"What happened to him?" He seemed too groggy to understand what was really going on.

"He got hit with a mortar this morning. Don't you remember?"

"How bad is it?" He seemed irritable.

"He's still got a compress on it. Can't really tell. He said he thought it would be alright, though. I think he should go back."

The lieutenant shrugged his shoulders in half-agreement, and turned back to a message-form in his hand.

"We're going to need him if he can make it. If he can't, send him back. This just came in from regiment."

I looked at the slip of paper that said we were to move on up north to help hold a pass open for French and Netherlands troops to pull through.

"We'll have trucks here in about ten minutes to take us up to the area," he continued. "Better brief your men and get ready to move out."

I went to talk to Dickson about getting the platoon organized. When he learned we were moving up again, he became furious.

"Damnit, we haven't had a rest now for three days. What are we, mechanical monsters or something? You just can't keep going night and day!"

"Keep your voice down, Dick. You'll get the men all excited. Hell, if an outfit's in a jackpot, we've got to help them out, don't we? Besides, some of our division's 23rd Regiment and a Ranger company are caught. They've got to move back They can't just stay there and get clobbered!"

"How long will it take?"

"No way of telling, but it's just a holding action. Shouldn't take too long. Tell you what. As soon as we get into position, you grab some shuteye. When they start pulling back or something breaks, I'll let you know." Even though I was platoon leader, I felt strange in giving orders to Dickson. He'd had nearly 5 years of war, counting World War II.

He had asked if we were mechanical monsters. I thought about that as I got what was left of the company organized. It would have been of tremendous help if we were mechanical. I searched out Jennings.

"How's the leg?"

"Pretty sore, but it feels better if I keep moving. Where are we going, anyway?" He kept flexing his leg, just slightly so it would be loose when he began the walk. Blood was soaking through the compress and his pants leg.

"According to the message-form, we're going up in the vicinity of Kun-Mun-gol. There are some buildings around there. If nothing happens maybe you can bed down there. Are you sure you don't want to go back?"

He said he didn't, and hobbled over to get his weapon and load onto one of the trucks that had arrived. I picked up a piece of machine-gun belt to tie a blanket and sweater around my waist and hopped on the last truck as it pulled out. When we arrived at the end of the run we found the mountains standing directly in our path. Ski was over at an ammo trailer.

"What's the latest word on the situation?"

"There've been a few snipers reported in that vicinity." he said, indicating a small rise, or hump on the ridge to our right front.

I was stacking grenades in the front of my shirt and picking up carbine clips at the same time. The lieutenant gave me a wry grin.

"What do you think you've got there, candy?"

"Better than that, sir, *poison.*"

I had learned long before that grenades were much more effective than rifle bullets.

"How many have you got there?"

"About eight grenades and four hundred rounds of carbine ammo. That should be enough to last for a hour. Then I'll have an excuse to bug out." We both laughed at my reply.

He explained the situation further and said we were to take the hills on our right and hold the pass open for the men who were with drawing. I went over to talk to Dickson.

"We've got to get out of here and move up pretty quick," I said.

The urgency of that statement was punctuated by an artillery shell that came screaming in. We all hit the dirt and fragments whistled above us. Then a helluvva loud bang came right next to me. I thought it was a grenade and that we had been ambushed, but when I raised my head, one of the trucks had a flat tire, a piece of shrapnel as big as my fist jutting out the other side of it. Before we could determine just what had happened, a barrage of 120's came in, sending the earth skyward and twisting it, making our entrails ache from the concussion.

"We've got to get the hell out of here," Sokolski said, crawling to my side. "They've got this pass zeroed in and don't want it kept open. Let's go."

The formation fell into a single file and moved through the draw. The artillery still boomed through the night air, but we didn't get any more rounds in our immediate position. The sweater and blanket bumped against my buttocks as we climbed.

About fifteen minutes later we met the Dutch retreating. I was reminded of a picture I once saw of Washington's troops at Valley Forge. We didn't have any snow and cold wind whipping down upon us, but the wounded far outnumbered those who could make it under their own power. There was a pitifully small troupe representing a battalion of men. Not more than a fraction of a company left.

Jennings turned to me. "It must be pretty rough if someone as tough as the Dutch are forced back."

No remarks, except words of encouragement were made to the Dutch as they passed us. Usually, whenever we met someone pulling back, we had a lot of things to shout at them, jokingly. No one joked now. One of the Dutch was heard to mumble, "You can't fight 2000 with 200. *You can't do it.*" His voice was lost in a groan of pain as he struggled to stay on his feet. Another howling round of artillery came in with a murderous crash. Then all was silent, save the constant rush of projectiles intended for other people.

When the initial roar had passed, I looked back to see how the Dutchman had made out. The two men who had been helping him were trying to lift him from the ground. I went back to help.

"No need trying to help him," a sergeant said, "he wouldn't have made it anyway."

A jagged hole ran from his shoulder to the base of his skull. His brains were seeping out in a mass of pink-tinted fluid. We rolled him over and I could not stand the sight of what was left of his face where the fragment had burst out. His body flinched spasmodically a couple of times, and fell motionless. "You can't fight 2000 with 200," he'd said. Our column moved on up.

About a quarter of a mile further we crossed a stream and passed one or two houses. Every man's mind was sober. Artillery increased in fury until the earth staggered from its incessant torment. A man-made earthquake was ensuing.

The night air was getting cold by the time we were able to take a break.

"What happened back there?" asked Dickson, referring to the Dutchman. "Someone said you were hit.".

"No, it wasn't me, it was some philosopher."

"Some what?"

"Nothing, just a guy who had the right idea, I guess." I changed the subject. "Don't you think we should put a couple of guards here before we move out?"

"I asked Lieutenant Sokolski about that a minute ago. He said to wait until we get to the top of the ridge. Put them out there."

"Okay. Did he say anything to you about switching the marching order of the platoons around from here on up?"

"Yeah, he wants the fourth platoon; then the third, second and first."

We sat there for a few minutes just resting. We couldn't smoke, nor could we talk above a whisper, even though the artillery was deafening. Too often it would suddenly, and for some unexplained reason, stop. That's usually when we would be talking in a loud voice to get a point across. Too dangerous. Too many Chinks around. I grew progressively chilly from the perspiration which was drying on my body.

"Think I'll put my sweater on." I said, rising to my feet.

It was as if someone had zeroed in on me. No sooner had I gotten to a standing position when another round of artillery came whistling in. I hit the dirt at the same instant as the explosion. The earth was there to meet me and I ran a tooth into my lip.

Dickson thought it a terrific joke. "Looks like the Chinks don't like the OD sweaters any better than we do."

Another barrage had passed before I was finally able to get into the sweater. We began our climb up the hill. My legs ached and I was tired. Too tired to think, only climb like a robot with an objective—but climbing unobjectively. We reached the ridgeline and put two men on guard. I told Jennings to stay there. His leg was giving him trouble. I suggested that his partner on guard give him a chance to rest. Both of them needed it, but Jennings was wounded. He smiled weakly and wished me luck. Plucky kid.

The acrid fumes of burnt gunpowder choked the air. My lungs ached and I gasped for breath. "One breath of fresh air," I said to myself, "would be worth all this stinking land. One breath of fresh air."

We could hear shouting on a hill north of us. Shouting that was the mixture of Oriental sing-song and American cuss words. Suddenly Sokolski began shouting from the front of the column 100 yards away. He was calling for us to move up fast.

I rushed to him. "What's happening?" I asked above the steady beat of bursting shells.

"Tie in with the first platoon, quick!"

"What's the scoop?"

"I think that's a Chink attack forming in the valley. That could be their patrol on our right, off that finger. Tie in and tell the men to get into the foxholes."

We were fortunate that the hill had been occupied before and the previous occupants had been there long enough to have foxholes. No one knew what was happening. We got into our holes and waited.

Joe Buckholtz, Dickson and I were in the same one.

"What in the diddle-be-damned hell is going on?" Joe asked.

"I was about to ask you the same thing. I don't know." I was laying my ammo out in a pattern so it would be readily accessible. "Ski says he thinks there's a Chink attack on the way in. The way I figure it is that you can't tell the Chinks from anybody else in a fracas like this."

"What kind of rifle have you got, Herb?"

"Carbine, why?"

"Wantta trade me? I've got an M-1. Too heavy."

"Sure, I'll trade you. How much ammo have you got?" I was always a little more at ease with an M-1. "Do you have the bayonet?"

"Couple of hundred rounds—bayonet, too. Do you have one with the carbine?" he asked.

I thought about the bayonet's use at Kuneri before replying, "Are you kidding? You'll never catch me without a bayonet on my rifle. It's life insurance. Trade you even."

"Sold to the man in the bullet-lined foxhole!" he quipped.

We could hear the jabbering of the Chinese as they crept closer. From our right a grenade exploded. "Someone jittery and can't wait for them, Buck."

"Just as long as they don't fire their rifles and give their position away." he whispered.

"It's so damn dark I can't tell our own positions, can you?"

"No, but I know none of us speak Chinese, so they must be the real natives of Shanghai climbing the hill."

We sat and waited, hardly daring to breathe for fear of missing a whisper that would tell us where they were. Unexpectedly, the searchlights came on. Their beams bounced from the clouds and illuminated the valley like the inside of a ball park. I glanced around and discovered that we were in a hole right smack at the center of a "T", just as a figure appeared silhouetted on the ridgeline about twenty yards away.

"Of all the places to be," I bitched,, "right on a finger. Hell's fire, you might as well be trying to talk the Chinese out of using their main line of approach."

Buck and I let go of grenades about two seconds apart. The figure twisted and fell back. Just then we heard a clinkety-clank a little more to our right and saw about fifteen Chinese pulling a machine-gun mounted on iron wheels up the hill.

"Let's get them with grenades." Buck said.

"Okay, but don't you think they should work some more, first?"

"Right, let's wait until they're just about ready to set it up. Then we'll both cut loose on them."

We gave them a couple more minutes, and when they looked like they were ready to stop, we threw two more grenades. The fragments made loud cracks and zinged off into the air when they hit the steel parts of the gun. The Chinks fell back, dragging their dead. Then all hell came our way.

Screams of, *"Monsoo—sonsofbitches,"* from the fanatical bunch charging up the hill, and calls for the medics were all mixed up in the night.

A grenade fell into our hole, and Buckholtz picked it up, throwing it back at them. It exploded in mid-air.

"Hey, we've got air-burst cover. Did you see that?" he called out over the noise.

I didn't take time to answer. Five more grenades fell into our hole in the next few minutes and Joe was kept busy tossing them back.

"We've got to get out of this hole if we're gonna fight," he yelled, "it's too big and they've got us spotted."

Before we had a chance to, a concussion grenade landed in the hole and *blew* us out of it. Then we lay on the ground, firing at the figures as they came over the ridgeline toward us. My nose was bleeding from the explosion, and my head was pounding. Over on our right, "Self-Propelled" was, of all things, detail stripping a light machine-gun, just as calmly as if he were in the States, giving a demonstration to a class.

At that moment, three Chinks ran over the top of the hill, carrying burp guns. Before Joe or I realized what was happening, they emptied their guns into the hole we had just been blown out of.

Buckholtz was loading his rifle and couldn't fire at them—he just shouted, "Look Herb, gettum! Gettum!"

Dickson and I started shooting together. One of the three died fast, his head half torn off by Dick's automatic carbine. Another fell to his knees, screaming at us in Chinese and frothing at the mouth. But he continued firing, and then pulled the pin on a grenade, threw it at us and dropped to the ground. Before the grenade could go off, Buckholtz had bayoneted him and the third one. Then the explosion came. Something hit me in the arm, and at the same time, the hill teemed with Chinese. Everything disintegrated. It was every man for himself. I was slashed across the arm by one of the Gooks before I was able to bayonet him.

"Let's get the hell out of here and try to regroup further down the hill!" Buck and Dick both exclaimed. That was the only way we would ever be able to stand them off, so we backed down, trying to check the tide until we could fathom what recourse we had.

Lieutenant Sokolski was having a private fight all of his own. Perhaps it was his confused state of fatigue, or maybe it was an example of one's refusal to cease this instinctive struggle for self-preservation. In any event, the Chinese were paying dearly for every inch of ground they were getting from him.

As regularly as if ejected by a machine timed for the job, grenades were raining in on him. The Chinese must have felt that he, and he alone, was responsible for delaying them. Their army in its entirety was dedicated to but one purpose—the elimination of Lieutenant Sokolski. But they were having a rough time accomplishing it. A grenade would no sooner touch the ground before he'd scoop it up and throw it back in their laps. It was obvious that he couldn't keep up much longer. There was nothing we could do to help him. We were too far away with too many Chinese between us.

Not satisfied with grabbing the grenades from the ground, he began snatching them from midair, like a spirited end in football making a fingertip catch. With a quick flip, he was returning them to their owners. Then a grenade exploded behind him. He was knocked down, wounded. Dragging himself to one knee, he continued to pick them up and heave them back. They couldn't kill the guy. He was on his left elbow now, on the brink of collapse. One more grenade came in. In a final, desperate move, he lunged for it. He had it in his hand and was about to whip it away from him when it exploded. His right arm was blown off, and when help got to him and rolled him over, they found that his right eye was gone, too.

If Ski made it back and is alive today, that dauntless spirit he displayed on this hill is still with him. The loss of an arm and an eye couldn't possibly keep him down. *He had too many guts to become a defeatist.*

When we reached the valley. Chinese mortars and artillery swamped us. It became one continuous scream and explosion. We had to keep down to avoid being hit by fragments, but when we did raise up to see what was happening, we spotted the Chinese through their own fire, some dropping as they were hit by their own artillery, but others still trying to get to us. We could fire about two rounds and then duck again. As soon as it would let up for a second, we'd try to get further back, toward battalion.

Somewhere along the line and in all the excitement, I became separated from Buck and Dick. I found myself with Ryan, our platoon medical aidman, and King.

"We're going the wrong way!" Ryan said.

"No we're not," I replied. "This is the draw we came through getting here. I remember."

"But there's fighting going on ahead of us too. We must be going the wrong way!"

We discovered the battalion was being hit. That meant we were completely encircled! The searchlights went off, leaving the night to surround us in a protective cloak of darkness. But it also hid the Chinese. At that instant a bullet passed through my left leg just above the ankle, chewing flesh, but narrowly missing the bone.

We came to the point where Jennings and the other man had been posted on guard. There was no one there. A little further down the hill we came across seven other men from the company.

"Where's everyone else?" I asked.

"I was about to ask you the same thing. I don't know what the devil's going on."

"So who does? It's a cinch we can't stay here though, there must be a million Chinks after us." The numbness in my right arm was beginning to leave and it was aching. My fingers were stiff and barely movable. I asked King if he'd been hit. I noticed he was limping.

"Got it in about three places, I think. No bones broken, just flesh wounds."

"Better have Ryan take a look at it."

"It's alright, I had another medic bandage it up before we fell back."

"When did you get hit?"

"I don't know. As hour or so ago, I guess."

We walked on through the night, hitting the ground every now and then when rounds of artillery came our way. We couldn't hear the Chinese behind us any more. They were probably stopping to reorganize. I couldn't figure out how they could need reorganizing when they had so many men to overrun a position. We were staying close to the hill to avoid being seen.

Some of the men got to discussing the best way to get back to battalion. One of them said, "We're gonna get clobbered out here in the open. Why don't we take off down the river? At least we'll have some cover if we use the brush on the bank."

"Did you ever stop to think that the Chinks might have the same idea, Jerk?" Someone answered.

"At least you'll have someplace to hide, in the underbrush!"

I was too tired to get into the conversation and I had no intention of going down the river-bed, so I let them fight that out for themselves. My left arm was beginning to swell from the bayonet wound.

"You know as well as I do," the argument continued, "the Chinks will have something up there waiting."

"Well for crap's sake, you guys, if you're gonna go, go!" I griped, "Don't foul us all up with that yapping! We're having enough trouble without you causing more."

Three of them stopped, talked it over for a second and headed down the river toward the battalion. Ryan was the next to come up with an idea.

"I think we'd better wait until morning before we get back to battalion. We're liable to be mistaken for Chinese by our own men and get shot that way. I think I'll wait until daylight."

"Where are you going to hide out?" King asked.

"I saw some brush back there a minute ago. I think I'll duck under some of it and wait for daylight. Anyone with me?"

One man said he would go, so that left King and three of us to make it on through. A burp-gun opened up over on the river. The Chinks had set up an ambush, waiting for someone to come down that way. They did.

The whoosh of big shells accelerated. The Chinese were catching hell now from our own batteries. It gave us reassurance to hear it purring overhead in support. King and I agreed that we would not be taken prisoners. We'd die first. I remembered too well, the short time the captain and his men had been prisoners. It seemed years ago.

We hit the pass about 200 yards above the battalion, and had about concluded that we were in relative safety when King grabbed my arm. I winced when he touched it.

"There's a Chink at a machine-gun up there!" he exclaimed.

"Where, I don't see him?"

"Just to the right of that pile of ammo cans, you can see the muzzle of the gun."

He was right. The Chink was there, but he looked as if he were asleep. We stopped and were turning around to double back when shooting broke out on the river again, behind us. We decided we couldn't turn back.

"Do you suppose if we talked a little 'gook' he might think, we're part of a patrol and let us pass?" King questioned, hopefully.

"Sure, it might work. How much 'gook' do you know?"

"Enough that I made out with that babe back in Uijongbu."

"Do you want to proposition him?"

"Who?"

"The Chink on the machine-gun."

"Hell no, I know a little more than 'how much' and 'come on' though."

"Okay, it's worth a try, let's go." I said, beckoning for the other men. We stretched into a single file and walked past the machine-gun, trying to assume the air of a patrol looking for separated Americans. King said something to the Chink who gave him an answer in three syllable Chinese words and we walked on by. He moved his machine-gun. It squeaked, ominously. The hair stood up on the back of my neck. In a moment we were around a bend in the road and saw battalion headquarters, established in a group of buildings that had once been a town called Kun-Mun-gol. We thought we were free and had escaped, but we had just infiltrated through the outer ring of the major trap.

Battalion headquarters was surrounded, and fire was zipping into the buildings from everywhere. About a hundred yards behind it was a river, but what had been a lazy stream before, was now alive, crawling and black with Chinese. To the north were the mountains we had just left, swarming with Chinks. South we were cut off from our units and to the east where our mortars had been set up in a rice-paddy, were more Gooks than is possible to visualize.

We lay huddled in their midst, watching for our chance to get to the buildings. The firing stopped and we dashed for a house. We burst through the door of the building nearest us. A frightened kid who had been standing at the window shooting the Chinese, wheeled around, his M-1 clicking emptily.

"I thought we were finished," he explained nervously, trying to reload his empty rifle. "I thought you were Chinks. Good thing I was out of ammo."

Over in the corner, a major was trying to get through to the tankers for support. I went over to where he was talking on the radio.

"How many of you are there, Sergeant?" he asked.

"Five, sir, we got cut off and made—"

I was cut off by the crackling voice on the radio. "It will be impossible for us to get through until daylight," it said. "We've got to break through, and there's no use trying unless we know what they've got and where they are. Try holding—over."

"It's not as easy as that!" the major screamed into the mouthpiece. "I doubt if we've got enough ammo to last an hour. Do the best you can, but hurry!—over and out." The radio fell silent and the skies burst into red brilliance. Light fell through the windows, showing the hollow tiredness of the major's face. "Here we go again," he said flatly.

We rushed to the windows of the room just as a wave of about four hundred Chinese came up out of the river bed, charging toward us, firing on the run. We fired at them as fast as we could; reloaded and fired again. That couldn't stop them and some were hit by as many as three or four rounds of 30 cal. fire, but they continued to the window, trying to break through. They would fling themselves toward the open space and we would bayonet the ones who reached us. After about ten minutes of this, they fell back. All that broke the stillness of the night was the never-ending rumble of artillery.

"How long has this been going on?" I asked the kid who had tried to shoot us.

"For about an hour. They attack in waves like this, then pull back. A few minutes later they get another red flare and, that's it. Got a cigarette?" he asked.

"No I don't have, sorry. Don't smoke. How about a stick of gum?"

"Thanks, I could use it."

His hand was covered with blood from a shoulder wound and the sleeve of his jacket was soaked. I tried to help him unwrap the gum, but my own arms cried out in painful anger.

A lieutenant came to us.

"How do you men feel about surrendering? Do you want to?"

"Hell no!" both of us said in unison, ' Don't do that!"

"That's the way I fed," the lieutenant replied. "The way the Chinks are worked up now, they'll never take prisoners anyway. They'd bayonet us first. I've been talking to the major and he said to find out how you men feel about it."

'How many of us are there all together?"

"I should say about a hundred and forty, counting everyone in the other buildings. We could make a bayonet charge on the Chinks. We might not make it, but at least we'll die like men, agreed?"

We assented and the lieutenant began asking the others. I knew without a doubt that we were all going to die. For a moment, time was at a standstill. I was close to God, possibly closer to Him than at any time in my life. I was a man completely isolated from a world of hurt and turmoil. There were just the two of us; a humble individual and his Maker.

I held my rosaries and prayed. I didn't pray to get out alive, it was too late for that. I told Him I wasn't sorry for the things I'd done, because I had said that many times before and invariably had broken my promises about doing better. I tried to think of the things I would have done differently, if I had another chance. The majority of the atonements were related to my mother. I apologized to her through God, then asked that I die fast. No lingering deaths like some of the prisoners we'd seen captured by the Communists. Better it should be like the Dutchman got. I wanted to be shot. It was quicker that way. Complications set in because I couldn't decide how or where.

I thought of the head and didn't like that. I considered the stomach and hated it. The chest wasn't good, either. The hand seemed the only decent place to get hit, and that wouldn't kill me. I just up and damn well decided I didn't want to die, period.

I looked for King and found him in an empty building, hiding in a hole. The hole was filled with manure that was running out from the edges onto the ground from his body, which pushed it past capacity. I could hardly stand the damn smell, and here he was, down in it.

"Cripes man—you stink!"

He returned, "Brother, when it saves your life it smells like a rose garden!"

I told him to climb out of the hole and get ready to meet his Maker. It did not register. I explained what the rest of us had talked over. He said it sounded all right to him, so we went to where the lieutenant and the major waited. They said we would attack with bayonets the next time a flare hit.

One hundred and forty of us; the remaining elements of the 23rd; the 38th; the 1st Ranger Company and the 38th's Headquarters' Company, sneaked outside the buildings and waited. We waited for the signal that would unleash the Chinese against us again, so that we might attack *them*.

Our ammunition was all but gone, anyway. It was just a matter of time. A red flare burst. *That was the signal!* We left our cover to charge at them as they came toward us.

They came across the rice paddy screaming, *"Banzai, bastards, sonsofbitches,"* and many unintelligible words. Our meeting them was just the thing they didn't expect. We encountered them half way across the rice paddy. It shocked them so that it was almost funny. Some dropped their weapons and deserted. Others started shooting and we began bayoneting. It was just like a movie, only we knew it would not end with us walking off the set.

For every Gook who ran, twenty remained to replace him. The odds were stacked at four to one, and in the darkness, it was next to impossible to determine friend from foe. They were climbing over us, like a pile-up in a football game, sometimes three men jumping on one of us. We were slashing anything that dodged around us. At one time, a Chink was climbing over my head, biting my ear and neck. Another was biting my hand, both of whom drew blood. Somebody saw them and slashed down with his bayonet on the one hanging onto me. His guts spilled down the front of me, over my face. The one biting my .hand was disposed of in the same way. This happened several times. Before we got through them to an escape route down the river, I was as soaked with blood as I could have been had I been dunked in a vat of it. As a walked, my boots squished from the blood inside them. Some Was my own, but mostly it was Chinese. My hair was sticky with it.

Upon reaching the river wc cut south and ran into a second group of them. Their guns were turned the other way. We got them from behind. They probably died thinking they were shot by their own men. Some of us were dying, too. Chink white phosphorous began coming in, hitting some of the men in the face. They dived screaming, into the river, hoping the water would squelch the burning. Two of them drowned. We were re-attacked, and bayonets flashed again. Our own men were falling from bayonet wounds and others were killed while trying to take care of phosphorous bums.

I saw one fellow in trouble and went to help him. As I did, several Chinese came to help *their* buddy. I was bayoneted through the side. Then I lost my weapon and in looking for another, found the major lying on his back, wounded. He told me to take his pistol, that he wouldn't need it anyway. He said to get out of there and save myself.

The major was just a small man, maybe five feet, five—but he was guts from the soles of his feet to the ends of his hair. I couldn't think of a braver man with whom to die. Besides, I couldn't take his pistol and leave him there. It would be unorthodox. I helped him across the river and laid him under some brush. Then I left' to join some GIs who had made it that far.

Further down the river we came in contact with a Chink machine-gun. It was firing from above and to the left of us. King got hit in the leg again. He could barely walk. I asked a couple of men in our group to cover me. I went after the gun. Chink guns were normally manned by one man. If I could get behind him, I could catch him by surprise. I had two grenades and a rifle with a bayonet I'd found. Painfully, I crawled up the hill. My arms ached and my hands felt ablaze from the bites. From time to time the gun would fire. I could tell from its muzzle-blast where it was. Other than that, visibility was zero. My arms buckled and I fell, again and again. Eventually I was above it. I could make out the man on the gun, but that was all. I was in luck. Only one man in the hole. Slowly, cautiously, I creeped nearer. When I was within striking distance, I leaped. The bayonet plunged clear through him, into the dirt wall he learned against. He screamed, and suddenly the hole came alive. *The man an the gun had not been alone!* There were two others with him. With all the strength left in me, I pulled the bayonet from his back and jumped out of the way of a charging Chink. My blade found its place. The third one swung his rifle. It caught me full in the mouth. Blood ran down my throat. I was strangling on it. The world was spinning. Unable to use the bayonet effectively any longer, I swung the rifle like a baseball bat. It smashed against his skull. He went down. I was about to bayonet him when I was struck in the back by one myself.

A fourth Chink had sprung from the darkness and was in the corner of the hole behind me. His blade protruded from my side, in front. Not knowing how many there were, and fighting desperately against dying, I whirled. The bayonet broke from his rifle. It stuck in me. In turning, the butt of my rifle had made contact with the Chink. He reeled, and that instant of shocked immobility was enough. I beat his head in. Then I pulled the blade from my back.

I tried to hurry back to King and the others before I passed out. King said I looked like hell.

"Then I look just like you smell," I replied, too weak to do anything but stumble along. It was an effort to put one foot ahead of the other.

We ran into small groups of Chinese for the next mile and a half. As it began turning daylight, they pulled back. About a half mile further we came around a bend in the road and found a contingent of Americans. We spoke of the major hidden in the weeds. A lieutenant with a jeep load of Rangers took me to look for him. We found him still in the weeds where he'd been placed. He was alive. They took us both to the aid station.

King was still at the battalion aid when I was taken in. I didn't stay conscious very long. King was next to me on a litter. My lips were swollen and split. I could barely speak.

"How many of us made it, do you know?" I couldn't understand what I was saying, but King did.

"Eleven of us made it, Herb. Eleven out of a hundred and forty. Here, the doc told me to give you this." he said, extending his hand.

On his palm he held a piece of shrapnel about the size of a half dollar.

"What's that, a souvenir?" I asked.

"Sort of. It was stuck in the wool fiber of your sweater. What do you think of that?" His face was etched with the fatigue eating at his body. His tired eyes, red from lack of sleep, deepened.

"I don't know what to think, King. Maybe. . .maybe we all think too much. Why don't we try to forget a little more often instead of remembering?" It was difficult to speak and I was too exhausted to care. The morphine I'd been given was taking effect. Numbness blacked out everything.

CHAPTER NINETEEN

SIX VERY BADLY WOUNDED men lay next to me, moaning. The bunker hospital danced crazily in a hazy translucence. Standing in the doorway were two medics, trying to figure out where to put the man they were bringing in on a litter. Conspicuously oldtimers at the game of patching up the wounded, they patiently bade time until others could take a minute from their own work to make room. I asked for King and was told he had gone back to the company.

"How could he go back when he was hit like he was?"

"They need everyone they can get. He's bandaged up tight. If they don't get hit, and he takes it easy, he'll make it alright," the medic explained.

"How about me?"

"You'll probably be evacuated to collecting. Maybe not, though. Like I say, they need everyone they can get."

King had gone. He'd left me behind. He could've at least waited for me. If I was needed, I wanted to be there. These people had no right to keep me from the outfit. I watched for an opportunity, and when no one was paying any particular attention, I struggled to my feet and groped my way out of the aid station. It wasn't long until I'd grabbed a ride in a truck. When he once got a good look, the driver didn't want to take me. The aid station was not out of sight before I passed out. He backed the truck up and the medics carried me back to my litter. As things developed, it was some two weeks and a lot of blood plasma later before I did return to the company.

In a way, it seemed like the old outfit. At least there was a familiar line of garbage flowing. I came up behind a jeep where some men were batting the breeze. A voice was sounding off.

"So the old man asked me if I liked to fish. Says I, 'Who, me? Best damn fisherman in the whole city of Brooklyn. I used to go fishing up north in the wintertime,' I told him. Then I asked him if he ever did any ice fishing. He acted like he never heard of it. Asked me how it was done. Told him it was very simple. . . 'Just cut a hole in the ice and when the fish sticks his head out, pow! Kick him in the *ice-hole!* Get it?" he slapped his leg and roared with laughter. Sonofabitch! That could only be one guy. Birnstein!

"*Dave!*" I shouted excitedly.

"*Tony,* bless your cotton-pickin' guts! Hell, I thought sure you'd be dead by now."

"Who in the hell's gonna do it?" I pumped his hand.

"I thought sure since I wasn't around to look after you you'd get it.

Give it a little more time. What happened, they boot your ass out of the hospital?"

"Didn't have enough chow."

"Tell me what happened. You can trust me."

"Whattya mean?"

"Buck and Dick tell me you bugged out on them."

"Buck and Dick? Are they back here?" I was elated.

"Yeah, they made it okay. Dick's around here someplace. Saw him about half an hour ago. I hear this *Massacre Valley* was pretty rough."

"Is that what they called this last brawl?"

"Yeah."

"Brother, it was rightly named, I'll clue you. So what are you doing here? Back in the company?"

"Never happen! Been assigned to battalion. No more of this lower echelon stuff for me. Headquarters material, that's me."

"What do you do back there, rear-echloner?"

"Rear echloner hell! I spend more time up here than I do back there." he pouted.

"Doing what?" I challenged.

"Chogie-man. Bringing up supplies and ammo, besides courier stuff. I've had two trucks shot up already. Didn't scratch old Davey boy, though."

"You driving a truck?"

"What's wrong with that?"

"Hell, you wouldn't know how to drive a baby buggy."

"You don't think so?" How would you do it?"

"What?"

"Drive a baby buggy."

"I was only kidding."

"That's just what I thought," he smiled wisely, "you don't know how to drive one yourself. S'very simple. Just tickle his feet!"

He was accorded the necessary courtesy laughs from the men around the vehicle. Some of them I might have seen before, but for the most part, they were new faces. I asked Dave about Buck, Bugs, Dick and King. Dave told me where I might find the first three, but that King had been evacuated to the States. The medics wouldn't let him stay in the company. Birnstein overheard someone wondering out loud who I was. "Him?" Dave asked. "He'll be your hancho now. He's been here a long time. Since Ridgway was a lance-corporal as a matter of fact."

He got ready to leave. "By the way, Tony. In case you're dead the next time I come up this way. 'Sbeen nice. And see you 'round. . . like a toilet seat?"

"Get the hell outta my area. Birnstein."

"You'd better get out of my way before I run you down."

We parted, laughing. It was great to be back, but I seriously wondered about the others. What had happened to Jennings and Ryan? There were only three remaining from the original platoon, unless Crandell came back. I doubted that he would. The bullet that caught him in the shoulder had broken a bone, so he was probably in Tokyo by this time. When I found the others, I also discovered that Annus had returned. The whole bunch looked fit as a fiddle, and they had a lot to tell.

"The new CO is one of these *'fairy'* nice guys, I think." Buck volunteered. "Name's Thimmes. What a difference between him and Sokolski." said Dick. I learned that this lieutenant had been a Marine. "He faints all the time. I suppose he should carry a handkerchief under his watch band. Then he could put spirits of ammonia in it, or flip it invitingly at them he likes."

"How about non-coms?"

"Got an SFC in named Carlson. Helluvva nice guy. Quite a difference between him and Pickens, too. You'll like this sergeant."

"I'd like to meet him."

"You'll get your chance." Dickson replied.

I asked about Jennings and Ryan. Nothing was ever heard of either of them. I had already checked at battalion aid myself. They never got there.

"By the way," Bugs said, "you know this friend of yours, Jordan, in George Company?"

"Right."

"He was over the other day to see you. I told him I didn't think you'd get back here. He said he'd check when he got a chance. You two are having a helluvva time getting together, aren't you?"

"We sure are, but we'll make it one of these days. Are Greer and Valdez still around?"

"Yes, but between you, me, and the fence-post, I still think they're a couple of bad apples."

"Why?"

"I don't know, it's hard to tell. Nothing you can put your finger on. Only, I heard one of them, I don't know which it was, saying something about getting even with you. The other one told him he wouldn't have the chance. That's when we thought you weren't coming back. Better watch them."

"Thanks for the tip. Next time I put grenades in their hands I'll throw the pins away. That's probably what they're all shook up about. I'd still like to know how you guys got back from that hill before *Massacre Valley?*"

"So would we."

I was introduced to Sergeant Carlson. He was a big man with a thick chest and wide, square shoulders. Blonde curly hair extended above his jacket which was open from the top three buttons. His voice was rich, heavy and friendly. The kind of smooth flowing resonance that makes you comfortable just to hear it. He appeared to be the quiet type, not one to talk much. His helmet was in his hand, and the pock-marked face perspired freely. Almost white hair encumbered by a receding hairline completed the picture of a soldier. A soldier named Carlson.

"Glad to meet you, Herbert, I imagine it's good to get back. Or am I being cynical?" he laughed.

"Not at all. It really is good to be back."

"Thought you might like to know that I've already talked it over with the lieutenant and the platoon is yours again. I know what it's like to come back to your old outfit and find someone else in your job. It's pretty hard to work under those conditions. The platoon's yours."

"I wasn't worried about that."

"I don't imagine you were, but it's the only way I'll work it."

"What goes with you then?"

"I'll be your assistant. I'll have the benefit of age, and experiences from a different place and you will have the edge on me on Korean action. I think that together, we can make a pretty good combination. How does that sound to you?"

"Good. Good deal. Thanks."

"Okay. See you later."

I came in contact with Greer and Valdez three times this particular day. Speaking to them promoted only a sullen, curt salutation. Whatever was bothering them had really worked its way in during the past couple of weeks.

The Imjim River flowed south of us, and the division had a good foothold. New men in the company brought us up to about half-strength. In a few weeks it would be autumn. An autumn without football games, hayrides or the million other things that constitute life back home. 'Home' meant peace and tranquility. When they spoke of the war they spoke in the terms of savings bonds, and blood drives, and 'How soon is Johnny coming home?' The war was not there, though. It was here. And so was I.

As I lay thinking of the progression of events I felt lucky; lucky because when so many of the men with whom I had grown very close were being killed or captured, I had not been in the right place at the right time, so to speak. I wondered about Jennings. Captured or killed? For the second time since the Korean War began, his mother and father would get a telegram from Washington, '*We regret to inform you that your son. . . .*' It would be hard for them.

Soon I felt, I must talk at great length to someone, about a lot of things. Bugs had confided in me about his wife and their baby and how he fought because of love for his country. To talk with him might get him to thinking about his family too much. Not that he didn't anyhow, but too often in more recent weeks whenever he was on a break or things let up, he'd dig the faded old picture of his wife and kid from his billfold and study it. It wouldn't be long before he'd be on his way back to the States. Maybe two or three weeks would do it. Rotation was his life-saver. You can't go on forever. Somewhere in the centrifuge of shrapnel and bullets there is one with your name. You don't have to look for it, it finds you. No sense worrying about that at such a late stage of the game. Before long the war would be over and bullets would stop chewing the sky. We would never know which one had been intended for us. We could live without that knowledge.

Buck snapped me out of my association of ideas. "Bugs wants to know if you'll go on a patrol with him."

"Does he have one?"

'Yes, about a five or six man job. You don't have to, he just thought since you've been gone for a couple of weeks and we were in a new area, you'd want to get the lay of the terrain and everything."

"Might be a good idea at that. What time is it?"

"The patrol?"

"Yeah."

"Right now. He's getting the men ready now."

"Daylight patrol, huh?"

"Yeah, it's just a daylight recon."

"Oh. Who's going on it?"

"I don't know. Don't know that much about it. I was just headed this way and Bugs asked me to ask you if you wanted to go."

"How about you?"

"Beg your pardon?"

"You going, too?"

"That'll be the day when you catch me going on patrols when I don't have to."

"Hell! You've done it a million times before."

"That was different."

"How?"

"Case of necessity."

"Guess you're right. Yeah, think I will go with him. I feel a little rusty."

Bugs smiled a big welcome. Eagerly, he stuck his mitt out. "Gimme some skin, man! Wantta play cops and robbers?"

"Whattcha gonna do out there?"

"Only look. No touchee merchandise."

"No contact?"

"Hawa-no"

"Dye-jobee, Joe...let's go."

"Gotta wait a minute for the others." His face grew a little taut. He appeared worried about something. "I didn't tell you, but Greer and Valdez are going on this one."

"So what?"

"They don't like you."

"I'm sorry, but I'm not going to lose any sleep over it."

"I admire your bravery, suh, but I didn't expect you to be scared. I just think it would be better if I'd get someone else in their places. They don't seem to me to be above shooting someone right in the back if they don't like them. They're just liable to plunk one into you if they get the chance."

"No, hell, they wouldn't go that far."

"You never can tell. I still think I'd better replace them."

"No, don't do that. I'm the one who's out of place. If anyone's to be dropped, better let it be me. If anything happened and you had had them replaced, it would be just my luck that the guy who got it would be one of the replacements. I don't want that on my conscience. Either they go or I won't."

"You're not being stubborn?"

"No, hell no. I don't think I should go anyhow. I'm liable to foul you up."

"You're not going to pull, 'my old wounds are acting up' deal, are you?"

"What you think, GI?"

"I think it's time we got patrollin'. Where in the hell are those guys?"

"Who else is going?"

"Annus and Dickson, I think. Annus .went back for him. Here they come now. Only, I don't see Dick."

Three figures made their way toward us. Greer and Valdez spotted me and hung back behind Annus. They were talking. Annus came up to Bugs and me.

"Dick can't go. Something in personnel he had to take care of. Looks like Tony's taking his place."

Bugs turned to me. "Wanna lead the patrol? You've got rank on me."

"I'll shit in your mess-kit if you talk like that again."

Bugs laughed. "Tell him what the chow up here's been like lately, will you Annus? 'Twould't be anything new, b'lieve that."

"Wellll," Annus smiled, "it hasn't been the best."

"Anyone died from it?"

"Not from the chow."

"Then don't worry about it. I haven't got anything. Only gangplank fever."

Greer and Valdez had remained silent. I spoke to them and in return, got a discourteous, "Hello."

CHAPTER TWENTY
"Bugs"

OUR COMPANY was hidden behind a series of hills. Here on the banks of a ravine, our patrol waited. If we saw nothing, we would advance a little farther. So far, so good. The underbrush was thick on the banks, and it offered good cover. A few feet ahead of us the ravine dropped off abruptly where it met a stream, which was not at its normal depth because of the recent lessening of rain. It made a quiet, unhurried noise, like a breeze stirring a lone tree. We could hear it as we lay listening and watching. 'No Man's Land' was often this quiet.

I fondled a little purple flower; a wild flower that I'd seen hundreds of times, growing in abundance on the hillsides. I had often wondered what its name was. It looked like a violet in a way, but then again, it resembled a miniature daisy. Silly how a man wastes time when he's just lying close to the earth with nothing to do but wait. The earth is a good friend to whom you can cling. In trouble, you kiss the earth as if to woo her. We advanced further, and stopped at the stream. It was shallow, the water a soft rusty color which darkened at the shoreline. One by one, we crossed it and held up again. Bugs beckoned that this was far enough. We could see from here, and if we couldn't see well enough, there was no reason to go behind their lines..

On one side of the ravine were Greer and Valdez. A little ahead of them, Bugs scanned the countryside, searching. Annus and I were on the opposite bank. To our left, a dried and parched rice-paddy lay unused. The burned remains of a thatched-roof hut stood silent guard over the once proud farm, waiting for its tenants to return. Perhaps someday they would. Probably they wouldn't.

The Korean hills, known only by military number or pet names vested by GIs wanting something to remind them of home, shimmered in the hot summer air. The hills extended as far as the eye could see, and became engulfed in soft, cottonish clouds at the horizon. It was all hills and valleys, everywhere. It was difficult to remember, graphically, what plains looked like. In the shade of the brush and scrub pines, it was cool. Occasionally a big black crow circled overhead and cried out, petulantly. Even their calls sounded Oriental. The solitude was conducive to relaxation. I regretted that we were not on an outpost. I felt for the first time in many months, that at this moment, I could sleep; untroubled, undisturbed. Annus tapped my shoulder. He pointed to Bugs.

Bugs clipped a signal to lie low and to be quiet. He had spotted something. It was a Chink patrol, making its way down the banks of the stream. We wriggled around so that we faced the water we had just crossed, and watched them. They moved toward us, much less cautiously than we ever would have ever dared conduct a patrol. Maybe they assumed that since it was daylight, and they were so close to their own lines, they were safe. They were, if we weren't spotted. We were on recon— not supposed to make contact. But if we were discovered; that was something else.

There were eight men in the group, six of whom swaggered with the arrogance of Chinese non-coms. It didn't seem right that the Chinks would have that many non-coms on a patrol. This outfit didn't look like a reconnaissance force, though. They were heavily armed all right, but they were searching for bodies, not information. Maybe they were planning to infiltrate the lines this night. That happened quite often. Once they got in back of the lines and changed clothes with a ROK, you couldn't tell one from the other. I wasn't sure whether these were Chinks or Koreans in the stream. They were in Korean uniforms, but it was hard to distinguish. I was certain the Chinks were on the line, but they may have switched around. Oh well,

I shrugged, it didn't matter. What did matter was that they were here, and we had to keep from being seen.

The patrol came to the stream's junction with the ravine. They held up to have a look-see before crossing the opening in the bank. Bugs hugged close to the ground under some brush. So did the rest of us. Valdez wasn't satisfied with his position. He shifted. An alert eye caught the movement. Gooks scurried like rats disturbed in an empty barn. There was no choice but to fire on them. Bugs opened up, and we followed suit. Six were killed in the initial burst. None of us got hit. But what of the other two slant-eyes? In a moment they reappeared, one to the right of Annus and me; the other from the left of Bugs and his men. We waited for them to get to their journey's end and cut loose. They died in their tracks without firing a shot. They had tried to get behind us. It didn't work.

A patrol had been wiped out, but there was still work to be done. Maybe one of them was alive. If so, we could take a prisoner. If not, perhaps on a body there would be some papers of value to intelligence. We started searching them. Bugs placed Greer as a watch at the peak of the bank overlooking the stream. We trawled on our bellies. One Chink was still breathing, but he was done for. I bayoneted him, just in case he was playing games.

Whatever we were going to do, had to be done fast. We frisked the pockets of the bodies. Bugs found what appeared to be a map. That was the fruit of the labor. Greer hissed to attract our attention. Someone was coming. Bugs gave the signal to hide again. We utilized the nearest camouflage, the bodies of the men we had just killed. Annus and I were, under the same clump of brush, with a Chink between us. The smell of garlic from the body was putrid.

From upstream came the sounds of boots sloshing through the water. What a stupid bunch of bastards, I thought, to be coming the same way the last patrol came. We were all on one bank, so we didn't have to worry about getting caught in our own crossfire when we opened up on them. Greer was on the opposite bank, but in such a position that he didn't get in the line of fire. If we had any ideas of ambushing, they vanished when the Commies came into view. There were at least forty of them. When they spotted the dead strewn over the stream's bed and on the banks, they halted. Something in Chinese was spoken, and they assumed a formation. They approached our position.

I was lying next to the bank's edge with my right hand lying on the ground. As each Chink stealthily moved past, his boots came closer and closer to the hand. I dared not move it for fear of disclosing that I was alive. As it was, they evidently thought we were casualties and that the main ambush party had moved back toward our lines. The last of the file passed. I began breathing again. They were gone and we were safe; for the time being, at least.

But the great tragedy of war is that it takes not only the body of man, it takes his mind as well. I had seen men's minds snap under fire, but never when things were going his way. War itself is unpredictable. So are the men who fight it. An American voice shouted, "Hold it!"

Annus touched my arm and pointed to Greer. Across the stream, Greer was rising to his feet and pointing his rifle at the patrol. He was trying to capture the forty-some Chinese! They stopped and turned to look at him.

Slowly, the front of the column doubled back and they stood as a group; burp-guns slung over their arms and yellow, cracked teeth showing through parted lips.

"Drop your weapons!" Greer demanded. *"You're prisoners."*

They looked at one another and smiled. Someone said, "Yeah, Joe, yeah."

"Well don't just stand there, drop them!" He sounded less convincing this time. *The crazy, brave sonofabitch.*

The Chinks grinned a couple of times and began walking toward Greer. He made a couple of half-hearted gestures for them to remain in place. Seeing that they had called his bluff, he flung his rifle to the ground and raised his hands. This was his chance to be a hero. He had gambled and lost. At least he was taking it like a man. The only trouble was, Greer was not a man.

"Get them over there, too. They're not dead. They're just pretending." He pointed to us. Valdez got to his feet and dropped his rifle. He joined Greer. Bugs began getting up and spoke rapidly in English so that the Chinks would not understand what he was saying. They would think he was cussing about what had happened.

"You guys stay down and watch your chance to get away." He spoke so fast that it took a couple of seconds for it to soak in. We lay motionless, Annus and I. I never felt nearer to any living man than I was with Bugs at that moment.

He walked to the middle of the stream and confessed, "I'm the leader of the patrol. We three are the only living ones." He spoke slowly and very distinctly. He was being understood. "I ordered them to lie down here. The others are dead. Let's go," he encouraged.

They started to move, but Greer wasn't going to let it go like that.

"Those two are still alive." He pointed to Annus and me. "C'mon you guys, you might as well give yourselves up. They know you're not dead. The one is a sergeant," he proudly informed them.

A Chink started across the creek. "Watch your chance!" Bugs yelled. He was immediately grabbed by his captors. They twisted his arm. Since I was nearer, I was approached first. The Chink jabbed me with the snout of his rifle and rolled me over. At the same instant, Annus jumped up and smashed him in the face with his steel helmet. The Gook dropped, and we ran. We heard Bugs calling. *"Go, go, go!"* Then firing opened up in the creek bed.

Annus and I raced at top-speed across the rice paddy we had seen in its virgin calm not long before. Now the symmetrical pattern of the furrows were causing us trouble. It was difficult to run without falling.

The Chinks were not chasing us, but they were firing everything they had in our direction. We zig-zagged to spoil their aim, and had almost reached the thatched-roof hut when Annus stumbled. "I'm hit!" he panted, "Keep going!" I grabbed his arm and half-dragged him behind the Korean house. The Chinks had left the stream now and were coming across the rice paddy after us.

"Where'd you get it?"

"In the back."

There was blood on the front of him. "Gut wound," I said, "Came clear through. The longer we lie around here the worse you're gonna get. They'll expect us to head for our own lines to the left here. Let's go to the right, and when they leave, we'll make it back okay."

"I don't think I can make it."

"Sure you can. I'll help you. Let's go."

"You go by yourself."

"And leave you here? Would you do that to me?"

"That's different."

"Like hell it is."

"Where are they now, can you see them?"

"They're about halfway across the paddy. Maybe two hundred yards out."

I picked his arm up and put it around my shoulder. My rifle bumped him. I was the first time I'd realized I had it. I thought sure it was back on the bank of the stream. I transferred it to my right shoulder. Annus clutched his stomach. His arm over my shoulder was placing a strain on him. I was at least a head taller than he.

Behind the house lay another stream with high banks. It circled around to the left and joined the one we had just vacated. We slid down the bank and turned to the right, then ran.

Some two hours passed, and Annus was vomiting blood. It would soon be dark, and I didn't know this area. Bugs had wanted me to come with the patrol so that I could know it better. How ironic the day had developed. There was no sign of the Chinks. Annus was nearly unconscious. It would be useless to ask him the way back.

Chances were, he would not know anyway. We began walking again. I was too weak to carry him.

I remembered a road we had crossed a thousand yards or so away. If we could find that, it should lead back to the company. We stumbled along and did find it. There were no vehicles in sight. It was hot and dusty. Ahead lay a curve. I didn't remember seeing it on any maps.

I shifted Annus to my right shoulder. The left one was getting tired. When the curve was rounded, we were keeping in the shadow of the hill the sun was ducking behind. When I looked up, directly ahead of us was a fork in the road. Sitting there, not more than twenty five yards away was a Chink with a machine-gun. It was aimed straight at us. To try to get my rifle would have been useless. It was slung on my right shoulder between Annus and me. I couldn't run and leave Annus. Even if I'd tried, the machine-gunner could have cut me down before I'd travelled five feet. I raised my left hand in surrender and pointed to my buddy. The Chink nodded, but still looked down the sights of the gun. He knew Annus was wounded.

After a second's pause, he gestured to our right. The right fork. That meant we would be taken prisoners at his company. This was the eternal fork in the road I'd heard of so many times. Which one should we take? We had no choice, but the one to the left meant freedom. The one to the right...who knows? If we decided to go down the opposite one, he'd shoot us. If we did take the right one, he'd probably shoot us anyway. As if the decision itself was not enough, we were walking straight into the jaws of death. The machine-gun looked as big as a 155 mm. He kept us in his sights, and as we turned to the right, so did the gun. It groaned and squeaked, rustily. Don't look back, Herb, I told myself. If you're gonna get it, it's better not to see it when it comes. What a blast in the ass, I growled. Captured.

I regretted having dragged Annus into this. He would have been better off if I'd left him where he got hit. Then again, maybe they'd take care of him when we surrendered. The gunner was completely behind us now. The urge to run was welling up. But, you can't outrun bullets. We continued walking, and twenty minutes later we walked into our company area! A *Chink* had saved our lives by sending us away from his own troops!

Annus was carted off to the hospital. He'd make it. I reported to the new CO. After telling him what had happened, he dispatched a crew to get the machine-gun we'd passed. The next men might not be so lucky. He made out a report which concluded: *Hoover, Robert E., MIA.*

Bugs was gone. I was convinced that he was dead. The firing that was going on when Annus and I took out across the rice paddy was not directed at us. It was intended for someone else. Who else but the prisoners? Not more than ten hours ago, Bugs had stood almost in this same spot and said that Greer and Valdez were bad apples. They were vindictive, and had proven it. They had their revenge on me, but how? By killing Bugs and wounding Annus. And I had given them credit for not being cut from the same pattern as Pickens. They were the lowest of vermin.

I didn't know if it was an act of God or sheer luck that brought me through, but I knew it was miraculous that I was alive. I whispered a prayer of thanks to my God, and promised I would say a Rosary for Bugs everyday. It was a promise I would keep.

I had been granted one of the many strange breaks that in wartime alter the destinies of countless people, but with Bugs' loss, something inside me withered. I choked with loneliness.

Bugs.

CHAPTER TWENTY-ONE
July, 1951, "The World's A Stage..."

WAR'S INTRIGUE was gone. Even though Birnstein still came to the company every few days, the platoon was not the same. Buckholtz and I were the only ones left from the old platoon. Dickson had recently caught a fragment in the chest from a stray artillery round. He was sent Stateside. I made another attempt to see Jordan, but he had taken someone back to the aid station. His CO told me that he had put Bill in for a commission. He would make a good officer.

Guerilla warfare became a major concern. The renegades had been doing a pretty thorough job on a lot of people in the few weeks just past. We lost four replacements the very day they joined the outfit. The guerillas' rifles left neat little round holes, right in the head. One minute they were sitting around eating, when, *'pttsuingg'...*gone.

It was generally conceded that the farmers' line was the cause. Refugees brought back to their farms to put crops out, were harboring North Koreans or ROK Communists who mainly came out at night, and hid in the hills in the daytime. No place was safe, on the front line or behind it. A lot of house-burning patrols had been run recently, but so far, I had been able to stay off them. I wanted nothing to do with burning people out of their homes. It was bad enough to be killing as we were, without sending people out to die of starvation.

Killing; cheezus, was there nothing different to think about? Carlson was across from me. I had to talk to somebody about something more sensible.

"Carlson?" No answer. I didn't want to disturb him.

He was sitting on a rock, holding his steel helmet in his right hand. Occasionally he'd lift his other hand and shoo away a persistent fly. It had been bothering him for some time, but the quiet comfort he found in the sunshine was compensation .enough for the little insect's harassment. Carlson was the most reserved of the whole bunch of us, and was a damn good soldier. He didn't look like it, though. A soldier, I mean. He just didn't look the part. I wondered then, how this man who must have been every day of forty-five years old could be chogie-ing these hills and keeping up with the younger ones. He appeared deep in thought and unconsciously reached up to swat at his fly friend as it attempted to duck into his ear or buzz around his nose.

The two of us were alone. It would be a good time to get better acquainted. I'd waited long enough now that I could bother him again.

"They tell me you're a veteran of World War II, Sarge. Is that right?"

He turned to me slowly, wearing a sardonic grin. I had broken his train of thought. He bounced the helmet a little toward the ground from the chin strap he was holding, like a yo-yo on a short string. "That's right. As a matter of fact, I had three years of this crap in Europe." He started thoughtfully. "How about you? Were you in the big one?"

I was embarrassed for a moment, with the thought that I had been just a kid. "No, I was only fifteen when it ended. I tried to get in, but they said I was too young. How can you be too young to fight? If you're big enough and you want to, why won't they let you?"

For several seconds he sat motionless as if trying to think of the answer, then he asked, "How old are you?"

"Twenty."

' How old do you think you'll be when this is all over?"

"I don't know. I haven't given it much thought. Why?"

"I just wondered." Taking a cigarette out of his pocket, he lit it and sat with the smoke curling out of his mouth, allowing it to be caught in the wind and whisked away. "How old do you think I am?"

"About thirty-five or forty at the most." I answered, knowing full well he must be closer to fifty.

"Forty-seven, what do you think of that?"

What was I to think? So he was forty-seven—was that an accomplishment in itself? He took the cigarette from his mouth and even though it wasn't half gone, dropped it to the ground. He put his helmet on, doubled up his knee and held it in folded hands.

"Before you ask why I'm back in the Army and how long I expect to stay, I'll try to answer that for you. It's a long story, but maybe it will help you to make up your mind about staying in or getting out when the time comes to make that decision. We've all heard a lot of men talking about others staying in because, 'they never had it so good.' That's true, isn't it?" I agreed, and he continued, "A lot of people usually laugh when you say that. Most of us say it jokingly, but deep inside, we really mean it. I do. For one thing, I saw men from World War II who got shot up and when they got back to the States, they were heroes. Parades in their hometowns— the red carpet. Then just as soon as they got back into civvies, bingo! Those who were unfortunate enough to have been crippled or shot in places it would show, like in the face, were regarded as cripples. Luckily, those with guts realized they were still useful to themselves, and to other people.

"Sure they were crippled, but it wasn't from falling off a curb when they came staggering out of a saloon. A lot of them gave their lives and weren't lucky enough to get back, while others gave years of their lives.

"Personally, I gave only the years. But when I got back to civilian life and took my old job over again, I found that I missed the excitement of being with young men. Sounds funny, I suppose, but when you reach my age, and you're in good shape—and I am—you'll find that you have to detach yourself from older folks. They don't think of work like you do. There's something about the Army that makes you hold your youth. I find that by being with younger men and competing with them, I don't get old. You haven't seen me falling out anywhere along the line, have you?"

"No, I haven't."

"And you won't, either." he concluded.

"How does all this look to you?" I asked before he had a chance to begin giving me hell.

"What, the war? It doesn't look good. I've heard you talking about it ending soon. You're not the only one, either. The papers from home are filled with it. Everyone thinks it will be over soon, but let me tell you something... there's no chance that it'll end for at least two years. I've seen too much of these Orientals. They won't quit that easily." He sounded as though he had lost all confidence in himself, and everything around him.

I shook my head as if to restore his optimism. "We've made out pretty well so far. Before you know it you'll be back home blowing out the candles on your fiftieth birthday cake." I smiled encouragement.

He half-laughed, "Funny you should say that—it's what I've been sitting here thinking about. My sister writes me letters all the time, and damn if the one I got yesterday wasn't about that. Seems everyone thinks about reaching the age of fifty, but she's already passed it and is fifty-two now, or will be this month.

"Her letter got me to thinking about my own chances of being her age.

What is it about war that makes you think of longevity? God knows you're old enough before your time, only with her, she has her husband and children. She takes a pretty good view of life. I wish I could see it through her rose-colored glasses. Like to see the letter?"

I protested, feeling I'd be intruding into something that was intended for him personally. He reached into an envelope and pulled the letter out, handing it to me. It was typewritten and she told him about their new home and all the things she felt he would be interested in. Then on the second page she began:

Saturday was Jim's birthday—55th, And I will be 52 next month. There must be some mistake somewhere. Like falling down elevator shafts and catching tropical diseases and marrying flag-pole sitters, fifty is something that happens to other people. When you're fifty, you're through, finished; kaput. I remember when I was twenty, and that was only yesterday.

Funny, there wasn't any of this feeling of finality in turning ten, twenty or thirty. I can't be fifty yet. I'm not ready. Middle age seems so stuffy and remote. I still have my enthusiasms, my desires, and my own teeth; and I continue to cling to all the sweet, persistent and foolish illusions, like love and friendship, and the chance of changing the world. These are the things you're supposed to outgrow at this stage.

At the age of ten, one is sweet and solid, and life seems awfully simple. If I ate my carrots, was kind to animals and held my stomach in, I was automatically guaranteed curly hair, the admiration of my fellow men, and a handsome fellow of my own with whom I'd live happily forever after.

Only nobody said on what, now that I think of it. Or how. Or haw much tact it takes. But on tenth birthdays one is not burdened by reason or reflection. At ten you think only with your hands. You make doll dresses and push little boys off jungle-gyms and make things out of sponges and otherwise prepare yourself to meet life head-on. At twenty you think with your heart, although there is no light to signal the change; no milestone to mark the end of the tomboy, the gawky, susceptible, despairing schoolgirl. All you know is that you are vulnerable with hope and enchanted to be alive.

But now I am cm equal footing with the rest of the adult world and there's no getting around it. Accomplishments are no longer extolled, but simply expected. I'm playing for keeps now. Everything is counted. At twenty you can squander time and emotion and there is always more there. All manner of roads are available, all endless with possibilities; and there is endless time to explore them. When a detour turns out to be a blind alley, you can always start out fresh. But at fifty you can't forever begin anew, you know that then.

I'm allowed a minimum of detours; a modicum of wasted motion. At fifty, failures are called by their proper names, and you know genuine regret for things you might have done and didn't. Perhaps perspective is what sets this time apart from all others. Friends still matter a good deal, but I feel I need fewer of them, value them more and make them less easily. I still feel the need to love, but I find I don't have to talk about it as much or hold it up to the light as often.

At twenty, I looked at a man and saw only the shape of his head, and the cut of his jacket, or the way he danced. At fifty, I see the width of his heart, the shape of his courage, and wan\t him not for what he could be—but rather for what he is. I suspect I am less cynical and less lyrical. I still warm to each new scheme of salvation, no matter how doomed or daft, although I am no longer very hopeful of its outcome, nor do I move as quickly from ecstasy to disillusion.

At fifty I am no longer intent on burning with Mr. Pater's hard, gemlike flame, nor do I believe that, to maintain this ecstasy is life enough. I know it can't be done, nor do I have much interest in doing it. I am finally willing to accept the fact that I am an imperfect person in an imperfect world, and to lower my sights accordingly—because I know there are other kinds of success, less volatile, more enduring. Today I know that only love and work matter, and I think with my head and feel with my heart.

I felt uneasy. Her words were pleasant and reassuring, yet they had such an air of finality about them—as though fifty-two was the time to pay your debts, take stock of your blessings and wait. "Good letter. Does she always write this way?"

He was looking at the ground, making indistinguishable tracings in the dust, then for no apparent reason, wiping them away. He didn't even look up when he replied, "Not always. Maybe the letters I've been writing her started it. Wonderful philosophy, don't you think? I mean, people go on and on, never trying to live today to its fullest. They don't get all they can out of it. Or maybe that's the trouble—they try to get everything out of it instead of contributing to it."

"What do you mean?"

"I don't know if I can explain it—but—it only stands to reason, doesn't it, that we have to know life and how to, as my sister put it, realize that, 'we are imperfect people in an imperfect world, and to adjust our sights accordingly?' Much of the difficulty in the world today lies in the unwelcome truth that none of us really know these things; the little things, like being imperfect."

'You mean we feel that there's no room for improvement?"

"I suppose many of us, yes. Certainly not everybody, thankfully."

He stood up, stretched himself for a moment and sat on the ground, using the rock he'd been sitting on, for a back rest. "You remember in the letter how she mentioned that she was continuing to learn, even at fifty-two? She's smart enough to know that you never stop learning, even if you live to be a hundred years old. Some of the knowledge that goes into our brains, leaves just as quickly. A man's extremely lucky if he retains even a particle of the knowledge he's absorbed through the years.

"The sum and total of something even as great as human evolution, is simply, when you stop learning—you stop living. When you stop learning, you become stagnant—dull and tired. Then you become tiresome to yourself and to the people around you, because when you stop learning, you might as well say you're giving up. There's no need to continue the battle for existing. And it is a battle, let no one tell you differently. It's a fortunate and a wise man who arrives at that conclusion. . .that a man never lives so long that he cannot benefit from everyday experiences. That a man has never seen so much, or so little; that he cannot see something new, or something familiar, in a different way or with a different concept. Fortunately, the occasion seldom occurs when any of us stop learning. Follow me?"

"I'll buy that, but there seems to be a lot of men in the Army, right here with us who don't seem to feel that way."

"Well, we can't use them as a criterion. Even in the cases of brazen youths, who supposedly having seen and heard what they believe to be life, second hand; firmly believe they understand existence itself in all its varied complexities. Even in their cases, they're learning. Since it's nothing more than a stage they pass through, they gain something—consequently, they have learned that much more, when they emerge from it. I think it's safe to say that every man who serves in the Army learns. He learns something, even if he simply learns that the military is not his choice of a lifetime's profession. For instance, a man is sent thousands of miles from home, across his own country and miles and miles of water, to a strange land. Then he discovers that traveling is not the fascinating pastime he imagined it was, but actually is something whereby the confusion can outweigh the pleasure. The way you travel in the Army, it couldn't be anything but confusion. It's a pleasure when the trip is over, regardless of where you're going.

"I remember a fellow in my outfit during the last war who had been on the front so long that he believed—he *really* believed—that there was nothing left for life to teach him. It might sound silly, but it can happen to a man who stays on the line too long. Anyway, one day a situation occurred that required someone to stand cover for a small advance unit which was trying to get back to our lines. It was under fire. Everyone agreed that the mission was at best, a fatal one. At least in this case it was.

Who do you think volunteered? Our know-it-all friend. None of the men were surprised by this, because volunteering for such things is pretty common.

"I knew this fellow pretty well and I know why he volunteered and what he was thinking. He had resigned himself to the notion that this was to be his *last* job, but that was alright, because life had nothing more to teach him. That was his attitude."

I was learning myself, listening to him talk. If nothing else, I was discovering a new personality in the platoon. "How'd he make out?"

"He made it okay. They all got back, but something happened to the man who felt there was nothing more to learn. For the first time since I had known him, he finally admitted that he had gained something new. He had learned it in a manner so subtly, so strangely, and so powerfully, that he began to think seriously. And oddly enough, he began to care for life. He suddenly felt that there was so much of life that he had not known before, and so many things he had to learn, that instead of giving up—he began to live again."

"Why, was the action that bad? If they all made it out, it must not have been. What caused this. . .this about face?"

'That's probably the most confusing part, it's hard to say. We all react differently under the same circumstances. Right here in Korea, we all know that death lies just across a rice-paddy. But the reaction within one man when faced with the real thing may very well differ from someone else's. It's a very strange thing what a man can do when he's working under pressure. The things he'll do are not a part of his nature, as a rule. It's something deeper than that. A peculiar ingenuity comes to aid him—an ingenuity which he never, physically or through conviction—possessed.

"I suppose some would call it the sub-conscious, like a boxer getting up from the floor at the count of nine after he had received his opponent's knockout punch, and going on to win the fight. Who can explain *why* it happens? We brush it off with something about subconsciousness, probably from the lack of a better answer. Whatever it is, we have seen it happen many times. All of us have seen people do impossible things. Things that they were completely incapable of doing under normal circumstances. Why? Sub-conscious?

"There are those who will stand firm that this peculiar ingenuity has its origin not alone with the man himself—but it is a further indication of a power we don't really understand, but somehow, it's there. It's Divine Providence. What else?

"I know it and you know it, but there are many who don't. However, I think most soldiers in danger believe in this guiding power. A lot of times a man does something spontaneously, without any reason, so to speak. Like a corporal I heard of who bent down to tighten the laces of his boot, even though they didn't need tightening—and a fraction of a second later, shrapnel went flying over him, killing two men who were directly behind him. We pass it off with, 'luck.' Luck or not—he was safe."

"A lot of men get killed or wounded through their own fault, though. The worst part about this whole war—I suppose I shouldn't say it—is that it's not necessarily the men who are over here in it, but their children who suffer." I replied.

"Don't confine that to their children. Sure, there's no doubt that it'll be rough on them from the standpoint of having no fathers, but the children in the country where war rips *through,* suffer even more. Look at the children we've seen so far."

I had been thinking of them as he spoke. Little kids with arms missing, or hobbling on makeshift crutches, serving as the legs they had lost. Blind babies, tied onto their mothers' back while she scraped particles of rice from a gutter where it had somehow fallen. Starving babies with no cover, no heat, save for that from their mothers' body. Indescribable, heart-rending hardships.

"We can't take on the problems of the world ourselves," he began again, "I know that. Even as much as we'd like to, we can't." He had grown very serious and his hands gestured, indicating the futility of world turbulence. "Even though many of these victims are not Christians, as such, they're still human beings. They're being killed, maimed and subjected to every conceivable discomfort. Families are completely destroyed, and some of us say they didn't care about human life anyway. I don't believe that. Don't forget, they're defending their country and we'd probably be the same way under even lesser circumstances.

"The thought that they don't care about living is certainly not confined to them, either. A lot of *us* are that way. Men right here in our own outfit. We do things we wouldn't do as rational, thinking humans, probably with the thought that if we get by with it we do, if we don't—we die.

"Take yourself, for example. You may feel you don't have a great deal to live for. I doubt if you do feel like that, but you might. You're young, and you've got everything to live for. Some of us older ones don't. I'm not married and I don't imagine I will ever be, so I don't necessarily fall into the category of having a lot to live for, really."

"That means you'll probably make it and I won't, is that what you mean?"

"According to the book, that's the way the movies would make it, but this isn't a movie. I'll take that back... in a way it is. The only difference in many respects is that you won't get up an hour from now and have the conclusion of the story. The only way a man can do his job in a bastard-war like this is to pretend it is a movie and that *he's* the main character."

"Why the main character?" I questioned.

"Because the main character never gets killed, it's always the bit players. The world's made up of bit players who die prematurely. If you keep the attitude that you're the main character, you can't miss."

"As simple as that?"

"As simple as that."

"Why don't you take that attitude? Then you wouldn't have any worries about making it."

"Because I know I'm not. You probably are, but I'm one of the bit players and won't get back. I know it, whether you do or not."

"What was it you said about the man with the fatalist conviction? You've resigned yourself to the same thing lie did. It's the same attitude you condemned in him."

"I was the one I had reference to."

"In the story?"

"Yes. I was the one who stood the guard and had resigned himself to death. I've had so many close calls I feel like a fugitive from the law-of-average. No, I'm not supposed to have that birthday cake with fifty candles. I'll be lucky if I have forty-eight. It's a cussed premonition I've had so many times before, but it never seems to materialize when it comes right down to it. I accept it. You just keep in mind the idea that you're the main character and you can't get killed. Remember that and you'll be alright."

There was a particle of truth in what he said. I had been in the War long enough to know that a great deal depended upon luck, the split second or mere inches that had you at another place when something happened. Like the time Buckholtz, Dirkson and I had just left our hole as the Chinks came over the hill, emptying a burp-gun into the hole we'd just left. Or *Massacre Valley,* where eleven of us from one hundred and forty got out alive.

The same thing always occurred in the movies, come to think of it. A hero would climb over a wall in the thick of battle and suddenly the earth erupted behind him, swallowing everything—only he wasn't there. He'd left just a second before. The object now, was to be sure to move before, and not after 'that happened.

"Tell you what, Sarge, let's both be the main characters. There's no room for small parts." I tried to inject some humor into it. Apparently I was successful, because he stood up, grasped my arm in his hand and said, *"Okay, it's a deal!"*

CHAPTER TWENTY-TWO
Carlson's Prophecy

WITHIN THREE DAYS, sniper fire had grown to such proportions that it was hardly safe to be exposed. Five or six guerillas wormed into the hills overlooking our positions and constantly took pot shots. Occasionally a courier returning to battalion never got there. The brass became concerned. They ordered more village-burning patrols. Carlson had been saddled with the job. He said he would do it, and I didn't want to. Although normally an extremely considerate man, he suffered no qualms in running these people away from their homes. I couldn't understand it. He mentioned one day that in Europe, he'd lost two very good friends through guerilla warfare. His sentiment was that the same thing would happen here.

The day did not pledge anything. Another such razing-group was going out, but I had other duties. The front line was static and it looked like the end of the war was again in sight. It was a comforting thought. But at once, the whole complexion changed. A crack of a rifle broke up a burning party that was getting ready. A man shouted for the medic. I sprinted to the scene of excitement.

The regular curious ones were crowded around a prostrate man who was sprawled in a depression. There were those who wanted to know what happened, and the more advised, who knew. They exchanged questions and answers. All were oblivious of the probability that the sniper would fire again. No one had thought to go after him. I yelled for them to get out of sight. They scattered, and the medic moved in to make an examination. He clucked his tongue.

"He'll make it if we get him back quick enough. At least, I think he will."

I moved to help. A small rivulet of blood was falling from the jacket which had been opened by the aidman. Reddish-blonde hair on the man's chest was stained with it. *It was Carlson!* He had a bullet hole through his lung.

"How you makin' it, Sarge?"

He opened his mouth to speak, but blood came instead of words. The medic told me not to make him talk. Carlson smiled. I understood. They took him to battalion aid, but the patrol still had to go out. I asked for the job.

"You've tried to get out of them before," the lieutenant returned, "why do you want to go now?"

"Carlson could be the answer. Do I get it?"

"Sure, sure. I wouldn't recommend you going after the sniper himself, though. They travel in bands. There might be five or ten of them up there."

"Is it okay if I do go after them?"

"It's okay, but I wouldn't recommend it. It's up to you. I couldn't care less."

"Who have I got for the job?"

"Whoever volunteers."

"I don't mean for the snipers, I mean the burning job."

"Oh. You'll have Bedoc, Sparks and Redskin. Good men."

They were good men. The last shipment of replacements had brought them all in together. Bedoc was Hungarian, which accounted for his nickname, "Hunk." A strapping man who was constantly giving his close friend, Sparks a hard time, Bedoc had been a steeplejack in civilian life. He had nerves of steel. I had pulled several ambush patrols with him. He was rough.

Sparks was a poor man's imitation of Birnstein. He rode Hunk until the big guy thought he was going to lose his mind. Bedoc promised the little guy more than once that someday he would get drunk and blow Sparks' head off.

"What's the matter with doing it sober," Sparks asked, "or don't you have the nerve?"

"You skinny little bastard," his friend retorted, "you're as worthless as tits on a boar hog!"

"Yeah, and you go for me like a hog goes for slop, don't you?"

"Shut your cotton-pickin' mouth, man."

"Make me." Just about the time Sparks would say that, Hunk would tear after him. It wouldn't take him ten seconds to run him down. He'd have him screaming, "Uncle Hunk," until the surrounding hills cringed from the reverberations. Just as soon as Bedoc would free him, Sparks would hit him on the arm and run like hell. Time and again this would happen.

But on patrols, they were inseparable. Quite a team. The four of us talked over the idea of going for the guerillas. Redskin insisted that he had seen at least one of them leave a hillside and head for the village we were going to work over.

"We'll try there first, huh, Herb?"

It sounded okay to me. The man called Redskin was an Indian from a Minnesota reservation. He was one we'd have sneak up on guards when we were out on prisoner patrols. He used some sort of a unique Indian headlock that put them to sleep. Five prisoners were captured this way. His main fault was that he was always hunting for whiskey. We hoped to hell he never found it. There were too many stories about the way Indians acted with a belly full of firewater.

The village looked tranquil enough. Only four houses had stood through the war. Families were living in each of them. An old mama-san was beating clothes on a rock at the side of a stream. Papa-san was watching her. From time to time he would grunt something. She would stop beating the clothing and hold it up for inspection. Not satisfied herself, or being unable to please her master, she would resume pounding the material. When they saw us, she jumped from her squat and ran into the house, wiping her wet hands on her apron as she went.

Papa-san bowed and scraped, offering us a seat on the ground. What was the old woman in such a rush about? We started for the house.

The Korean jumped in our path, smiling and jabbering away. His scraggly beard and unkempt clothing were obnoxious.

"You have Korean GI here?" we asked. The reply was a tirade of Korean double-talk. "GI. . .you know? Korean GI. . .havva-yes?"

"Havva-no." he clipped.

"Bullshit!"

"No bullshit, GI. Havva-no."

"Get out of the way. We'll take a look." We walked around him. Again he stood in our path. "Two of you guys go around to the back." I directed, "something stinks here, and it's not *sakana*."

"*Sakana* havva-yes." The old man hissed.

"I don't want any of your damn fish. No want, understand?"

"*Sakana* havva-yes."

"Get the hell out of my way, will you? I'd hate to have to clobber you."

"GI want *sakana*?"

"Come on, Redskin, this guy's stalling for some reason."

We pushed around him into the doorway. When it was evident we were not taking 'no' for a answer, the crummy old man pulled a 'Hank Snow.' He moved on, and mama-san was left holding the bag. The first room was small and dirty. The next one was even smaller and filthier. Piles of paper served as a bed. Tiny bits of it were scattered about, probably chewed up by rats. Shouts came from Hunk and Sparks outside.

"We've got him, Herb! We've got him."

Redskin and I left by the back door. Our strategy had paid off. While we were busy at the front of the house, the old woman had warned the young Korean who was inside, and then left by the rear door. The prisoner looked sullenly. "Watch him." I warned, "You never know what they'll do." Redskin was standing behind him. Gook-boy would have a hard time getting away if he did try.

"You have ID card?"

He looked dumb.

"Card, cardo havva-yes?"

Still he looked dumb. "Search him, Sparks."

As Sparks moved forward, the Gook grabbed for his pocket. He whipped out a knife, but that was his funeral. Redskin made a thrust. The bayonet was plunged deep into the Korean's back. It shot out the front, right in line with the buttons on his GI fatigue jacket. He was still clutching the knife and attempting to stab Sparks with it. The bayonet remained in him, shining clean. It glinted in the sunlight. Redskin gritted his teeth and with a squeal of delight, twisted his rifle. The blade turned in the Gook's body. Something snapped. He fell to the ground.

"Search him, Sparks. He's done for."

He had no ID cards, but he was identified. In his pocket was a Chinese soldier's cap with a red star.

The Indian and Hunk went to search the house. Sparks and I continued to another. At the last hut, some twelve people stood watching. Papa-san from the first house wormed his way to the crowd's hindmost. He didn't want to be seen. We had already decided what to do with them. None of the huts yielded any more guerillas, and with the search completed, we motioned for them to gather their things from their houses. Some did; others glared, defiantly,

"Last chance. Everything havva-yes?"

They wouldn't answer.

"Alright, lets all make torches and start a bonfire," I instructed. "Get some of that straw and set it on fire. Get 'em burnin.' "

The four remaining houses were soon ablaze. It didn't take long for them to bum. They were as dry as tinder. At the last minute, four young men came running out of two of them. Where they had hidden was a mystery. The houses had been practically turned wrong side out during the search. An old woman started into her hut just as it was about to crumble. "Chop-chop," she said. She had fallen to her knees, tugging at our pants legs. We dragged her back. She begged and pleaded for us to let her go. Just as we decided to, the house fell in. It sent a shower of sparks skyward.

We directed our attention toward the men the fire had run out.

None of them had farmers' cards. They were soldiers, on one side or the other. Anybody's guess was good as to which one. Redskin was holding the four of them with one rifle. Maybe they had seen him with the other prisoner. We wouldn't get any trouble from them if they had.

"Get everything together. We're movin'." The Koreans did not budge. "Damnation I hate this pidgin-English! You catch, okay?" I grabbed one by the hand and placed it on his belongings. *"Hayaku!"*

He called his woman to him, and lifting the huge, blanket-wrapped bundle, he put it on her head. She staggered for a moment before gaining her balance, and began walking south. The others followed suit. -The men walked beside them, puffing on pipes two feet long. From time to time, one of the women would drop her cargo. Her old man would give her hell. It was her burden to carry. Although each man carried an A-frame, it had no cargo. Before we formally left the village, their three head of cattle were rounded together. They joined the procession. It must have been an amusing sight, this patrol with point-man out; another behind him, followed by refugees and cattle.

The Koreans squinted with distaste. Their eyes spit at us. "You must really hate us, old people." I apologized. There was hatred in their ogling. There were looks of revenge from the young men, too. It was their own doing that the whole thing was taking place. Too many men had been lost because of the guerillas that these people were. They probably figured we were the most ruthless men in the world, but they were hiding and feeding the very ones we were fighting. They had to leave.

Upon reaching the spot where another company was entrenched, we turned the refugees over to them for shipment further south. The younger men were sent to battalion for interrogation.

Birnstein was in the company area when we returned.

"I saw all of you down in that valley, Sergeant Herbert. I've been trying to figure out if they were trying to catch you with a butterfly net or if they were your keepers. Which is it?"

"You're nuts."

"Reminds me of the psychiatrists' convention. Ever hear the story of the two who met on the street?" He didn't wait for an answer. "You know how they're always analyzing people for everything, and how whatever you say means something to them? Well, one passed another on the street, tipped his hat and said, 'Good morning.' The first one stopped, scratched his chin and said, 'Now, I wonder what he meant by that?' " He waited for my approval. "Crazy doctor, huh?"

"I want to go see how Carlson made out, Dave."

"He's dead."

"No, I don't think so. The medic said he'd be okay."

"I just came from the aid station. He was dead when they got him there."

"Holy hell."

"Bullet must have grazed his heart or something."

"I don't think he really wanted to live."

"Why say that?"

"Just the way he talked when we got together a few days ago. He was convinced he was gonna get it."

"Did he give you odds?" I thought I detected mockery in his voice. "It's not funny, Dave."

"Nobody said it was. I'd give you odds on your chances."

"Really? What kind?"

"Let me think a minute."

"You're smart, Dave, how much longer will I be here?"

"Hell, that's simple. I told you before. 'Til you die."

"So Carlson was a *bit actor* after all." I mused.

"What you mumbling in your beer about?"

"You wouldn't understand. I'm not sure I do myself." I got up. "Why don't you stick around for chow?"

"I have to. Got some stuff to take back to battalion, later."

"Okay, don't eat on my invitation then."

"Reminds me of a girl back home. Got invited to, a fishing party with a bunch of her college friends. She went, alright, but it turned out to be a necking party instead. She came down with syphilis and was kicked out of school because of it. Got to her home town and called her mother. 'Mom,' she says, 'I don't know how to tell you this. . . but, I've got a case of syphilis. Is it alright if I come on home?' The old gal came right back with, 'Heck yeah, bring it home, I'm tired of Schplatz Beer anyhow.' "

Hunk, Sparks and Redskin were not at chow. After we had eaten, Dave and I began looking for them. We didn't have to look far; we traced them through boisterous singing. They were sitting in the back of Dave's truck. Sparks was croaking a song. . .

> Ohhhhhh, the pitter patter of little feet
> Means the First Cav's in full retreat,
> They're buggin' out. . .
> They're buggin' out.

"That's not the way it goes, you simple shit!" Hank bellowed. "I'll sing it for you."

We came around the corner of the tailgate and they spotted us. Hunk had his mouth open to sing, but the words hung inside.

"Wanna drink, Sharge?" He was loaded.

"Have you guys been drinking?"

"Not sho's syou could tellit. Wanha drink?"

"Where'd you guys get whiskey?"

"Ish that whattit ish?" he giggled, "I was beginnin' to worry 'bout what kindda rot-gut we been drinkin.' "

"Where'd you get it?"

"Now, Sharge, don' get all hot-tuh-trot," Sparks butted in. "Nobody's gonna know duh diffrunsh unlesh you tell 'em."

"Hell! The Commies probably know you're that way from all the noise you knuckleheads are making. Where did you get it?"

"We foun' it inna Korean manshun—tuh-day."

"You got it this afternoon?"

"Yup. Didn' know that, did-juh?"

"For God's sake, don't let Redskin know you've got it."

"Redskin?" Sparks roared with laughter, "Redskin's out. There." He pointed to the corner of the truck. The Indian lay huddled in a heap. "He's had it."

"Brother, are we gonna have our hands full with that guy when he wakes up."

"Why?" Dave asked.

"One of his buddies told me what he's like when he gets drunk on *American* whisky. What the hell's he gonna be like on this Korean garbage?"

"That's your problem."

"Give me a lift, Dave." He boosted me up into the truck. I tried to stir Redskin.

From a drunken stupor he growled, "Noooooo." I bent over closer and shook him. An arm flailed out. It caught me just right. I went sailing backward and landed on the ground, completely out of the truck.

"You're a puny runt, aren't you, Herb?" Dave laughed.

About that time Redskin came to. He staggered to his feet and got to the tail-gate. Then he folded up and fell to the ground with a thud. He looked up and Hunk was standing over him.

"Get outta my way, you Hunky bastard!" he slobbered.

"Who'sha Hunky?"

"Now just who'n hell you think I'm talking tew?"

"Let'sh fight about it." Hunk invited.

"Here we go." Dave said. I unslung my rifle and turned it around, holding it by the barrel.

Redskin stood up, using the truck as a support. He rolled up his sleeves and was just about to hunch his back to fight when Sparks crashed down on his head with a carbine. Redskin fell to his knees, then scrambled to his feet. Sparks stared in disbelief at the shattered gun-stock. Redskin snarled at him, and the kid jumped from the truck, running like a scared rabbit. The Indian turned around to Bedoc.

"Where d'ya want the pieces sent, Hunky?" he jeered. He didn't sound quite as drunk as before.

"Don' chu worry 'bout thuh pieces, Injun', I'm out fer yer scalp. Whattcha waitin' fer?"

"I'm gonna kill you, Hunky." The Indian meant it. "Right now!" He lurched past me and as he did, I smashed him over the head with my M-1. The stock broke in two. For the second time, Redskin lay sprawled on the ground. He brought his eyes to focus on me, rubbed his head and rose to his knees.

"I thought you were my friend, Herb," His feelings were hurt.

"I *am* your friend, Redskin."

"Then why'd you hit me?"

"Can't let you kill Hunk, can I?"

"You're not mad at me?"

"No, I'm not mad at you."

"Sure you're not mad at me, Herb?"

"I'm sure."

"I don't want you to be."

"I'm not."

"Sure?"

"Sure. But I'm gonna be if you don't crawl back up in the truck and sleep this off."

"Can't I kill Hunk first?"

"No, you can do that afterwards. . .maybe tomorrow. That okay with you, Bedoc?" I whispered to him. . ."If you don't go along with this, I'll kill you myself."

"Tomorrow'sh okay with me, but he'll have tuh be drunk to do it."

"What'd you say?" Some of it got through the drunken haze in Redskin's head. "Who'd have to be drunk to do what?" He was ready to go again. There were no more M-1s handy.

"Will you shut the hell up while you're ahead, Hunk? C'mon Redskin, he was talking to me." I implored.

"Let me kill the Hunky first, then I'll go to sleep. My head hurts."

"Yeah, I should think it would."

"I'm tard."

"Well then let's go to sleep, whattya say? C'mon, into the truck."

Between Dave and me, we got him back into his corner. He dropped off, slobbering and muttering about killing Hunk, 'first thing in the morning.' Sparks sneaked back. He was more sober now. Breaking a rifle-stock over a man's head and seeing him stand back up had had a sobering effect.

"If you weren't from my home town, I'd kill you," Hunk shouted, "I'd da clobbered the Injun if you hadn't hit 'im."

"The hell you say!" Sparks returned.

"I wantta go home," Bedoc was dejected, "I don't like it over here."

"I don't either. Let's both go home."

They sat discussing the possibility of going home together. Bedoc decided he'd rather kill himself. Sparks wanted to do it for him.

"Would you?" Hunk asked, quizzically.

"For you? Hell yes!"

"Get my rifle." Badoc demanded, dramatically. *"Fetch my lethal weapon!"*

Sparks got it and handed it to the big guy, who forthwith pushed it against his chest and held it with both hands. "Pull the trigger!"

Sparks stuck a finger in his ear and grimaced. Dave and I laughed. Sparks pulled the trigger and there was a muffled explosion. A shell was ejected from the chamber and the rifle jumped out of Hunk's hands. Our faces fell from smiles, to looks of astonishment. The rifle had been loaded! Hunk was shot in the chest. He didn't speak.

"Oh, my achin' back. Here's five years of paper work now." Dave slapped his forehead. "I didn't see a damn thing."

We got the medic, who immediately started the trip to battalion aid. We had to take Sparks to the CO. Thimmes couldn't get a thing out of him. He became exasperated. Grasping Sparks by the hair, he shook him until the soldier's teeth were about to fall out. "Now, you tell me how all this happened!" he shouted.

"Yessir. It all started back in 1948 when Hunk and I joined the Army together. We served our year and went home. We both liked to dance but no one would dance with us, and we reenlisted. And that's how it happened."

Thimmes gritted his teeth and rattled the head hanging in his hand more vigorously. Its eyeballs registered, 'tilt.' "Goddammit, Sparks, you tell me how this happened or I'll snatch your head off!" Sparks groveled on his knees. "Yessir. It all started back in 1948 when Hunk and I joined the Army together. We served a year, got out, and none of the girls would dance with us and we came back in the Army, and that's how it happened."

Thimmes was raging. "I'll give you one more chance, Sparks. Either you tell me what happened or I'll get a firing squad ready right now."

Sparks jumped to his feet, and snapped to attention. "You don't have to do that, sir, *I'll take all the blame.*"

"You'll take all the blame?" the lieutenant said, sweetly. "Now isn't that nice? WHO in the hell do you think's gonna take the blame anyhow?"

The ringing of the telephone interrupted him. The company clerk took the call. He talked for a moment and with a bewildered look, said, "This is battalion aid, sir. They report that Bedoc's body has come up missing. He wasn't dead, though. They say the gun was held so close to his chest that the gas pressure built up in front of the bullet and deflected the gun away from him. The slug skipped off a rib. They said he'd be alright, but now he's missing. What should I tell them?" Thimmes let go of Sparks' hair. "Tell them he's their baby, not mine. He's out of the company now. It's their problem. We've got paper showing it."

"Yessir."

"And," the CO added, "you can tell them if they find him, to keep him until he's sober. We've had enough of him for one night."

The clerk turned back to his duty. He had just hung up when the sound-power phone from an LP rang. Thimmes took the call.

"This is Corporal Redskin, sir, on LP 14. Would you give us a mortar concentration on B-coordinate-650, please?"

"What have you got spotted?" the lieutenant asked.

"Ten vehicles."

"On their way, ten rounds. Get that dope to the mortar crew, will you?" He added hurriedly, "Better alert the company. Might be an attack breaking."

I shot the information to S-3. They said mortars would be coming. Dave and I looked at each other. Puzzled expressions, to say the least. We left the hut and double-timed it to the truck. Redskin was gone.

"That crazy bastard is gonna get himself killed up there." I exclaimed.

We went back to the CP. Thimmes was talking to Redskin. The explosions were sounding over the phones. "Call off the mortars, sir. This is Corporal Redskin attacking."

"He's drunk, sir."

"He is?" Thimmes asked. "Why didn't you tell me he was drunk, too?"

"Didn't see any reason to. He wasn't bothering anybody."

"Well he sure as hell is now. Redskin, you get back to the CP!"

"Too late for that, sir. Just call off the mortars and *I'll go clear to the Yalu.* We'll get this war over in a hurry. What's the matter, don't you *want* it to end?"

"Get back here, I say!"

"Okay if I sleep on it? I'm tired."

"If you go to sleep, yes. No more of that messing around up there. Got it?"

"Good night, sir."

When he finished talking with the Indian, Thimmes told the company clerk to send ten men to the outpost and get him back. I suggested he make it fifteen.

Dave was in his truck ready to leave when we heard a voice down in the valley, singing away...

Ohhhh, the pitter patter of little feet
Means the First Cav's in full retreat
They're buggin' out,
They're buggin' out...

"That Hunk on his way back here?" Dave asked.

"Must be."

"Gotta shag, boy. Be seeing you."

"What's the hurry?"

"Is it always this quiet up here?"

"Sometimes, why?"

"I was just thinking. You must get awfully bored."

CHAPTER TWENTY-THREE
September, 1951

AUTUMN'S CHILL signaled the advent of winter. The rainy season was running rampant, and our gradual but heavily opposed push northward, continued. Casualties mounted. Lieutenant Thimmes found it impossible to endure. The constant threat of patrols and eventual skirmishes with an armed enemy were too much for him. Invariably, when called upon for a job which involved any semblance of contact, he fainted. He was pulled off the line and relieved of his command.

Nameless hills with only numbers to give them distinction, were added to our list of priceless Korean possessions. We struggled for the high ground to keep Joe Chink from towering over us. Artillery pieces screamed, as each projectile belched from their seared, burnt throats. The war grew.

In a jeep, riding to battalion where I had been called for a mission, the torrent of rain whipped around my body. I was drenched. Streams of water coursed their way from the hills to inundate the valleys beneath them. The vehicle sent showers shooting from either side as it hit the currents. It was a dark, miserable night, so typical of Korea. The mission would be a patrol. Under these circumstances, what else?

Inside battalion headquarters were two staff officers waiting to begin the orientation. With them were three lieutenants from other companies. It took but a moment to get down to business. One of the battalion officers, in a voice of authority, acquainted us with the task at hand.

"I'll try to be as straight with you on this as I can," he started, "Each of you has been in Korea for about the same length of time. That means all of you will be going home about the same time, too.

When that will be—is your guess as much as mine. You have every reason to believe it'll be soon, I do know that much. For one of you, to be decided by yourselves, the war in Korea will be past, very shortly." We glanced at each other approvingly. He continued, "There's a patrol going out tonight, and I want a volunteer. However," he held his hand up to hold off the deluge of shouts which did not come, "however, I must make it plain that it'll be a rough one."

A lieutenant with a scar on his check from a recent wound asked where the patrol was to run. Our informant lifted a green cloth covering the contour map of our sector and pointed to a ridge well into enemy territory. The stem of his pipe stabbed, "This is it, *Hill 982.*"

The lieutenant scratched his chin. "Kindda stuck out there, isn't it?"

"Yes it is, and definitely occupied by the enemy. That's why whoever takes the patrol, will be rotated. That's a promise. No more patrols for that man. Call it compensation. It's pretty dangerous."

"How many have been up there and what have they run into?" another of the three lieutenants asked.

The officer briefing us shrugged his shoulders. "It's virgin territory. We haven't had any probes out onto that particular peak. Now. . . who wants to tackle it? How about you, Lieutenant?"

Scarface did not take long to ponder his decision. "I'd like to, sir, but I'm afraid that with a cold I've been getting, I'd just be endangering the lives of my men. I pass."

"Lieutenant?" He turned to the next one.

"That's a pretty high ridge to be climbing around on with my back the way it is, sir. I wrenched it the other day and have put off going to the medics. I had planned on going in tomorrow. I'd rather not, if it's alright."

"And you?" he directed to the third officer, who in the meantime had taken a handkerchief from his pocket.

"Sir, I've been sneezing all day. Sure as anything, if I get out in this downpour, I've had it. I don't see how I can. Of course if it's an order—"

"This is a volunteer job, I told you that when I started." He looked at me, "How about you, Sergeant?"

I had heard the three lieutenants alibi their way out of the mission. They had exhausted all routes of escape. I could not think of anything to have wrong with me. "Yessir, if I'm the only one left, looks like I'll have to take it."

"You don't *have* to, but there isn't much time to spare. We've got to have certain answers as soon as possible. We can't be piddling around trying to find volunteers. It's yours. You're dismissed, Lieutenants." He fell far short of courtesy with them. They departed before he changed his mind.

I studied the map while his pipe was being reloaded. Satisfied with the way it was burning, he resumed discussion on the hill. "This is an important ridge to us, Sergeant. We're going further north and we need it. So do the Chinks, but we're going to take it away from them, and the sooner, the better."

"This just a regular probe for contact?"

He hesitated for a minute and pursed his lips. "Regular in one sense, yes, but in another, no. If you're able to get on top of the hill and hold it, we'll immediately send in an entire company to cinch it."

"How many men do you want in on this?"

"I think it had better be a twenty to thirty man operation. You shouldn't get too many. Besides, you'll have a company in readiness."

"What's on the ridge?"

"So far as we've been able to determine from reports we've gotten, there's an outpost with five or six snipers. That's all, as far as we know. We have to know more about it."

"There are a lot of Gooks between here and the base of the hill."

"Yes, you're right there, but under the cover of rain, you won't have much trouble getting through."

"How about getting back?"

He grinned, "You've always been able to get back so far, haven't you?"

"Sure, but there's always the first time for anything."

"Don't worry about that part of it. If you make it to the top of the hill and can hold, the company'll move right in. If you can't get that far, you'll still have darkness and rain to come back under."

"That about it, sir?"

"As far as I'm concerned. How about you?"

"The only question I might have is, 'why in the hell did I volunteer for this?' "

The radioman was a replacement named Nelson. Assistant patrol leader was Buckholtz, who really didn't want to go, but did anyhow. I tried telling him he didn't have to. He insisted.

From our own positions, a long, crooked finger extended to a road. The road led to Hill 773 which was a connecting-link with 982. It was about a mile's walk. The rain subsided, and almost instantly, it became foggy.

Redskin, Sparks and Bedoc were directly behind me as the procession moved in single file down the finger, across the valley and onto Hill 773. Nelson radioed in.

"White GP, White CP, this is Able-three, over."

Static crackled and popped. The answer came, "Able-three, this is White CP. Go ahead, over."

"We're at check-point November, over."

"Got it. Everything alright? Over."

"So far. No report, any instructions? If not, over and out."

"Hawa-no, Roger, over and out." The radio fell silent. I remembered my first night out in Korea. It was on an outpost. I had compared the frontline troops with the crew of a train, whose engineers wearing stars, directed the fight from the caboose. Tonight, it assumed the form of an octopus extending a long tentacle to grasp an ice cream cone. Suction cups under the tentacle were soldiers moving toward the hill, that to a degree, resembled an inverted ice cream cone. Swiftly, the vision was destroyed. A long knife lashed out and chopped down. The tentacle was severed. We would be in a hell of a spot if that happened to us.

Not a sound was heard. No words were spoken. We were in Chink territory, behind the lines. No gates to pass through, no guards to stop us, only fog which was delaying our journey. If we were going to get to the hill's summit, we wanted to be there and out by daylight. Redskin grabbed my arm and pulled me his direction.

"There're Gooks cooking *gohan* over there, see?" he pointed. About twenty-five yards to our right and partially out of sight in the mist, were about ten of them around a campfire, cooking and eating rice.

The Indian cupped his hands around my ear. "Let me sneak over and get one of them, will you Herb?" I shook my head. "Why not? We could find out what they're doin' without climbing the rest of the way up this damn hill." Still I refused. He gave up, disgustedly.

The Chinks were behind us, the right of us, to the left and dead ahead. We were crawling under a blanket of fog which lay about two feet from ground level. Thick, slimy mud allowed us to slide on our stomachs. We were almost to the top. The first level had been passed. In a matter of moments, the second peak would be reached and our objective conquered. It was a long, hard filthy climb, but at last we were nearly there.

Nelson contacted the CP and used the head-set so the operation would be soundless. He whispered their reply, "They said to stay here and find out as much as we can. They sounded surprised that we made it. What's that matter with those people?"

"Beats me. Did they say anything about alerting the reserve company?"

"Huh-uh."

I sent Bedoc to the right of the approach we had used, and dispersed the other men. Sparks went with Hunk. Together, they were to count all the enemy they could see. I was on the left, with Nelson. A Chink was heard walking toward us. We crouched a little deeper into the mud and held our breaths. The hill was haunted. This was no place to be discovered. He passed in the swirling fog and was lost. We had been unable to see his face because he was shrouded from his knees up. In a moment, this one was followed by another, and then still others. There were more than any five or six men holding an outpost on *this* ridge. An endless column of Gooks made their way past, some within three feet of us. When it appeared that the last one had gone by, Hunk crawled across the path.

"How many did you count?" he asked.

"I got one hundred and fifteen."

"I thought you'd be counting this trail, so I got another one. We're right at the fork of two of them."

"How many did you see?"

"Ninety-six."

"Hell's fire, that's over *two hundred!*"

The Chinks began returning. Soon most of them were back in their own positions. I told Nelson to contact the CP and tell them we were on our way home. We had determined how many were up there and it was a sure fire cinch we couldn't hold anything in the face of the odds. It was pointless to stay. Nelson didn't get a chance to relay that message. One of the excitable members of the patrol stirred around. He made contact with a mine. It blew sky-high, taking him with it. Shouts went up from the Chinks. A machine-gun cut loose. Bullets zipped in our direction.

"We've had it! Get CP and tell them to start that company on its way!"

Nelson shot the dope through. "They said to hold on, the company is standing by."

We immediately established a perimeter of defense. The worst could be expected now. Twenty-three men were not very many to be fighting off unknown hundreds of Chinks, but that was about to take place. Less than two dozen men trying to make a stand until a company could come in to relieve us. The man who had stepped on the mine was killed. He had been our medic. Redskin was itching to go after the machine-gunner, and since this sort of thing was his specialty, I okayed the idea and he left. In about a minute or two, from within the scud which had swallowed the Indian, the gun fired sporadically, then stopped. The quiet was broken by an exploding grenade. A few minutes later *Gung-ho* crawled back. His right arm was shattered from machine-gun slugs, but he smiled, "I got the sonofabitch. There's another one up there, though."

"Let's put a tourniquet on that arm. If we weren't up so far, I'd send you back."

"Like hell you would. My chances are better staying right here than they would be trying to get through the Chinks below."

"There's nothing you can do here with that arm."

"I can pass ammo."

"Okay, Molly Pitcher."

We ducked our heads as the machine-gun fired again. "I thought you said you got that gun, Redskin."

"I did, they'll never fire that one again. I jammed a grenade in it. That's the other gun I told you about."

"They've got us zeroed in alright." Through the mist, we spotted dark shadows moving. "Here comes a banzai!" I shouted.

Our BARs served as machine-guns when the attack broke loose. About fifty Chinks charged us but they fell almost at our feet. Those who did not get hit turned to run. We cut them down in their tracks. "Nelson, for God's sake tell battalion to send those reserves in!"

"I already have. They say to hold."

"How much longer do they think we can do that?"

"I give up, I say let's get going while going's good."

"We can't do that. We're supposed to stay here until the company comes."

"What if it doesn't?"

"We stay here forever."

"Very funny."

"It wasn't intended to be."

The banzai had served at least one good purpose for the Gooks. It had given them our exact location, and they took advantage of the information. They unleashed their mortars.

The first barrage caught about half of our men. Many were hit so badly that their chances of making it out were double-zero. The echoes had not subsided before the next banzai was organized.

Nelson was pleading with the CP. The answer was, "Wait one."

"Wait one, hell! Nelson," I ordered, "bust that goddammed radio up! It's not doing us a bit of good."

"*Hell* no. We'd be cutting our own throats. Besides, who would go on the statement of charges?"

There was no time to argue the point. Mortars tore at us in preparation for the second banzai. They really had us in the palm of the hand. Through the haze of fog and smoke, red streaks of tracer bullets whined. Ear-bursting cracks of mortars deafened us. Dirt and mud smacked our faces. My ears, nose and mouth were filled with mud. I gagged on it. Before the barrage had stopped, the Chinks came running through the holocaust. We fired again and again. They lay heaped in front of us; a pile of at least one hundred.

"*Get that goddammed CP on there and tell them to send that company in, Nelson!*"

"What the-hell do you think I've been doing? They keep saying, 'Wait one.'"

I was just about to smash the radio with my rifle butt when it stopped squawking. A chunk of shell saved me the trouble by going right through it. At the same time, another machine-gun cut loose. Number *three*. They had power on this ridge, and it was time for us to leave. "*Let's go you guys!*" I didn't have to yell twice. We re-organized, and a quick check disclosed that every one of us left living, without exception, was wounded. Buck had a fragment in his chest. He found it difficult to breathe or talk. Both Bedoc and Sparks had been wounded in the back and legs. It was a tattered, ragged looking bunch of men who started for the valley. In very short order we ran into more resistance. The Chinks had been encircling us. Had we stayed where we were for another five minutes, the game would have been over. As it was, there was *one spot* where the encirclement was not yet complete. We headed for it, but were held up there. The three more seriously wounded; Buck, Sparks and Bedoc, crawled for the aid station. They needed medical attention. . .bad. The fog was lifting rapidly as daybreak came. We formed a double column and fought our way through their lines. The last part of the trip was murderous. In addition to being wounded, the men found it was almost impossible to remain standing, because of the slippery under-footing. They decided that the easiest and fastest way to get down the hill was to cooperate with the law of gravity. Many just squatted, and slid down the hill, while others pitched forward and floundered as best they could.

When we reached the road, the Chinks were still chasing us, but not for long. As soon as we got into what was considered to be our own territory, they returned to their lines. Of the twenty-four who began the patrol, only twelve remained. Three had gone to the aid station, but nine stayed on the hill, dead. We couldn't bring them out. Nelson sat on a boulder about the size of a basketball, worrying about the radio. "What're you gonna tell them about it?" he asked.

"To hell with the radio. They're pulling something on us. If those reserves were coming in to help us, where in the hell are they? They should be on this route *right here*. Nine men dead are more to worry about than that damn radio."

"Here come the engineers looking for mines in the road," Nelson said. "Shall we tell them we've been over this route twice and there aren't any?"

"Hell no, let them earn their pay."

They approached us as we rose to resume our journey. Nelson got off the rock and walked away. An engineer, searching for traps, rolled the rock over. An explosion was his reward. A release type mine which had been under the rock, completely ripped the man's head from his shoulders, and chewed his body to pieces. Nelson almost fainted.

The moment we were comparatively safe, the tension was broken. Suddenly I was very tired. Where was that reserve company? We found it in its staging area, with the men writing letters home and cleaning equipment. For a company alerted to jump off, they were doing little in preparation. *They had not been called on for a thing.*

With the wounded from the patrol checked in at the aid station, I was ready to report on the night's operation. However, I wanted to know how Buck, Bedoc and Sparks were.

"We don't have them on our list," the medic said. "You'd better let me take a look at your arm. What's in it?"

"Mortar fragment. It's alright. You must have those men. They started back about two hours ago. . .maybe three." I was a little grouchy with him.

"I tell you I don't have. Were they in Chink-land?"

"Yeah."

"Maybe they got captured."

"I doubt that."

"They could have been."

"They might have wandered into another battalion aid."

"Could be. Why don't you check back after you finish at headquarters?"

"Good idea, and if they show up, will you give me a buzz there?"

"Sure thing. Good friends?"

"One of them in particular."

"Okay, I'll let you know."

I was certain that if nothing else, intelligence would be happy to know what we had learned about the fortifications on the hill. I was not greeted with pats on the back from anybody. The pipe smoker blasted me.

"Why did you come off that hill, Sergeant?"

I was astounded. "There was no other choice, sir. All my men were wounded and they had us surrounded. We had to fight our way out."

"What were your orders?"

"To get to the top of the hill, which we did."

"Did you establish a perimeter of defense when they hit you?"

"Yessir."

"Then there's no excuse for them cracking it! Once you get a perimeter established, *no one's going to break it!*"

"Twenty-four men can't hold off that many Chinks!"

"How many were there?" It was a captain standing off the side who asked it.

"We killed at least a hundred."

The captain scoffed, "Really?"

"Really. What happened to the company that was coming up? You said they would move in on the hill."

The pipe-smoker was quick to reply, "We're going to take that hill in the morning. I didn't think you'd be able to get to the top of it. We wanted you to feel them out for us."

"You didn't think we'd make it back then?" It was disturbing to think that we had been singled out as a sacrificial gesture.

"Oh, we thought you'd get back alright, but it's surprising you got to the top of the hill."

"It's more surprising we got *back*. Why wasn't that company sent up like you said it would be?"

No answer. They side-stepped it.

A second captain inquired about what happened to the radio. I told him it was knocked out by a mortar round. "Are you sure?" He was doubtful.

"As much as I can be."

"How many do you think are up there, Sergeant?"

"At least a battalion."

"Oh, no, there can't be that many up there."

"You asked me what I think, didn't you? That's what I think."

"What makes you think there are that many?"

"I know there's more than a company."

"*How* do you know?"

"For one thing, we were fired on by three machine-guns, and they don't have that many in a company."

"How do you know there were three?" I was asked from another side.

"*Hell, I might be stupid, but I can count!* There were three of them. Corporal Redskin got one of them himself."

The first captain asked sarcastically, "What kind of machine-guns were they?"

"Heavies." My head was turning from side to side as though I were watching a table-tennis match. I had difficulty keeping the answers directed toward the proper questioner. They were more like accusers.

From the corner of my eye, I saw Jordan leaving the other end of the bunker. I wanted to call to him, but couldn't.

"How do you know they were heavies?"

"From the sound."

"You can't tell from the sound what the hell they are!"

"Okay, I can't tell by the sound, let it go at that!"

"Goddammit, tell us the facts!" he shouted.

"Alright, dammit! They were firing heavy machine-guns. . .Maxims, and there were at least three!"

"How do you know they were Maxims?"

"They were heavier than our .30s, and that's what they're using up here isn't it? Maxims?"

"Well tomorrow morning," said the voice of authority, "we'll have a company go up and take that hill."

"They can't do it, sir. There are too many up there and they're in too deep. There's at least a battalion on that ridge."

The captain interjected, "I doubt it."

I turned to look him square in the eye. "Have you been up on that ridge, Captain?" He shook his head that he had not. *"Well, I have, and I know what the hell I'm talking about!* To send Easy Company, George Company, Fox, or any other four platoons up there will be murder. You haven't got a battalion in the regiment that could even begin to take it. *I doubt if the whole 38th could!"*

The three of them grinned to humor me. *"We'll take Hill 982 tomorrow, and . . . with one company."*

"Will that be all, sir?"

"Unless you have something more to add."

"Only that you'll lose all your men."

"That'll be all, Sergeant."

Outside the headquarters, I shook with frustration. After what we'd gone through to get them the true information, they would not believe us. They had had no intention of sending a company up in support. *We had been left there, high and dry.* I went in search of Jordan and was told that he had just left for his outfit. *Lieutenant* Jordan it was. That was the purpose of his trip to battalion. To get his bars pinned on. I wanted to be the first to boot him in the ass.

The aid station still had no report on Buck or the others. They had even called around for them. The three were picked up on the records as missing-in-action. The Chinks must have caught them. As I was leaving the battalion area, Birnstein came roaring up in his two-ton. "Hey, where you going?" he shouted.

"Just heading back to the company. Buckholtz, Bedoc and Sparks are MIA."

He looked startled. "When did this happen?"

"Last night, on 982."

"Cheezus. That must be the hill they were talking about up front. I just came from there, and one of the outfits is getting ready to jump-off, either tonight or in the morning. Everyone's pushing panic buttons."

"That's what I hear."

"So am I," he said in triumph.

"Where you goin'?"

"Rotating Stateside."

"The hell you say! When?"

"Tomorrow morning, 0500. Damn shame you have to stay over here and get knocked off."

I would trip him this time. "Not a chance of that."

"What makes you think so?"

"Last night's patrol was *supposed* to be my last one. Besides, it's a snap. If a simple bastard like you can make it, why in the hell shouldn't I?" It stopped him.

"Thanks Herb, I love you, too. You might as well stay here to have your last supper."

"Might as well." I hopped in the truck and we went to eat. It was several hours before I started forward to the company. Dusk was falling and the air was getting crisp. Dave and I had talked a lot, about many things. One thing was most obvious. I was the only one left of our original company. We shook hands, promised to look each other up, and repeated our goodbyes for the second time.

As we split, a friend of Dave's came over and asked for a cigarette. While Dave got it for him, I took the chance to leave without saying anything further. I walked away from them. The man asked for a light, too. I visualized the distorted expression Birnstein twisted his face into when he quipped, *"Want a kick in the lung to get you started?"* Dave would never change in a million years.

I hitched a ride part of the way up, but when the truck took a turn away from my own area, I got out. It was dark now, but the outfit was within walking distance. I wanted to walk and think, hard. This was indeed, a universe turned in upon itself. My stride was erratic. My arm hurt, and I became confused as to which way I was actually heading. I went to the side of the road and lay next to a man I recognized as being from the company. We spoke, and the conversation died right there. I lay parallel to the road, with my head almost touching his waist. He mentioned that he had leg trouble and wanted to lie with his feet propped by a small bank at the gravel's edge. We formed a "T", with his head toward the road. I was completely spent.

Sleep was fast in taking command. It was not a restful slumber, but one that skipped from an over-lapping chain of thoughts to another; none of which made sense. It was a cavalcade of nightmares. The earth was tremorous as tanks moving up to assist in the morning's assault, passed by.

"*POP!!!*"

It was the sound of a shotgun, but instead of awakening me, it plunged me deeper into this sequence of fantasy. *A shotgun fired at a rabbit back home.* "Jim" is dashing for it. He wags his long curly tail and playfully backs away while I reach to take it from his mouth. I place the rabbit into my hunting jacket. The dog barks his agreement that it is a nice fat one. We start for home, and "Jim" runs to an apple tree. Lifting his head upward, he howls for one. He hasn't forgotten in this long. I also pick one for myself. We are sitting under the same tree I had left months before. But I am swiftly carried from under the tree to my kitchen at home. It is warm and inviting. I toss my hunting coat into the corner and take out the rabbit we have caught. I go to the sink and begin cleaning it. I am not sure whether I like this peculiar odor of wild rabbit or not. Before, I did, but somehow I've changed my mind. It is distasteful. I turn my head from it, but it pursues me. It becomes vomitous. The rabbit is crawling over my face...wet and smelly!

But this is Korea. It is not home.

The rumbling of a tank passing dangerously near jarred me awake and presented the un-varnished truth. My face and chest were covered with matter. I ran my hands over my face and wiped, unable to identify the substance. I turned to the man sleeping beside me. He was the answer. The sound I had identified as a shotgun, was actually the sound of his skull being crushed under the churning treads of a tank. *I was covered with his brains!*

If this was living death, where was its end? Could it go on until eternity? If I were dying, why couldn't I live my life over; quickly, completely, as so many have said you do? I was perturbed that I could not. I could only continue until told to stop. But when would that be? A war was yet to be fought. I brushed myself off as best I could and picked a handkerchief from the dead man's pocket to finish the job, then covered his smashed head with it.

The attempt to take Hill 982 was waning as a faint, daybreak glow spilled on it. One company had been committed to the attack, and that company had been all but destroyed. The outfit was pulling back to regroup. They were calling in for an additional regiment. I went to see if I could be of help. I didn't know at that moment to where my own outfit had moved. I would look for it later. Right now, I wanted to find Bill Jordan. He owed me ten bucks and I wanted to pay him a swift kick in the posterior for getting commissioned. A wounded man was being carried down the trail. I stared at him. He resembled Jordan a great deal. I was mistaken for a minute. I thought it was he. The way I looked at him, the kid must have thought I was mentally deranged. Someone spoke to him.

"How's it going up there?"

It caused him pain to speak, but very feebly the words came out, "It's pure slaughter."

I inquired about Jordan. No one knew where he was, but a medic said I'd find him about twenty-five yards to the left. I searched, but Bill was not there. I was about to ask again, when my eyes glimpsed a carbine, that even though caked with mud, was clean. It could belong to but one man. I walked to the body next to the rifle and turned it over. *It was Bill Jordan!* At last I had found him. . .but too late. Jordan was *dead.* One shot in the forehead, just above his left eye, had done it. The tiny blue hole was the only mark of violence.

The tuning-fork of battle became lost in a din of nothingness. I sat in the center of a vacuum; motionless, suspended. Bill had carried his grain of sand, as had so many others, and flung it at the punch-pressed face of war. That offering had been ridiculed. War's shrieks of mockery defied resistance.

"*Herbert!*" The voice echoed a thousand times over, vague and hollow. "*Herbert, you're wanted at battalion. You've got another patrol to run.*"

I was unhinged. Numb. And yet, I shivered in that numbness. For the first time since its inception, Korea acknowledged its name, "*Land of the Morning Calm.*" Another Korean sunrise was here. Black hills clawed at the sky in tormented anguish.

I picked up Jordan's rifle and walked away. With luck, my war would soon be over.

Perhaps someday, somehow, this... this *conquest to nowhere,* would end.

— *The End* —